IN GOD WE TRUST-IN ROTH WE PROSPER

IN GOD WE TRUST–IN ROTH WE PROSPER

How Contributing Just a Few Dollars a Day to a Roth IRA Can Help You Live Large. A Must-Read for all Millennials and Generation Xers

ADAM BERGMAN, ESQ.

ISBN-13: 9781530818310
ISBN-10: 1530818311
Library of Congress Control Number: 2016905766
CreateSpace Independent Publishing Platform
North Charleston, South Carolina

TABLE OF CONTENTS

INTRODUCTION

JOHN MAYNARD KEYNES once said, "The avoidance of taxes is the only intellectual pursuit that carries any reward." If Mr. Keynes were alive today, he wouldn't have to work too hard to find a way to avoid taxes. Such a way is available at any local bank or financial institution. It is even advertised on the TV, radio, and the Internet and encouraged by the Internal Revenue Service (IRS). The tax-avoiding strategy I'm talking about is called a Roth retirement account, and it can make the difference between retiring rich and working for the rest of your life.

What is the secret behind the Roth retirement account?

Go to the personal-finance section of any bookstore, and you will see that there are as many theories about how to save for retirement and retire rich as there are books on the shelves.

As someone who has participated in and carefully watched the retirement-investment industry for many years, I can tell you that not all those theories and approaches have your best interests in mind. All experts and institutions have angles, interests, and points of view about your money that benefit them. So in the interest of full disclosure, I want to tell you about my point of view before we get started.

I believe

1. anyone can become wealthy by retirement if he or she invests in retirement-savings vehicles;
2. the earlier you start to set aside income and invest it for retirement the better;

3. it is totally unacceptable that nearly 40 percent of working households with members aged between twenty-five and sixty-four have no retirement savings;

4. if you are a millennial or generation Yer, this book can help you retire in style;

5. the Roth IRA or Roth 401(k) Plan is the best way to build tax-free retirement wealth;

6. it's never too late to start; and

7. the Roth IRA and Roth 401(k) are the best remaining legal tax shelters available.

Accordingly, the companies I've built, IRA Financial Group and IRA Financial Trust Company, are designed to help you save for retirement through retirement-savings vehicles, such as an IRA or Roth IRA, that you can establish, manage, and control. The fact is that according to a 2014 Gallup's annual Economy and Personal Finance poll, conducted April 3–6, a firm majority of Americans, 59 percent, are worried about not having enough money for retirement, surpassing eight other financial matters. What is interesting is that the 59 percent figure did not just cover the elderly or baby-boomer generation, but included a broadly defined group of middle-aged Americans—those aged from thirty to sixty-four. This book is about educating America—especially young professional millennials and generation Xers and even the baby boomers—about the enormous tax advantages and retirement benefits of using a Roth retirement account to build retirement wealth as well as the importance of committing to retirement savings. For purposes of this book, the millennials, generation Xers, and baby-boomer generations will be categorized as follows:

Millennials: born 1979–1996

Generation X: born 1965–1978

Baby boomers: born 1946–1964

Baby boomers are people born during the demographic post–World War II baby boom approximately between the years 1946 and 1964, giving an age range between fifty and sixty-nine as of 2015. Even though baby boomers are in many cases business and professional leaders and are reaching their maximum earning potential in 2015, many baby boomers are concerned about their level of retirement savings. The Insured Retirement Institute 2015 survey found that 27 percent of baby boomers are confident they will have enough money to last through their retirement, down from 33 percent a year ago and 37 percent in 2011. Only six in ten boomers report having any retirement savings, down from roughly eight in ten in previous surveys.[1]

Generation X is the generation born after the Western post–World War II baby boom that grew up in an era of emerging technology. Like their parents and the baby-boomer generation, generation Xers are arguably equally ill prepared for retirement. In fact a J.P. Morgan Asset Management report makes the argument that generation X is likely to be worse off in retirement than the baby-boomer generation—making the cohort the first postwar generation to be more ill prepared for retirement than the previous one.[2] One fact working in the generation Xers' favor is that they will inherit the bulk of the boomers' wealth, which can greatly help them during their retirement years. Nevertheless, generation Xers generally understand the importance of saving for retirement but have been somewhat unsuccessful in getting started. A recent report by the nonprofit Transamerica Center for Retirement Studies (TCRS) indicates generation X workers know they have to save a lot for retirement, but generally they have hardly started. The report notes Gen Xers "are concerned Social Security will not be there for them and more than 85 percent feel they will have a harder time achieving financial security than their parents."

Millennials, the generation of Americans born between 1980 and the mid-2000s, is the largest generation in the United States, representing one-third of the total US population in 2013. In the first quarter of 2015, millennials

---

1 Insured Retirement Institute, "Boomers' Confidence in Secure Retirement Sinks to Five-Year Low," April 2015 (Washington, DC).
2 Greg Iacurci, "Gen X Lags Boomer Generation in Retirement Savings: Study," October 2015.

became the largest generation in the US labor force, with 53.5 million workers.[3] The millennials is the first generation to have had access to the Internet while growing up. Millennials also are unique because they comprise the most diverse and educated generation to date: 42 percent identify with a race or ethnicity other than non-Hispanic white, around twice the share of the baby-boomer generation when they were the same age. About 61 percent of adult millennials have attended college, whereas only 46 percent of the baby boomers have done so.[4] Unlike baby boomers and many of the generation Xers who benefitted from the workplace offering lifetime pensions and benefits after spending an entire career at one company, millennials are dealing with a less robust 401(k) plan, and face a larger burden in saving for their own retirement.

Whether one fits into the baby-boomer, generation X, or millennial generation, the one common trait is that all three generations have not done enough to save for retirement. I do understand the obstacles facing many millennials and generation Xers when it comes to juggling financial responsibilities with the need to save for retirement. There is no question that income levels have not yet revived from the 2008 recession while college-tuition costs, rent, and many living expenses have all escalated. As of 2015, the median personal income of millennials is just $57,000,[5] making saving for retirement somewhat challenging. No one is saying that all millennials and generation Xers are neglecting retirement saving, but the fact is too many of them are incorrectly assuming that they are not able to save for retirement or that it is just not possible. This book hopes to show that almost everyone with income can start saving for retirement even if it is just one dollar a day, which can turn into hundreds of thousands of dollars tax free down the road with the right investment choices. With nearly 40 percent of working households with members aged between

3 Richard Fry, "Millennials Surpass Gen Xers as the Largest Generation in U.S. Labor Force," *Pew Research Center*, May 2015.

4 Decennial Census and American Community Survey. Data for millennials are for those fifteen to thirty-four years old in 2012. Baby boomers' comparisons are for when they were fifteen to thirty-four as surveyed in 1980.

5 B. Rubell, "Are Millennials Saving Enough for Retirement?" *Reuters*, July 2015, New York, NY.

twenty-five and sixty-four having no retirement savings,[6] our country is facing a real retirement-savings crisis, especially among the millennials and generation Xers. This book hopes to show millennials and generation Xers that their best asset is their age and time, and making annual retirement contributions on a consistent basis is possible for almost all income earners and can really mean the difference between retiring and having to work the rest of your life.

JOHN F. KENNEDY AND THE POWER OF EDUCATION

President John F. Kennedy, who died long before most generation Xers and millennials were born, once said, "The goal of education is the advancement of knowledge and the dissemination of truth." I agree with President Kennedy, and yet his statement exposes one of the main reasons why more Americans are not using a Roth account to save for retirement—a lack of education.

Americans love to spend and hate to save. When all households are included—not just households with retirement accounts—the median retirement-account balance is $2,500 for all working-age households and $14,500 for near-retirement households. Furthermore, 62 percent of working households ages fifty-five to sixty-four have retirement savings less than one time their annual income, which is far below what they will need to maintain their standard of living in retirement.[7]

Americans have one of the lowest savings rates for developed countries. Americans are the ultimate consumers, and that definitely plays a role. However, I believe that education—or its lack thereof—is a big factor. Most people don't understand the basic concepts of retirement planning and how crucial it is, largely because it's not widely taught in our high schools or even our colleges and universities. The goal of this book is to educate Americans, especially generation Xers and millennials, that starting young is the key to retiring rich and the Roth account is the best way to accomplish this. For

---

6 N. Rhee, "The Retirement Savings Crisis: Is It Worse Than We Think?" *National Institute on Retirement Security*, July 2013 (Washington, DC).

7 Ibid., 1.

example, if millennials began funding individual retirement accounts with $3,000 per year at age twenty and continued through age sixty-five, they would wind up with $2.5 million at retirement (assuming they earn the long-run annual compound growth rate in stocks, which was 9.88 percent from 1926 to 2011). Not a bad result for investing only $3,000 a year or about $8 a day. Imagine then if they learned that in school. But young people are not alone in lacking full awareness of the benefits of the Roth IRA or 401(k) plan, and they are not to blame. I graduated from law school and have a master's in taxation and not once was I ever taught about retirement accounts or their benefits. I must have taken hundreds of university and law courses, but no one ever explained to me the value of retirement savings or the power of the Roth IRA. How can we expect Americans, especially young Americans who are just starting out in their careers, to take advantage of retirement savings if they are not taught about the benefits? I have talked to tens of thousands of retirement-account holders and am always amazed how many people say, "I wish I had started saving for retirement earlier" or "I wish I had understood the benefits of a Roth account fifteen years ago." While I am not the most sophisticated investor, I have a diverse tax and investment background, but I only learned about the benefits of using a Roth account to make investments through research I'd done for a client.

Since then, I've helped a number of tax partners that I used to work with—one who even went to Harvard Law School—who were unaware of the enormous tax and retirement benefits of using a Roth retirement account.

IS THIS BOOK FOR YOU?

I've written this book for people—especially young people—who want to learn how they can take charge of their retirement by saving just a few dollars a day and building tax-free wealth.

Specifically, I have written it for people who

1. are between twenty and fifty-five years of age who are seeking ways to build their retirement wealth and are looking for a tax-efficient way to do this;

2. have very little understanding and knowledge of how retirement accounts work, especially the Roth IRA or Roth 401(k) plan;
3. may not have tens of thousands to put into a retirement account but are still intrigued with the idea of retirement saving;
4. are interested in understanding how saving just a few dollars a day can turn into real tax-free wealth when they retire; and
5. are excited about being more active, thoughtful, and deliberate in building their retirement wealth.

On its own, this book will not make you rich. But it will give you the tools you need to take charge of building your retirement wealth, and it will show you how easy and fun that can be. It is up to you to be committed, consistent, and patient when building your retirement wealth. But with some good investment decisions, you can have a million dollars-plus tax free in a Roth retirement account when you retire. The Roth retirement account is a golden ticket to tax-free retirement wealth and the best legal tax shelter out there. Starting a Roth account can become the most important and valuable decision a generation Xer or millennial will ever make. In terms of financial security and happiness, it can quite be as important as graduating or buying your first house. This book will show you how easy and attainable saving for retirement can be. In fact, saving just a few dollars a day—or one less Nonfat Grande Cappuccino from Starbucks per day—can make you a millionaire when you retire.

I understand it may be hard for someone in their twenties or early thirties to start thinking about retiring, especially when there is so much interesting stuff to check out on Facebook, Instagram, or Twitter. I also understand that millennials and generation Xers have expenses to worry about, such as rent or mortgage payments, car payments, credit-card debt, student debt, entertainment, and other miscellaneous costs, but I do believe that the majority of millennials and generation Xers can find a way to save a few dollars a day especially once they are shown that it can lead to a million dollars tax free when they retire. The fact is that new technology and smartphone apps are making it easier and easier for Americans to save for retirement seamlessly and cost effectively.

Most of all, this book will show how saving for retirement does not have to be scary—and it is never dull. In fact, it is exhilarating and empowering to know that something simple and easy you can do at a young age can directly impact future wealth and quality of life. The ability to secure your retirement wealth is at your fingertips. In fact, the IRS and Congress have given all of us the tools we need to retire wealthy—the problem is that too many of us are not aware that these tools exist and how they work. This book may not be as exciting as the Hunger Games series of novels from Suzanne Collins or have as many beautiful pictures as *People* magazine, but this book may end up making you rich when you retire or at least explain the path of getting there and how rewarding taking those steps can be.

1

How Amy First Heard of the Roth IRA

Wealthy people sure make living well look easy, don't they? Picture a husband and wife in their midsixties driving a nice car to the beach for the day or having a leisurely lunch over a nice bottle of wine.

Whatever the story, the people who are generally well-off and enjoying their retirement years have worked hard, been successful, and have saved for retirement. College prepares you for the "real world," and a second degree can help you become a professional, such as a lawyer, doctor, or architect, but we are all on our own when it comes to learning about how to save for retirement. This is a fundamental flaw in our educational system especially since our retirement system is privately funded and not supported by public funds, such as in some European countries. We spend a lot of time learning in school about a variety of very important subjects, such as political science, history, philosophy, psychology, sciences, mathematics, law, economics, finance, some of which will help us land jobs, start businesses, or go on to a higher level of education. However, the one area that can directly contribute to attaining a level of wealth needed to retire comfortably is ignored. I'm talking about learning about the different types of retirement accounts and the advantages of saving for retirement. I was lucky, because my father was a very wise man and always believed in saving, which rubbed off on my sister and me. However, not everyone is so well informed about the importance of starting to save for retirement at a young age. It's hard to imagine that someone can go to college for four years and never be taught the importance of retirement savings, especially because that knowledge can be more financially rewarding than a philosophy, psychology, history, or political-science class.

Let me tell you about someone who was taught at an early age the importance of retirement savings, the wonder of tax deferral, and the power of the Roth IRA and Roth 401(k) plan. I'll call her Amy.

THE STORY OF AMY

Amy is a thirty-three-year-old woman who is newly married and has no children. She lives in New Jersey with her husband, Steve, who is forty-two years old and is a dentist in a large practice. Amy owns her own Internet-marketing firm and has been quite successful. In fact, Amy first started in the Internet-marketing world way back in 2000, the summer before she started university. Amy had always been interested in computers and staying on top of all the new Internet trends. She was fascinated with Internet start-ups and spent a lot of time reading about the way the Internet would reshape the US economy and how businesses interact with their clients. Amy took a job at one of the first Internet-marketing companies in New York City in the summer of 2000. She was paid quite well and made close to $4000 that summer. Amy started university that year and continued to work with the Internet-marketing company on a part-time basis.

One Friday night during the summer of 2000, Amy was having dinner with her parents and their friends John and Mary when she mentioned that she was not sure what to do with the money she earned during the summer. John, who is a tax attorney, mentioned something about a new retirement account that was just established in 1997 called the Roth IRA. Amy had no idea what he was talking about but was interested to learn more. After dinner, Amy went up to her room and dialed into the Internet and started researching the Roth IRA. She was able to learn that the Roth IRA was named after Senator William V. Roth Jr. and that it offered her the ability to make after-tax contributions to a retirement account so that the money could grow without tax. Amy was intrigued but didn't really understand much of the terminology or the benefits it offered. Specifically, she read on a financial website that if someone just invested $2000 in a Roth IRA starting at eighteen every year until they reached seventy and the Roth IRA was able to generate an 8 percent annual return, which didn't seem so tough in light of the Internet boom, the Roth IRA would be worth around $1.45 million when she reached seventy. The number blew her away, and she couldn't believe that just $2000 a year from her Internet-marketing job could be close to $1.5 million tax free when she reached the age of seventy.

That was all Amy needed to convince her that the Roth IRA was the way to go. The very next day she went to a local bank to open a Roth IRA account. She was initially concerned about what would be needed to open the account but was delighted to find out that the account could be opened in mere minutes. Amy was ready to deposit the full $4000 she had earned from her summer Internet-marketing job into the Roth IRA account, but the bank representative mentioned that the Roth IRA limit for the year 2000 was $2000. Amy was a bit disappointed because she had thought she would be able to contribute more to the Roth IRA, but nevertheless she agreed to deposit the maximum of $2000 to the Roth IRA account. The bank representative asked where she wanted the funds invested, but she did not have the faintest idea. The bank representative suggested she talk with a financial planner and he set up an appointment for her the next day. Amy returned to the bank the next day and spoke with the bank's financial advisor. The financial advisor mentioned that since Amy was quite young, an aggressive investment approach might make sense, and he provided her with a list of mutual funds that he suggested she purchase with her Roth IRA. Amy did not have much of an investment background other than watching CNBC with her dad a couple of times, so she decided to bring the paperwork home with her and discuss further with her dad.

At dinner that night, Amy talked with her dad about her new Roth IRA and the mutual-fund options the financial advisor had recommended. Amy's dad read the list and recognized a few of the fund names from watching CNBC. He selected two mutual funds he wanted Amy to purchase with her $2000 Roth IRA. He suggested that Amy invest $1000 in each mutual fund from her Roth IRA. Amy's dad mentioned to her how proud he was of her taking saving for retirement so seriously at the young age of eighteen and suggested that she continue to make Roth IRA contributions each year. Amy agreed and promised that as long as she had a job she would continue making Roth IRA contributions.

Amy didn't lie. From eighteen through twenty-two, she contributed $2000 to her Roth IRA from the income she earned from her part-time job at the Internet-marketing company. In 2005, Amy graduated from university and took a full-time position with the Internet-marketing company she was working for. Amy received an annual salary of $37,500, which allowed her to get an apartment in New York City with two of her best friends. She always remembered her promise to her dad, and in 2005, she contributed $4000 to her Roth IRA, since the maximum Roth IRA contribution amount had increased to $4000 from $2000. Amy continued to make Roth IRA contributions in the amount of $4000 through 2014.

In 2014, Amy was starting to get the itch to branch out on her own and start her own Internet-marketing company. She had just gotten engaged to Steve and figured that before any kids came along, this was the time to pursue her dream of starting her own business. She knew she could do it. She had close to fourteen years of experience in the industry and many great contacts. Amy's only fear was losing her $78,000 annual income and the amount of goodwill she had put into the company over the last fourteen years. Amy spoke with Steve at length about the decision, and they finally agreed that this was the right move.

In the summer of 2014, Amy gave notice to her employer of fourteen years and started her own Internet-marketing company. Amy rented a small executive-office space in a nice building in midtown New York City. Amy's business started taking off immediately, and in her first year she generated close to $100,000 in profit. Amy couldn't believe it, and was very excited with her decision.

Around holiday time toward the end of 2014, Amy and Steve went back to Amy's parents' house for dinner, and lo and behold, John and Mary were also invited. Amy remembered that John was a tax attorney and was excited to be able to ask John some tax questions about her new business. Amy made sure to sit next to John at the dinner table and started talking with John about her new business. John remembered their conversation back in 2000 about the Roth IRA and asked if Amy had ever started one. Amy was surprised that John remembered their conversation from close to fourteen years ago and mentioned that she did take his advice and opened the Roth IRA account and that it was now valued at almost $100,000. Amy mentioned her promise to her dad and also that she had been diligent about contributing to her Roth IRA each year. Amy also mentioned that she had close to $135,000 in her former employer 401(k) plan, which did include some Roth contributions. John was really impressed and felt really good that he was able to offer Amy some valuable advice. Amy then mentioned that she had a really great year and had close to $100,000 in profits but wasn't sure what type of retirement plan to establish. John mentioned the SEP IRA, SIMPLE IRA, and Solo 401(k) plan. Amy had heard about the SEP and SIMPLE IRA but not the Solo 401(k) plan. Amy asked if she could buy John a coffee some time to pick his brain on retirement-planning options, including continuing to contribute to a Roth IRA as well as learning more about retirement plans for her new business. John was excited to help Amy, and they agreed to meet next week for coffee since they worked only a few blocks from each other.

2

RETIREMENT SAVING—FROM BABY BOOMERS TO MILLENNIALS

A week or so after Amy and John had met again at her parents' home for dinner, Amy emailed John about setting up a meeting to begin discussing various retirement-planning options for herself. Amy and John met up at a coffee shop located on the corner of 52nd Street and Third Avenue in New York City called Coffee Plus. Amy and John both ordered nonfat cappuccinos and found a quiet table toward the back of the coffee shop.

"I really want to thank you for taking the time out of your busy day and meeting with me to discuss retirement options," Amy said. "I know you are a really busy guy and to have some time to help me out discussing retirement options is really nice."

"It is my pleasure. I really enjoy discussing retirement-planning options with friends, especially young people who can really take advantage and leverage the nuggets of information I am sharing," John said. "I know a lot of people report that Americans are facing a retirement crisis. You have probably heard this said on TV or read articles online, and it is true, but I believe the real shame is that this perceived retirement crisis can largely be averted through education."

"Let me explain a bit more. Congress has given all of us the golden ticket to retiring wealthy. Specifically, when the Roth IRA was created in 1997, which I will be spending considerable time discussing through our conversations.

The Roth retirement account is a golden ticket to tax-free retirement wealth and the best legal tax shelter out there. Starting a Roth account can become one of most important and financially rewarding decisions of your life. However, before I dive into the nitty-gritty of how retirement accounts work and get into all the fun tax rules, I think it would be helpful to describe the three most popular categories of American generations: (1) baby boomers, (2) generation Xers, and (3) millennials in greater detail so we can better see how they have viewed retirement saving," John said.

"OK, that makes sense. Of course I know my parents are baby boomers, I am a generation X, and my little sister is considered a millennial, but I guess it would be helpful to learn more about each group to see how they have regarded retirement saving and what, if anything, can be done to learn from the past." Amy said.

"OK—let's start with the baby boomers." John said.

BABY BOOMERS

"According to Wikipedia, baby boomers are people born during the demographic post–World War II baby boom approximately between the years 1946 and 1964, giving an age range between fifty-one and sixty-nine as of 2015. Baby boom in the United States, referred to as the baby boomers, has been driving change in the age structure of the US population since their birth. This cohort is projected to continue to influence the characteristics of the nation in the years to come. The baby boomers began turning sixty-five in 2011 and are now driving growth at the older ages of the population. By 2029, when all of the baby boomers will be sixty-five years and over, more than 20 percent of the total US population will be over the age of sixty-five. Although the number of baby boomers will decline through mortality, this shift toward an increasingly older population is expected to endure. By 2056, the population sixty-five years and over is projected to become larger than the population under eighteen years."[8]

---

8 https://www.census.gov/prod/2014pubs/p25-1141.pdf.

On Jan. 1, 2011, the first baby boomers began turning sixty-five. For the next nineteen years, nearly ten thousand boomers will reach that milestone every single day.[9]

According to the US Census Bureau, the term "baby boomer" is also used in a cultural context. Therefore, it is impossible to achieve broad consensus of a precise date definition, even within a given territory. Different groups, organizations, individuals, and scholars may have widely varying opinions on what constitutes a baby boomer, both technically and culturally. Ascribing universal attributes to a broad generation is difficult, and some observers believe that it is inherently impossible. Nonetheless, many people have attempted to determine the broad cultural similarities and historical impact of the generation, and thus the term has gained widespread popular usage.[10]

As a group, baby boomers were considered by most to be the wealthiest, most active, and most physically fit generation up to that time, and among the first to grow up genuinely expecting the world to improve with time.[11] They were also the generation that generated high levels of income, which was perfect timing for the advent of individual retirement accounts in the mid-1970s.

"The baby-boomer generation was a remarkable generation that had an enormous impact on the social and economic development of the United States. Here are a few of the main characteristics of the baby-boomer generation:

1. Educated: More boomers are college graduates than any other generation before them. Compared to their parents' and grandparents' generations, boomers were far more likely to earn a college degree and hold white-collar jobs. All this is expected to have a positive impact on their ability to have a financially secure retirement.
2. Active: It is well documented that boomers desire to be active and maintain their well-being throughout retirement. In fact, the entire diet and fitness movement was born out of the baby-boomer

---

9 http://www.nytimes.com/2011/01/01/us/01boomers.html?_r&_r=0.
10 https://en.wikipedia.org/wiki/Baby_boomers.
11 Landon Jones, *Great Expectations: America and the Baby Boom Generation* (New York: Coward, McCann and Geoghegan, 1980).

generation, and it continues to play a huge role in the lives of most Americans across all generations.

3. Independent: The baby-boomer generation is fairly independent and understands that the world doesn't owe them anything. They are also free thinking. They grew up in an era of reform and believe they can change the world. They questioned established authority systems and challenged the status quo.

4. Hardworking: Baby Boomers are recognized as an extremely hardworking generation. They have been synonymous with long workweeks and define themselves by their professional accomplishments. Many baby boomers sacrificed a great deal to get where they are in their careers, and as a group they have been known as the workaholic generation. Interestingly, labor statistics indicate that nearly eighty million baby boomers will exit the workplace in the next decade. These employees are retiring at the rate of eight thousand per day or more than three hundred per hour. So where does this leave baby boomers when it comes to retirement savings?"

The baby boomers were fortunate to become the first generation to gain the advantage of contributing to a private or individual retirement account starting in the mid-1970s. That is not to say that retirement-savings accounts did not exist before. In fact, as far back as 1885, the American Express Company established the first private pension plan in the United States in an effort to create a stable, career-oriented workforce. By 1899, there were approximately thirteen pension plans in the country, and by 1919 over three hundred private pension plans existed, covering approximately 15 percent of the nation's wage-earning and salaried employees.[12] The growth of pension-plan coverage is generally credited to the desire of businesses to attract and keep workers.

---

12 Georgetown University Law Center, "A Timeline of the Evolution of Retirement in the United States," 2010, http://scholarship.law.georgetown.edu/cgi/viewcontent.cgi?article=1049&context=legal.

Just to be clear, these were pension plans established by businesses and not individual retirement accounts that could be established by individuals, which only came into being in 1975. In 1935 Social Security was enacted, establishing age sixty-five as the normal retirement age. By 1940, 4.1 million private-sector workers (15 percent of all private-sector workers) were covered by a pension plan. Similar to Social Security, pension plans were designed with the anticipation that they would need to pay benefits for a certain number of years after the retirement of the plan participants. In the mid-1950s, the IRS began issuing rules on various tax matters involving 401(k) plans. By 1970, approximately 26.3 million private-sector workers (45 percent of all private-sector workers) are covered by a pension plan. In 1974, the Employee Retirement Income Security Act of 1974 (ERISA) was enacted. ERISA is a federal law that sets minimum standards for retirement plans in private industry. One of the key components of ERISA was the individual retirement account, or IRA. As originally contemplated, taxpayers could contribute up to $1,500 per year and reduce taxable income by the amount of the contributions. By 1980, 35.9 million private-sector workers (46 percent of all private-sector workers) were covered by a pension plan, including many baby boomers.

"You would think that because baby boomers are educated and hardworking, they would have taken advantage of the increasing popularity of pension plans and the creation of IRAs, but all I hear people talking about is a retirement crisis," Amy said.

"You are right. The problem is that the average baby boomer has a goal of accumulating enough of a nest egg to have $45,500 a year in retirement income to live off, according to a 2015 report from BlackRock.[13] The average retirement portfolio, however, has just $136,200 in it as of 2015, which would provide an average estimated income of $9,129. That would leave the average boomer nearly $37,000 *per year* short of his or her goal.[14] However, the value

---

13 Blackrock, "BlackRock 2015 Annual Global Investor Pulse Survey," October 22, 2015, http://www.blackrock.com/corporate/en-us/literature/press-release/gip-press-release-2015.pdf.

14 Beth Braverman, "Baby Boomers Face a Shocking Retirement Savings Shortfall," October 23, 2015, http://www.thefiscaltimes.com/2015/10/23/Baby-Boomers-Face-Shocking-Retirement-Savings-Shortfall.

of the average retirement portfolio is only half the problem. Another hurdle faced by savers is the lack of a disciplined plan to save for retirement. Less than a quarter of Americans regularly set aside money for long-term savings, and just fourteen percent have a formal financial plan. Only twenty-one percent of Americans make regular contributions to retirement accounts through work, and the same amount save for retirement outside of their employer plan.[15] However, it isn't all bad for the baby-boomer generation. According to a 2015 J.P. Morgan Asset Management report,[16] baby boomers are entering retirement, bringing with them a median level of household assets considerably higher than that of their parents' generation and, in all likelihood, far exceeding that of the next generation as well.

"The baby-boomer generation certainly benefited from the growth in pension-plan participation but was only marginally benefitted by the introduction of the IRA because of its low annual contribution limit, which started at just $1500 and is now just $5500 or $6500 if over the age of fifty in 2016. It is hard to be critical of a generation's retirement savings in general because there are so many factors that come into play in determining how much one is able to contribute to a retirement plan. For example, the median net worth of those fifty-five and older is $34,760. This family is basically one small illness away from bankruptcy. The median annual income of those fifty-five and older is $18,932. That being said, there is still no excuse for many of the baby-boomer generation who neglected participating in employer-offered pension plans or even making an IRA contribution—no matter how small. When you think that nearly forty percent of working households with members aged between twenty-five and sixty-four have no retirement savings, you can understand why so many baby boomers are worried about how they will be able to retire, if ever. This leads to another related problem associated with a lack of retirement saving for baby boomers—the impact on the social-security system.

---

15 Ibid.

16 Benjamin Mandel and Livia Wu, "The Long and Short of Baby Boomer Balance Sheets," J.P. Morgan Asset Management, October 2015, https://am.jpmorgan.com/gi/getdoc/1383246462222.

"The majority of retirees with annual incomes up to $32,600 get two-thirds to all of their income from social security. Even at higher incomes (up to $57,960), social security is the single biggest source of retirement income, accounting for almost half. Only the top one-fifth of seniors, with incomes above $57,960, do not rely on social security as their largest source of income, and most of them are still working. According to a report from the Congressional Budget Office (CBO) in July 2015, Social Security and Medicare threaten to swamp the federal budget over the next twenty-five years, in large part because of the pending retirement of seventy-five million baby boomers born between 1946 and 1964. The fear is that with so many boomers soon entering retirement, there won't be enough coming in from the current workers and employers whose taxes finance the system to pay for retirees. Social Security won't have enough to pay all promised benefits somewhere between 2025 and 2035. Pretty scary stuff; although the likelihood that social security will be cut off for lack of funding remains quite low, there is a strong chance that social-security benefits will be somewhat reduced when it comes time for the generation Xers and millennials to retire."

"Wow! I was always under the impression that the baby-boomer generation was in a better position for retirement than they actually are. I know my parents have been very focused on their retirement savings and are almost always talking about their retirement portfolios. I guess the majority of baby boomers haven't been as focused, which will seemingly impact the social-security system as a whole for my generation," Amy said.

"Yes, it is too bad, because a lot of baby boomers had opportunities to contribute to employer pension plans and always could have made contributions to an IRA, at least beginning in the mid-1970s.

"You will soon learn that even contributing just $1500 a year to an IRA on a consistent basis can create retirement portfolio worth many hundreds of thousands with some good investments—an amount that would certainly help supplement any social-security benefits received and would hopefully allow for a more financially secure retirement." But enough about the baby boomers, let's get into your generation—the generation Xers," John said.

"Sounds good," Amy replied.

GENERATION X

"According to Wikipedia, generation X, commonly abbreviated as gen X, is the generation born after the Western post–World War II baby boom. The years for generation X vary from one historian, government agency, and marketing firm to the next. The United States Social Security Administration defines generation X as 'those born roughly between 1964 and 1979,' while another federal agency, the US Department of Defense, sets the parameters as 1965 to 1977. The term 'generation X' was coined by the Magnum photographer Robert Capa in the early 1950s. He used it later as a title for a photo essay about young men and women growing up immediately after the Second World War. In a 2012 article for the Joint Center for Housing Studies of Harvard University, George Masnick wrote that the 'Census counted 82.1 million' Gen Xers in the United States.

"When it comes to generations, it is often difficult to generalize about common characteristics and traits. With a generation of some eighty million people, generalizations are often inaccurate and unhelpful. That being said, here are a few common traits and characteristics that many commentators associate with generation Xers.

1. Technology savvy. Because the Internet was being developed and revolutionized at the time generation Xers began hitting the workforce, it isn't surprising that some of the most influential websites of today, including YouTube, Amazon.com, and Google, were developed by generation Xers.

Independent thinkers. As the divorce rate rose in the 1970s, in many instances generation Xers were left to look after themselves while both parents entered the workforce. As a result, many generation Xers developed independence and self-reliance. They prefer to do things their own way and thrive in casual, friendly work environments.

2. Educated. Compared to the generations that came before it, generation X is a highly educated generation of Americans. More than half of Gen Xers have attended college at one time or another. The one issue is that hardly any of the education being taught today focuses on the importance of retirement planning and saving."

"I agree. I bet that if my friends and I were taught for even five minutes about the basics of retirement accounts and how tax deferral worked, we would all be in better retirement shape than we are now. I am, like most of my friends and colleagues, educated, and we consider ourselves independent thinkers, but for some reason the value of retirement savings is not something that ever came up as something that we needed to focus on," Amy said.

"You are not alone according to a 2015 report by J.P. Morgan Asset Management,[17] 'Generation X is likely to be worse off in retirement than the baby boomer generation—making the cohort the first post-war generation to be more ill-prepared for retirement than the previous one.' According to the J.P. Morgan report, generation Xers who are thirty-five to forty-four years old today have a median net worth of approximately $47,000, compared with $102,000 for those of a similar age twenty-five years ago. These lower starting retirement balances are troubling because they could certainly create significant and wide differences by the time the generation Xer reaches retirement age. Making matters even worse, according to the report, the median generation X household would have to more than double its savings rate, to 17.5 percent, in order to follow a similar trajectory to the baby-boomers' assets. The good news is that generation Xers are young enough that they can work on fixing any past retirement-saving mistakes and hopefully have the opportunity to make up any deficiencies as they become more entrenched in the workforce. I truly believe that if explained, the generation X and millennials will embrace the novelty of retirement savings and position themselves to be more secure in their retirement years than the baby-boomer generation."

"That would be nice," Amy replied.

"Yes, it is my goal to help educate the generation X and millennials about the importance of retirement saving and especially the gift of the Roth IRA. To this end, I have established a not-for-profit organization called Roth & Roll that will help educate and inspire Americans, but specifically generation Xers and millennials about the importance of retirement saving and the beauty of the Roth IRA. My hope is that I will be able to team up with a number of popular banks and financial institutions in order to make establishing

---

17 Ibid.

and making IRA contributions as seamless and cost effective as possible," John said.

"That sounds really exciting, and I am sure you will be able to help a lot of generation Xers like myself as well as millennials get excited about retirement saving and the Roth IRA."

"I really hope so. I certainly believe that the generation Xers and millennials are smart and savvy enough to understand the benefits of retirement savings and the huge boost that comes along with starting early. I just hope I am able to reach enough of them and make an impact. That leads me to the millennials."

MILLENNIALS

"According to Wikipedia, millennials (also known as the millennial generation or generation Y) is the demographic group following generation X. There are no precise dates when the generation starts and ends; most researchers and commentators use birth years ranging from the early 1980s to the early 2000s. By 2020, according to a Brookings Institution analysis,[18] one in three adults will be a millennial. There are an estimated eighty million millennials, and they are becoming an important generation for various business and technology reasons. Many articles and blogs have been written about the millennial-generation characteristics and traits and what sets them apart from other generations, but I believe they can be best described by the following four characteristics:

1. Technology driven. They've grown up with digital devices that bundle communication, entertainment, shopping, mapping, and education all in one. From an early age, smartphone use has been the norm. Millennials have always had Internet at home and in school. While all generations have experienced technological advances, the sheer amount of computational power and access to information

---

18 Fred Dews, "11 Facts about the Millennial Generation," June 2, 2014, http://www.brookings.edu/blogs/brookings-now/posts/2014/06/11-facts-about-the-millennial-generation.

that millennials have had at their fingertips since grade school is unmatched. Computational processing power has roughly doubled every two years, and storage prices continue to drop. Under these trends, millennials have come of age in a world in which the borders of technology have appeared unlimited. At the same time, the costs of creating and distributing all kinds of digital content—from books to music to software—have fallen dramatically. This phenomenon has created opportunities for this generation to be innovators as well as large consumers of technology.

Technology has become far more user friendly during millennials' lifetimes, particularly when compared to what previous generations encountered. They tend to use their smartphones for everything, from Internet surfing, to shopping, and even managing their financial affairs. Technology has helped the millennials connect easier with friends and family as well as be more free and mobile, but at the same time, it has the risk of creating a layer of dependency where spending a day away from their smartphone could lead to withdrawal. All in all, millennials have the capacity of turning all the new technology they have embraced into a great asset for them personally and financially.

2. Social media. Millennials are a sociable generation. Almost anything and everything digital, mobile or online, is essential for this generation. The most frequently used apps for millennials are Snapchat, Tinder, Facebook, Messenger, and Instagram. It can be argued that almost every aspect of millennials' lives is now documented online. The use of social media and the rise of a selfie culture have become a dominating trait for millennials. As a generation born into social media, millennials are naturally well versed in the pros and cons of social media, and they're proving themselves to be highly selective and savvy about the social-media choices they make. Social media have helped millennials interact with friends and family and keep themselves in the loop with current events, hobbies, and special interests. Social media have become effective ways of bringing people together no matter where they are; however, it can also have some potentially negative impacts. Privacy concerns and the ability to lead

less-documented lives have contributed to some millennials turning away from social media. Overall, social media continues to help define the millennial generation and have the potential to help them save for retirement by using a variety of high-tech and social-media tools.

3. Collaborate and cooperate. Millennials are changing the status quo, of top-down management styles, which had been largely synonymous with the baby-boomer generation. Millennials and teamwork are at the core of this shift. Millennials value greater flexibility and team collaboration. Millennials generally believe that by working together, they can help develop better products and services or make better decisions, including investment and financial decisions. Millennials have looked to leverage their familiarity with technology and social media to help them collaborate and cooperate in business and other environments.

4. Highly educated but overwhelmed with student debt. While most young adults today lack a college degree, millennials are still the most educated generation to date, with thirty-four percent having at least a bachelor's degree.[19] One of the most important characteristics of millennials is that many of them have come of age during a financially troubling time, as the oldest millennials were just around twenty-seven years old when the recession began in December 2007. As unemployment swelled from 2007 to 2009, many millennials struggled to find a job. This helped contribute to many millennials turning to higher education as a way to help secure employment.

"The one drawback of having more millennials earning bachelor degrees is the level of student debt, which is piling up. Total student outstanding loan debt surpassed $1 trillion by the end of the second quarter of 2014, making it the second largest category of household debt. With the gap in earnings between college- and high-school-educated workers, both large and

---

19 Pew Research Center, "The Rising Cost of Not Going to College," February 11, 2014, http://www.pewsocialtrends.org/2014/02/11/the-rising-cost-of-not-going-to-college/.

growing, college-educated millennials are more likely to earn higher wages and be employed than those without a college degree. A four-year degree yields approximately $570,000 more in lifetime earnings than a high-school diploma alone, while a two-year degree yields $170,000 more.[20]

"Millennials are currently about one-third of the labor force, and, as a generation, they have faced some difficult challenges in entering the workforce during the most pronounced downturn since the Great Recession. However, research also shows that generally the most important factor of a person's income is their level of education. And as the most educated generation in history, this will tend to enhance earnings for millennials over the course of their lifetimes."

"Thanks so much for the very detailed summary. The information is really helpful in offering me some perspective of where the millennial generation stands compared to the two previous ones," Amy said.

"OK, great. What is important to remember is that no matter the difference in characteristics, personalities, skills, and makeup, all generations have several important features in common; all generations are interested in a healthy, safe, and financially secure life for themselves and their families. To this end, retirement saving is a common issue that impacts each generation significantly and continues to shape the manner and style in which all Americans live. The fact is that millennials and generation Xers, due to their higher level of education and embrace of technology, have a potentially higher degree of earning capacity than the baby-boomer generation, which if educated, should lead to increased retirement saving. Recently we have seen all kinds of exciting technology advances in the area of retirement savings, which were developed in order to make retirement saving and investing easier. For example, many major banks and financial institutions offer smartphone apps where a set amount of money is automatically contributed to an IRA from the individual's personal bank account, making retirement saving easy and seamless. In addition, there has been a strong push in the financial industry to offer more cost-effective investment products for retirement accounts. This coupled with the emergence of discount brokers and newly popular retirement

---

20 US Treasury, 2014.

products, such as the self-directed IRA and Solo 401(k) plan, now, more than ever before, there are no longer any valid excuses for anyone not having a retirement account or making annual contributions, no matter how small. I will show you how saving just one dollar a day in a Roth IRA can lead to several hundred thousand dollars tax free at retirement with the right investment decisions. It's not rocket science, and it doesn't have to be financially painful. The key is starting and starting early. My hope is that the millennials and generation Xers will see the light and embrace retirement savings in greater numbers than their parents. I just hope I can make a difference," John said.

"I think you will," Amy said.

"I look forward to our next coffee meeting so I can spend some time talking about the basics of the IRA and the Roth IRA, which may be a bit dry, but I believe important in helping you understand how the IRA can become your golden ticket to living large," John said.

"Me too," Amy replied.

3

IRA BASICS AND THE ROTH IRA

AMY WAS REALLY excited about having the opportunity to meet with John again to discuss her retirement-planning options. Amy met John at a coffee shop located on the corner of 52nd Street and Third Avenue in New York City and ordered two nonfat cappuccinos and two blueberry muffins. They sat down at a quiet table toward the back of the coffee bar. Amy immediately thanked John for taking the time out of his busy day to meet with her and chat about retirement-planning options for her and her business.

John responded, "No problem; I owe your parents a few favors, especially your dad for letting me win at golf a few times."

Amy laughed and said, "OK, let me get started because I don't want to waste too much of your time."

Amy started from the beginning and explained to John about her promise to her dad about contributing to a Roth IRA each year and the type of mutual funds she had purchased with her Roth IRA. Amy also mentioned the 401(k) plan funds she had with her former employer and how she was able to make pretax as well as Roth contributions to the plan. Amy then explained to John how she had always watched her expenses, but with credit-card and student-debt payments due each month and with her NYC rent and living expenses, saving had certainly become more difficult now than when she was in college.

Amy mentioned a *Wall Street Journal* article[21] where she read that the ability to pay off student loans troubles more than half of millennials, including 34 percent of millennials with annual income levels over $75,000 who doubt they will be able to replay their student loans. Amy then mentioned that although her monthly credit and debt payments were relatively low, many of her friends carried a credit-card balance, on which they were charged interest.

Amy moved on to discuss her new business and the relative degree of success she has had early on. She mentioned to John that her accountant had said her Schedule C income from 2014 would be around $90,000, and she expected to do better next year. John was impressed with Amy's new business and how well she was doing. John mentioned that in addition to continuing to making Roth IRA contributions, assuming she and her husband's income level did not exceed the Roth IRA limits, a Solo 401(k) plan, which has a Roth component, is something that she should look into as a retirement plan for her business.

"I know you have had a lot of success investing your Roth IRA and 401(k) plan into traditional investments, such as mutual funds, but I bet you didn't now that the IRS allows retirement accounts to invest in alternative assets, such as real estate, precious metals, tax liens, private businesses, hard money lending," John said.

Amy was intrigued and surprised because she didn't know much about the Solo 401(k) plan but was very interested to learn more especially because it had a Roth component, and she had no idea that you could buy real estate and make alternative-asset investments with retirement funds.

"You certainly piqued my curiosity into how I can potentially continue to take advantage of a Roth IRA while also having a Roth Solo 401(k) plan," Amy stated. "Can you tell me more?"

"Well, I happen to be a tax attorney who knows quite a bit. So yes, I would be more than happy to fill you in."

---

21 Anna-Maria Lusard, "Millennials, Debt and More," *Wall Street Journal*, November 2, 2015.

"Would you?"

"As long as you buy the coffee and those wonderful muffins the next time we meet, no problem."

"That's a deal. How do we start?"

"Where everything starts…at the beginning."

Everyone has heard of a traditional IRA (or Individual Retirement Account). This is the basic way that many Americans put aside a few thousand dollars of tax-deferred or after-tax income every year for their retirement. Many are also familiar with other variations of the IRA, such as the Roth IRA, SEP IRA, SIMPLE IRA, self-directed IRA, and Rollover IRA. Don't worry if these terms and the others I am about to use are not completely familiar to you or if you are, like most people, somewhat hazy on the differences. I will explain them simply and fully in the chapters to come.

Similarly, most of us have signed up for a 401(k) plan at some point in our working years. This retirement-savings vehicle is available to employees of companies that offer such a plan. The employee's contribution to their 401(k) amounts to some percentage of their total compensation and generally is deducted directly from their paycheck. That money is tax deferred or could be after tax in some cases and is often matched by the employer, typically at a 3 percent rate in order to take advantage of the Safe Harbor 401(k) plan ERISA (Employee Retirement Income Security Act) rules.

As of 2011, there were approximately forty-seven million IRAs in the United States. As of 2012, approximately fifty-one million people participated in 401(k) plans. A lot of the people I work with have a mix of approaches in their retirement portfolio. They often have a traditional IRA and a 401(k), and they or their spouse may also have a Roth, SIMPLE IRA, or some other variation. Together, these accounts represent their retirement savings.

"I know you have had a Roth IRA for a number of years and are probably pretty familiar with all its features, but I think it is important to get a detailed overview of all the features of a pretax IRA, also known as a traditional IRA in addition to the Roth IRA, since the traditional IRA may be an option for you down the road. Also, I know you have a sister that is in her twenties and has just got a job, so knowing the ins and outs of how a traditional IRA and Roth IRA work could prove very useful to her since she will now be able to start putting money away for retirement. So, if you want to study up on IRAs first, I suggest you listen as much or as little as you'd like. If not, let me know and we can start discussing the power of tax-free investing." John said,

"Thanks – but I think I would like to learn more about the basics of IRA," Amy said.

THE BASICS

IRAs exist in many forms. The most common type is the traditional IRA, also known as the regular or original IRA, to which any person with earnings from employment may contribute. These types of IRA plans are referred to as contributory IRAs. IRAs that are used to receive assets distributed from other retirement plans are called Rollover IRAs. Roth IRAs combine the features of a regular IRA and a savings plan to produce a hybrid that adheres to its own set of rules. SEP and SIMPLE IRAs are technically IRAs even though their rules are quite similar to those of qualified plans.

An IRA, like the trust under an employer's qualified 401(k) plan, is exempt from tax pursuant to Internal Revenue Code (IRC) Section 408(e)(i), and an individual maintaining an IRA usually is not taxed on principal or earnings of the account or annuity until they are distributed by the trustee, custodian, or insurance company. A deductible contribution to an IRA thus offers the same tax advantage as an employer's contribution to a qualified plan: deferral of taxation of the contributed funds and investment returns thereon until the funds are withdrawn at retirement.

IRAs can be invested in securities, real estate, or virtually any other asset except life insurance, artworks, precious metals, and other collectibles. An IRA is subject to some of the prohibited-transaction rules of IRC Section 4975, which impose excise taxes on self-dealing transactions and may be subject to the unrelated business income tax (UBIT) if it invests in a trade or business via a pass-through entity (i.e., LLC) or uses margins or a nonrecourse loan.

THE HISTORY OF THE IRA

In 1974, The Employee Retirement Income Security Act of 1974 (ERISA) was enacted, giving us IRAs. IRAs were created by Congress to encourage savings by employees not covered by qualified plans of their employers.

In doing so, Congress was trying to solve a simple but major problem. For many millions of employees, provision is made for their retirement out of tax-free dollars by their participation in qualified retirement plans. However, many more employees do not have the opportunity to participate in qualified plans. Often, plans are not available because an employer is not willing to incur the costs of contributing to a retirement plan since, in general, the employer is required to contribute funds that are in addition to the compensation otherwise paid to employees. Employees who are not covered under a qualified plan are disadvantaged by the fact that earnings on their retirement savings are subject to tax and grow more slowly than the tax-sheltered earnings on contributions to a qualified plan.[22]

Unlike a 401(k) and related salary-reduction plans, IRAs are not run by employers. The enactment of IRAs extended to workers without pensions the same kind of tax advantages already granted to pension funds and the self-employed.

Starting in 1975, individuals were allowed to set up separate accounts at financial institutions and deduct the value of their contributions from their current taxable income. Only employees without employer pension plans were eligible to contribute, and their annual contributions were limited to 15 percent of pay or a maximum of $1,500. The investment returns of these accounts were also excluded from taxable income in the year earned, but withdrawals were to be included in taxable income in the year they occurred. To encourage use of the accounts for retirement saving, ERISA set a penalty of 10 percent additional tax on withdrawals by taxpayers before age 59½.

The Economic Recovery Tax Act of 1981 expanded IRA eligibility and increased maximum contributions. Starting in 1982, all persons with earnings could contribute to IRAs, whether or not they were in a pension plan,

---

22 HR Rep. No. 779, 93d Cong., 2d Sess., reprinted in 1974-3 CB 244, 367–368. See HR Rep. No. 220, 105th Cong., 1st Sess. 775 (1997).

and the maximum contribution was increased to 100 percent of earnings or $2,000. In response, tax returns with IRA contributions jumped from 4 percent of all returns with wage and salary income in 1981 to 14 percent in 1982 and 18 percent in 1986. The Tax Reform Act of 1986 restricted deductible IRA contributions. Starting in 1987, the act allowed deductible contributions only by an individual who was not covered by an employer pension plan (and whose spouse was not covered), and who had adjusted gross income between $25,000 and $35,000 (or, for joint returns, $40,000–$50,000). Those not qualifying for deductible contributions could still make nondeductible IRA contributions, thereby benefiting from the exclusion of investment returns from taxable income. The restriction caused tax returns with deductible IRA contributions to drop to 8 percent of all returns in 1987 and to decline slowly from there, reaching 4 percent in 1997.

The Taxpayer Relief Act of 1997 substantially raised the income limits applying to taxpayers covered by an employer plan. Eventually, those limits would be $50,000–$60,000 for single taxpayers (2005 and after) and $80,000–$100,000 for married taxpayers (2007 and after). Even higher limits ($150,000–$160,000) were enacted for married taxpayers previously disqualified from making deductible contributions solely by virtue of a spouse being covered by an employer plan. The act also allowed individuals to elect backloaded IRAs, called Roth IRAs, in which contributions are not deductible, but withdrawals, assuming certain age and holding requirements are satisfied, are not taxed—a treatment similar to that of a tax-exempt bond. These IRAs are phased out between $116,000 and $131,000 of income for singles and $183,000–$193,000 for joint returns. All but the highest-income taxpayers will thus be eligible for some type of fully tax-favored IRA. Regulations imposing penalties on premature withdrawals were also relaxed so that the accounts may be used to save for higher-education expenses or the first purchase of a home.

The Economic Growth and Tax Relief Reconciliation Act of 2001 (EGTRRA) increased the maximum allowable contribution to both deductible IRAs and Roth IRAs. For taxpayers under age fifty, the limit would reach $5,000 in 2008 and then would be indexed for inflation. Taxpayers aged fifty and above are allowed to make additional contributions up to a limit that would reach $1,000 in 2006. In 2016, an individual could make a maximum pretax or after-tax (Roth) IRA contribution of up to $5,500 or $6,500 if over the age of fifty.

While the primary point of the IRA rules is to assist with the gathering of retirement savings, a set of rollover rules is also included, which allows funds to be transferred tax free from one IRA to another and allows employees to avoid tax on some distributions from qualified plans by contributing the distributed money or property to an IRA.

THE POPULARITY OF THE IRA

According to the Employee Benefits Research Institute, as of 2012, Individual Retirement Accounts (IRAs) are a vital component of US retirement savings, holding more than 25 percent of all retirement assets in the nation. A substantial portion of these IRA assets originated in other tax-qualified retirement plans, such as defined benefit plans (pensions) and 401(k) plans, and were moved to IRAs through rollovers from those plans. Thus, a sizable percentage of current IRA accounts are a repository for assets built up in the employment-based retirement system, as individuals hold money in them before or during retirement.

According to the ICI Research Perspective publication of November 2013, there were $5.7 trillion in IRA assets at the end of the second quarter of 2013. IRAs represented more than one-quarter of US total retirement-market assets, compared with 17 percent two decades ago. IRAs also have risen in importance on household balance sheets. In June 2013, IRA assets were 9 percent of all household financial assets, up from 4 percent of assets two decades ago. In May 2013, 46.1 million or 38 percent of US households reported they owned IRAs.

Traditional IRAs were the most common type of IRA owned, followed by Roth IRAs and employer-sponsored IRAs, such as SEP IRAs.

WHAT IS AN IRA?

An individual retirement account (IRA) is a trust or custodial account set up in the United States for the exclusive benefit of you or your beneficiaries.

THE TRADITIONAL IRA

A traditional IRA primarily is a tax-deferred retirement-savings vehicle. Tax is generally deferred on traditional IRA contributions and earnings until the year the IRA owner takes a distribution. A traditional IRA is essentially any IRA that is not a Roth IRA or a SIMPLE IRA. In general, if you have income from working for yourself or someone else, you may establish and contribute to an IRA. The IRA can be a special account that you can set up with a bank, brokerage firm, or other institutional custodian. Alternatively, it can be an individual retirement annuity that you can purchase from an insurance company.

Who Can Set Up a Traditional IRA?

You can set up and make contributions to a traditional IRA if

- you (or, if you file a joint return, your spouse) received taxable compensation during the year and
- you were not age 70½ by the end of the year.

You can generally set up a traditional IRA if you have income from working for yourself or someone else. If your only income is social security or passive income, such as interest, dividends, rental income, or capital gains, that income would not be considered earned income and would not be considered income available for purposes of making an IRA contribution.

TAX-DEDUCTIBLE CONTRIBUTIONS

With traditional IRA contributions, you have the ability to take tax deductions. This was designed to encourage saving for retirement.

When you take advantage of tax deferral by investing in your employer-sponsored retirement plan, you not only put off paying income taxes on the money you contribute, you may also save money on the taxes you eventually will pay.

The money you contribute to a traditional IRA is pretax, which means that the contribution is deducted from your gross income and goes directly into your retirement-savings plan, so you're left with a smaller dollar amount in your paycheck that can be taxed by the IRS. As a result, you'll pay less in your current-income taxes for the year, because according to the IRS, you've earned less money. This can help you reduce your income-tax liability.

The benefit of tax-deductible contributions is simple. For example, if you are in a 30 percent income-tax bracket and you contribute $5,000 to a traditional IRA in a year, that's $5,000 of your salary on which you're not paying taxes this year, so you will be able to reduce your annual income tax bill by approximately $1,500 ($5,000 × 30 percent). In other words, you will receive an income-tax deduction for the $5,000 contribution, which will save you approximately $1,500 in tax payments. By making tax-deductible contributions, you are essentially paying yourself to save for your retirement.

All earnings generated from traditional IRA contributions are tax deferred until distributed.

WHAT IS TAX DEFERRAL?

Tax deferral literally means that you are putting off paying tax. The most common types of tax-deferred investments include those in IRAs or Qualified Retirement Plans (i.e., 401(k)s). Tax deferral means that all income, gains, and earnings, such as interest, dividends, rental income, royalties, or capital gains will accumulate tax free until the investor or IRA owner withdraws the funds and takes possession of them. As long as the funds remain in the retirement account, the funds will grow tax free. This allows your retirement funds to grow at a much faster pace than if the funds were held personally, allowing you to build for your retirement more quickly. And when you withdraw your IRA funds in the form of a distribution after you retire, you will likely be in a lower tax bracket and be able to keep more of what you have accumulated. So, using a traditional IRA as a retirement-savings vehicle, not only are you not paying taxes on the money you invested, you could be paying them at a lower rate when you finally do "take home" your money.

As long as the funds remain in the account, they grow without taxes eroding their value. This enables assets to accumulate at a faster rate, giving you an edge when saving for the long term. "We will spend a considerable amount of time talking about tax deferral the next time we meet, but I just wanted to introduce you to the concept of tax deferral," John said.

What Are the Advantages of Tax Deferral?

By using an IRA to make investments, the IRA owner is able to defer taxes on any investment returns, thus, allowing the IRA owner to benefit in three ways. The first benefit is tax-free growth: instead of paying tax on the returns of an investment, tax is paid only at a later date, leaving the investment to grow tax free without interruption. The second benefit of tax deferral is that IRA investments are usually made when the IRA owner is in his or her highest income-earning years and is thus subject to tax at a higher tax rate. The third benefit is the ability to defer taxes on investments in the face of increased federal income-tax rates. With tax rates at a historic low (the highest income-tax bracket in 1986 was 50 percent and in 2000 was 39.6 percent), the likelihood of higher federal income-tax rates in the near future is significant, especially with the financial strain the baby-boomer generation is expected to have on the federal budget. Thus, the ability to defer tax on investments until the IRA owner is 70½ and likelier to be in a lower income-tax bracket makes an IRA a highly attractive investment vehicle.

Tax Deferral by the Numbers

The following examples illustrate the powerful advantage of tax-deferred contributions and compounding through a traditional IRA versus making contributions to a taxable account.

Example 1

Joe is forty years old and makes a $5,000 contribution to an IRA. Assume Joe is in a 30 percent federal income-tax bracket. Joe invests his IRA funds and receives a 6 percent average annual return. When Joe retires at age seventy, his $5,000 contribution would be worth $21,609.71. If Joe had invested the $5,000 personally, the account would only be worth $14,033.97.

Example 2

Jane is thirty-five years old and makes a $5,000 contribution to an IRA. Jane makes a $5,000 contribution to her IRA each year until she reaches the age of seventy. Assume Jane is in a 30 percent federal income-tax bracket. Further assume that Jane was able to generate a 7 percent average annual return on her investment. When Jane retires at the age of seventy, her IRA account would be worth $792,950.21. If Jane had made these $5,000 contributions though a taxable account, the account would only be worth $490,707.49.

TRADITIONAL IRA CONTRIBUTIONS

IRC Section 219(a) permits a deduction for contributions to IRAs, which is allowable only if the contribution is in cash, the contributor is under the age of 70½ at the end of the taxable year, and the contribution is not a rollover. Also, a deductible contribution may not be made to an IRA that was started by another person and acquired by the taxpayer as beneficiary on that person's death unless the taxpayer is the surviving spouse.

How Much Can Be Contributed?

Traditional IRAs may receive several types of contributions: regular, spousal, rollover, transfer, recharacterization, and catch-up contributions.

REGULAR CONTRIBUTIONS

To be eligible to make regular contributions to a traditional IRA, an individual must satisfy the age requirements for that year and have earned income.

Age

There is a maximum-age restriction on when traditional IRA contributions can be made under the law. IRA owners cannot make IRA contributions beginning in the year in which they attain age 70½. Therefore, IRA owners who reach their seventieth birthday before July 1 of a given year cannot make an IRA contribution for that year because they will be 70½ before the end of the year.

There is no minimum age for making IRA contributions; however, financial institutions may have rules restricting minors from signing contracts.

Qualified Compensation

Individuals must have qualified compensation in order to be eligible to contribute to an IRA. In general, individuals must earn income from personal services rendered. The personal services rendered must be performed in the year the compensation is received. For most individuals, the income is shown on IRS Form W-2, Wage and Tax Statement, or IRS Form 1099-MISC.

What Is Compensation?

Generally, compensation is what you earn from working.

- Wages, Salaries, and so on

Wages, salaries, tips, professional fees, bonuses, and other amounts you receive for providing personal services are compensation.

- Commissions

An amount you receive that is a percentage of the profits or sale price is compensation.

- Self-Employment Income

If you are self-employed (a sole proprietor or a partner), compensation is the net earnings from your trade or business (provided your personal services are a material income-producing factor) reduced by the total of

- the deduction for contributions made on your behalf to retirement plans and
- the deduction allowed for one-half of your self-employment taxes.

- Alimony and Separate Maintenance

For IRA purposes, compensation includes any taxable alimony and separate maintenance payments you receive under a decree of divorce or separate maintenance.

- Military Differential Pay

For IRA purposes, compensation includes military differential pay you receive.

- Nontaxable Combat Pay

If you were a member of the US armed forces, compensation includes any nontaxable combat pay you received.

What Is Not Compensation?
Compensation does not include any of the following items:

- Earnings and profits from property, such as rental income, interest income, and dividend income
- Pension or annuity income
- Deferred compensation received (compensation payments postponed from a past year)
- Income from a partnership for which you do not provide services that are a material income-producing factor
- Any amounts (other than combat pay) you exclude from income, such as foreign-earned income and housing costs
- Income from social security and worker's compensation

What IS and is NOT Compensation for Purposes of an IRA

Compensation includes...	Compensation does NOT include...
Wage / Salaries	Earnings and profits from real estate investments
Commissions	Interest and dividend income
Self-employment income	Pension or annuity income
Alimony and separate maintenance	Deferred compensation
Military differential pay	• Income from certain partnerships that does not involve [?] ° Any amounts you exclude from income • Income from social security and worker's compensation
Nontaxable combat pay	

What if Both Spouses Have Compensation?
If both you and your spouse have compensation and are under age 70½, each of you can set up an IRA. You cannot both participate in the same IRA. If you file a joint return, only one of you needs to have compensation for each spouse to open his or her own IRA.

CONTRIBUTION LIMITS
Under the IRA rules, a contribution is deemed to have been made during a taxable year if it is made not later than the due date of that year's return (not including extensions) and is "made on account of such taxable year." For a tax-payer whose taxable year is the calendar year, a contribution for any year can thus be made as late as April 15 of the following year. For example, for 2015, you will be permitted to make IRA contributions up until April 15, 2016.

Regular Contributions
A regular traditional IRA contribution is limited to the lesser of the annual contribution limit or 100 percent of the individual's eligible compensation.

Example 1
If Jim earned $25,000 in W-2 compensation in a year and is under fifty years of age, Jim would be permitted to make a $5,500 IRA contribution in 2016.

Example 2
If Jim earned only $4,000 in W-2 compensation in a year and is under fifty years of age, Jim would only be permitted to make an IRA contribution of $4,000.

For the year 2016, you may contribute a maximum of $5,500 each year or $6,500 if you will reach the age of fifty by the end of the year. If you are not covered by an employer's retirement plan, you may take a deduction on your tax return for your contribution. However, if you are covered by an employer's plan, your IRA may be fully or partially deductible or not deductible at all depending on how much gross income you have.

Catch-up Contributions
Individuals who reach age fifty or older before the end of the taxable year may be eligible to contribute an additional amount to a traditional IRA as a catch-up contribution. The maximum annual amount that individuals may contribute to a traditional IRA as a catch-up contribution is $1,000.

Spousal Contributions
If an individual has no qualified compensation income but his or her spouse does, that individual may generally make a contribution to his or her IRA based on his or her spouse's compensation. This is generally referred to as "spousal contributions."

To be eligible for spousal contributions to a traditional IRA, the spouse without compensation income must not have reached the age of 70½ in the calendar year in which the contribution is being made. Also, to be eligible, the spouse must have eligible compensation and the couple must file a joint federal income-tax return.

The traditional IRA contribution limits are applied to each spouse as a separate IRA holder. Thus, if both a husband and wife are eligible to make IRA contributions, the IRA contribution limit for the couple in 2016 is the lesser of $11,000 (plus catch-up contributions, if eligible) or 100 percent of the combined eligible compensation. However, no more than the individual IRA individual contribution limit ($5,500, plus catch-up contributions, if eligible) may be contributed to either spouse's IRA.

If a spousal contribution is made, the spouse without compensation must establish a separate IRA. However, the compensated spouse is not required to have an IRA in order for the noncompensated spouse to make an IRA contribution.

Example 1
Jim and Jane are married and both earn $25,000 in W-2 compensation annually. Jim and Jane are both under fifty years of age. Jim and Jane would each be permitted to make a $5,500 yearly IRA contribution for 2016.

Example 2
Jim and Jane are married. Jim and Jane are both under fifty years of age. Jim did not earn any yearly compensation, but Jane earned $50,000 in W-2

annual compensation. Jim would still be able to make a spousal contribution of $5,000 based on Jane's eligible compensation for 2016.

Can I Contribute Less than the Maximum Allowed Contributions?

You are not required to make maximum contributions to your IRA each year. In fact, you are not required to make any contributions to your IRA in any year. However, if contributions to your traditional IRA for a year are less than the limit, you cannot contribute more after the due date of your return for that year to make up the difference.

Example

Jim, who is forty-seven, earned $47,000 in year 2014. Although he can contribute up to $5,500 for that year, Jim only made a contribution of $3,700. After April 15, 2015, Jim cannot make up the difference between his actual contributions for 2014 ($3,700) and his 2014 limit ($5,500). He cannot contribute $1,800 more than the limit for any later year.

What Happens if I Contribute More than the Maximum Contributions?

If contributions to your IRA for a year are more than the maximum IRA contribution limit, for that year, you can generally apply the excess contribution in one year to a later year if the contributions for that later year are less than the maximum allowed for that year. However, a penalty or additional tax may apply.

In general, if the excess contributions for a year are not withdrawn by the date your return for the year is due (including extensions), you are subject to a 6 percent tax. You must pay the 6 percent tax each year on excess amounts that remain in your traditional IRA at the end of your tax year. The tax cannot be more than 6 percent of the combined value of all your IRAs as of the end of your tax year. (The additional tax is figured on Form 5329.)

Example

Jane is thirty-nine years old and single; her compensation is $25,000, and she contributed $6,000 to her traditional IRA for 2015. Jane has made an excess contribution to her IRA of $500 ($6,000 minus the $5,500 limit).

The contribution earned $10 interest in 2014 and $5 interest in 2015 before the due date of the return, including extensions. Jane does not withdraw the $500 and the interest it earned by the due date of this return, including extensions. Jane would be liable for tax on the excess contribution made.

What Happens if I Withdraw an Excess Contribution Made by the Due Date of Filing My Tax Return?

You will not have to pay the 6 percent tax on an excess IRA contribution if you withdraw an excess contribution made during a tax year and you also withdraw any interest or other income earned on the excess contribution. You must complete your withdrawal by the date your tax return for that year is due, including extensions.

What Happens to the Excess Contributions That Were Withdrawn?

If you made an excess IRA contribution for the taxable year and withdrew the excess contribution prior to the filing of your tax return, you would not include the excess contribution in your gross income if both of the following conditions are met:

- No deduction is taken for the excess contribution.
- You withdraw the interest or other income earned on the excess contribution.

You can take into account any loss on the contribution while it was in the IRA when calculating the amount that must be withdrawn. For example, if you made an excess IRA contribution and the funds were used to make an investment that has since lost value (there is a loss), the net income you must withdraw may be a negative amount.

What Happens to the Income or Interest Earned on the Excess Contribution?

You must include in your gross income the interest or other income that was earned on the excess contribution. Report it on your return for the year in which the excess contribution was made. Your withdrawal of interest or other income may be subject to an additional 10 percent tax on early distributions, which I'll discuss later.

Are All Contributions to a Traditional IRA Deductible?

Before 1987, IRA owners were allowed to deduct all eligible traditional IRA contributions on their federal income-tax returns. The Tax Reform Act of 1986 put restrictions on who may claim income-tax deductions for traditional IRA contributions, but it allowed IRA owners to make nondeductible contributions.

If I Have a 401(k), Can I Still Contribute to an IRA?

In the past, an active participant in an employer-sponsored retirement plan could not have an IRA. This restriction was removed in 1981, but it reappeared in modified form in 1986. Since 1986, the normal ceiling on deductible IRA contributions has been reduced if the taxpayer is an "active participant" of a qualified retirement plan and his or her adjusted gross income exceeds a threshold amount. In other words, rather than disqualifying all employees participating in employer-sponsored plans, the IRA deduction is phased out for taxpayers whose incomes exceed specified thresholds.

What IRA Contributions Are Deductible?

In general, an IRA owner is able to deduct a traditional IRA contribution, or a portion of an IRA contribution, depending on the IRA owner's active participation in an employer-sponsored retirement plan, such as a 401(k) plan; marital status; and modified adjusted gross income (MAGI).

Active Participation in an Employer-Sponsored Retirement Plan

An IRA owner is an active participant in an employer-sponsored retirement plan if he or she is participating in or receiving contributions from an employer-sponsored retirement plan, such as a 401(k) plan. In other words, an individual is an active participant for any taxable year during which benefits accrue to him or her under a qualified plan, such as a 401(k) plan maintained by his or her employer. If an individual is an active participant in an employer-sponsored retirement plan, the deductibility of an IRA contribution depends on the IRA owner's MAGI.

If I'm Married and Only One Spouse Is an Active Participant in a Plan, How Do We Determine MAGI?

If you file a joint income-tax return with your spouse, and only one spouse is considered an active participant, the deductibility of the traditional IRA contribution made by the spouse who is not an active participant in an employer-sponsored retirement plan is dependent on the couple's MAGI.

What Type of Plans Are Considered "Retirement Plans" for Deductibility Purposes?

An IRA owner is treated as an active participant in an employer-sponsored retirement plan if the IRA owner is an active participant in any of the following retirement plans:

- A qualified plan described in IRC Section 401(a), including a 401(k) plan
- An annuity plan described in IRC Section 403(a)
- An annuity contract or custodial account described in IRC Section 403(b)
- A SEP Plan described in IRC Section 408(p)
- A trust described in IRC Section 501(c)(18)
- A plan for federal, state, local government employees, or for an agency or instrumentality thereof (other than an IRC Section 457(b) plan).

What Is the Modified Adjusted Gross Income (MAGI) Threshold?

In general, for purposes of determining the deductibility of traditional IRA contributions, an individual's MAGI is calculated to be the individual's adjusted gross income without taking into consideration the tax deduction for traditional IRA contributions. An individual's MAGI can be found on the individual's federal income-tax return (i.e., IRS Form 1040, U.S. Individual Income Tax Return).

For an individual who is an active participant in an employer-sponsored retirement plan or is married to an active participant, the deductibility of a traditional IRA contribution depends on such an individual's MAGI as illustrated on the IRS Form 1040.

If the IRA owner's MAGI is equal to or below the annual minimum threshold, the IRA owner is eligible to take a deduction for the full amount of the IRA contribution up to the statutory limit (i.e., $5,500 if the individual is under the age of fifty). However, if the individual's MAGI exceeds the minimum threshold, the IRA owner will only be able to deduct a portion of the traditional IRA contribution until the maximum qualifying income level is reached.

What Is the Traditional IRA Deductibility Threshold for 2016?

In 2016, if you are single and covered by an employer's plan, your contribution is fully deductible if your adjusted gross income (AGI) is less than $61,000 and not deductible at all when your AGI reaches $70,000. Between $61,000 and $71,000 the deduction is gradually phased out. For married individuals, the phase-out range is from $98,000 to $118,000, if the IRA participant is covered by an employer plan. For an IRA participant who is not covered by a plan but whose spouse is covered, the phase-out range is $184,000–$194,000.

Why Is the Traditional IRA Deduction Threshold So Low?

It is believed that the relatively low ceiling on IRA deductions is intended to keep IRAs from becoming a significant alternative to qualified plans for highly compensated employees.

TRADITIONAL IRA NONDEDUCTIBLE CONTRIBUTIONS

An individual who is unable to deduct all or part of a traditional IRA contribution is still permitted to make a nondeductible traditional IRA contribution of up to the lesser of the applicable annual limit (i.e., $5,500 if the individual is under the age of fifty for 2015) or 100 percent of earned income.

An IRA owner who makes a nondeductible traditional IRA contribution must report the nondeductible amount to the IRS on Form 8606, which should be filed with the IRA owner's individual federal income-tax return (Form 1040).

Who Is Responsible for Determining the Deductibility of a Traditional IRA Contribution?

The IRA owner and not the IRA custodian is responsible for determining the deductibility of a traditional IRA contribution.

How Do the Contributions Limits Apply to Husband and Wives?

Generally, the husband and wife are treated separately under the IRA rules. If both spouses are employed, each can deduct contributions up to the lesser of the dollar ceiling or 100 percent of that spouse's compensation.

Can I Still Make IRA Contributions Even if I Earn More Money than the Phase-Out Limit?

A taxpayer phased out of making tax-deductible contributions is still allowed to make nondeductible contributions in the amount of $5,500 or $6,500, as applicable for 2016.

Distributions

The IRS's approach to helping people invest and save their retirement funds is a lot like a football game. If the quarterback takes too much time calling an offensive play, the team will face a penalty. Similarly, if a traditional IRA owner withdraws his or her funds too early from an IRA, the IRA owner will face an early distribution tax. On the other hand, if the quarterback calls an offensive play too quickly before his teammates are ready, the team will be in violation of the rules, just as you will face a penalty for taking an early distribution from your traditional IRA.

The required distribution rules are believed to have been designed by Congress to ensure that IRAs are mainly used as retirement-savings vehicles, not as a medium to build wealth for transfer to heirs.

In general, the distribution rules deal separately for distributions to IRA owners and distributions to beneficiaries after the death of an IRA owner.

When Can Distributions Be Taken from an IRA?

An IRA owner may take distributions from his or her IRA at any time. The determination of whether the distribution is taxed depends on the type of IRA (i.e., traditional or Roth); the age of the IRA owner; and in the case of a Roth IRA, the duration of time the account has been established.

Are Traditional IRA Distributions Subject to Tax?

Yes, the IRA owner is required to include traditional IRA distributions in his or her taxable gross income. The IRA owner who receives a distribution will report the distribution on his or her individual federal income-tax return (Form 1040) and pay tax on the distribution based on the individual's federal income-tax rate.

What Type of Transactions Are Exempted from the Traditional IRA Distribution Rules?

In general, the following IRA-related transactions are not treated as distributions subject to tax:

- rollovers;
- transfers;
- recharacterizations;
- revoked IRA within seven-day period; and
- the portion of a distribution relating to nondeductible traditional IRA contributions.

Early Distributions

In general, traditional IRAs are designed to encourage retirement saving and at the same time discourage people from taking money away from their retirement savings before reaching the age of 59½. The age 59½ was selected by Congress because it was believed to be the age when one began transitioning from active employment to retirement.

Are Early Distributions Subject to an Additional Tax?

Yes. In general, the IRS assesses a 10 percent penalty on the taxable portion of early distributions. However, the 10 percent early-distribution penalty does not apply in the following situations.

1. **Death of the IRA Owner**

   An IRA distribution to beneficiaries is not subject to the 10 percent early-distribution penalty. In other words, upon the death of the IRA owner, the distribution of the owner's IRA to his or her beneficiaries is not subject to the 10 percent penalty.

2. **Disability**

   Distributions received by a disabled IRA owner are not subject to the 10 percent early-distribution penalty. Prior to making the disability distribution, the financial organization may require written evidence from the disabled IRA owner to verify disability. The IRA owner can demonstrate this by using IRS Form 1040, Schedule R, Credit for the Elderly or Disabled.

3. **Rollovers and Conversions**

   Amounts rolled over to an IRA or properly converted to an IRA are not subject to the 10 percent early-distribution penalty.

4. **First-Time Homebuyer Expenses**

   Distributions taken for qualified first-time homebuyer expenses are not subject to the 10 percent early-distribution penalty. There is a $10,000 lifetime limit with this exemption.

5. **Return of Nondeductible Contributions**

   The 10 percent early-distribution penalty would not apply to the portion of a distribution that represents a return of nondeductible contributions or after-tax assets received through a rollover.

6. **Substantially Equal Periodic Payment**

   The 10 percent early-distribution penalty shall not apply to distributions that are part of a series of substantially equal periodic payments made at least annually over the IRA owner's life expectancy or joint life expectancy of the IRA owner and his or her beneficiary. The IRA holder must make a specific election under IRC Section 72 with the

IRA custodian to take advantage of this election. The rules that apply to this option are quite complex, so it is best to consult with a tax attorney or CPA.

7. **Health Insurance**

   An IRA owner who received federal or state unemployment compensation for twelve consecutive weeks may take IRA distributions to pay for health insurance. These distributions are not subject to the 10 percent early-distribution penalty. The IRA owner must take a distribution in the year he received his unemployment or in the year that follows. This exemption does not apply to distributions taken more than sixty days after the IRA owner regains employment.

8. **Medical Expenses**

   Distributions used for reimbursed medical expenses that exceed 7.5 percent of the IRA owner's adjusted gross income are not subject to the 10 percent early-distribution penalty.

9. **Higher-Education Expenses**

   IRA distributions used for qualified education expenses of the IRA owner, his or her spouse, or the spouse's child or grandchild are not subject to the 10 percent early-distribution penalty.

10. **IRS Levy**

    Distributions taken because of IRS tax levies imposed on the IRA owner are not subject to the 10 percent early-distribution penalty.

11. **Qualified Reservist Distributions**

    Qualified reservists (including National Guard personnel) called to active duty after September 11, 2001, for a period of at least 180 days or an indefinite amount of time, are permitted to take penalty-free distributions from their IRA. This applies to distributions taken between the date of the order or call to duty and the end of the active-duty period. **Note:** The distribution taken will still be subject to federal income tax.

REQUIRED DISTRIBUTIONS TO IRA OWNERS

The required minimum distribution rules (RMD) were created in order to guarantee the flow of IRA funds into the federal income-tax system as well as to encourage IRA owners to use their retirement funds during their retirement.

You don't have to be concerned about taking distributions from a retirement plan until the year in which you turn 70½. To avoid penalty, an IRA owner must comply with what are called the required distribution rules, also known as the minimum distribution rules. The required distribution rules require that an IRA owner take a minimum distribution amount from his or her retirement account each year, generally beginning in the year the IRA owner turns 70½. April 1 of the year following the calendar year during which the owner reaches age 70½ is the "required beginning date." The minimum distribution amount for a "distribution calendar year" is the owner's "account" for the year, divided by an "applicable distribution period." An owner's distribution calendar years are the years during which he or she reaches age 70½ and each subsequent year during his or her life. The "applicable distribution period" changes annually and is usually taken from a Uniform Lifetime Table found in the IRC. It is, for example, 27.4 for the distribution calendar year during which an owner reaches age seventy, 18.7 for the year of his or her eightieth birthday, and 11.4 for the year during which an owner turns ninety. The minimum distribution for the first distribution calendar year must be made by April 1 of the following year (the required beginning date), and distributions for the distribution calendar year containing the required beginning date and all other years must be made by the end of the year.

If your spouse is your beneficiary and is more than ten years younger than you, you will be required to use a different and more favorable table called the Joint Life and Last Survivor Table.

What Is the Required Beginning Date?
The IRA owner must begin taking RMDs in the year he or she turns 70½. The IRA owner may delay taking the first year's RMD until April 1 following the year in which they reach age 70½. This April 1 date is called the required beginning date (RBD). In all subsequent years, RMDs must be taken by December 31.

For example: Joe turned age 70 on June 23, 2013 and therefore will be age 70½ in 2013. Joe must take his 2013 RMD by April 1, 2014. Joe would also need to take his second RMD—the 2014 RMD—by December 31, 2014.

How Do You Calculate the RMD?

To determine an RMD for an IRA, the IRA owner will need to divide the December 31 prior year-end IRA balance by the applicable distribution period.

- IRA balance
  The IRA owner's IRA balance on December 31 of the prior year is used to calculate an RMD. Any outstanding rollovers, transfers, and recharacterizations must be added to the prior year-end balance.
- Distribution period
  The distribution period applicable to an IRA owner is a number that represents the average life-expectancy tables.

In general, during an IRA owner's lifetime, the IRS final regulations provide for a uniform distribution period equal to the joint life expectancy of the IRA owner and a hypothetical beneficiary exactly ten years younger. The life expectancy is determined using a Uniform Lifetime Table issued by the IRS each year. In order to obtain the applicable distribution period, simply use the age of the IRA owner in the year for which the distribution is being taken and refer to the Uniform Lifetime Table issued by the IRS.

Exception to Using the Uniform Lifetime Table

An exception to using the Uniform Lifetime Table arises if an IRA owner's spouse who is more than ten years younger than the IRA owner is named as the sole beneficiary of the IRA. In this case, the IRA owner may use a longer distribution period as determined by the actual joint life expectancy found in the IRS's Joint and Last Survivor Table. Note that the new IRA owner may take a distribution in excess of the RMD amount.

Who Is Responsible for Making the RMD Calculations?

The IRA custodian (the financial institutions) is required to submit reports to the IRS and to the IRA owner regarding RMDs. If an RMD is required to be taken from an IRA for a calendar year and the IRA owner is alive at the beginning of the year, the IRA custodian that held the IRA as of December 31 of the prior year must provide a statement to the IRA owner to report the due date of the RMD and, in most cases, the amount that is due. The IRA custodian is required to send this report to the IRA owner by January 31 of the year for which the RMD is required.

What if the RMD Is Not Made?
If an IRA owner's distribution from his or her IRA is less than the year's RMD amount, the difference is an excess accumulation, and the IRA owner is subject to a 50 percent penalty tax, which must be paid to the IRS. The IRA custodian does not assess or collect the penalty as the penalty is paid to the IRS with the filing of Form 5329, Additional Taxes on Qualified Plans and Other Tax-Favored Accounts. For example, if the IRA owner was required to take an RMD of $1,000 but only took a $500 distribution, the IRA owner would be subject to a penalty tax of $250 (amount of distribution shortfall less $500 multiplied by 50 percent penalty).

BENEFICIARY DISTRIBUTIONS
When an IRA owner dies, the financial institution holding the IRA account must follow certain procedures when making distributions to the beneficiaries of a deceased IRA owner. It is important to remember that if the IRA beneficiary does not take a required distribution, he or she will be subject to a 50 percent excess accumulation penalty. For example, if an IRA beneficiary was required to take a distribution of $1,000 but only took a distribution of $500, the IRA beneficiary would be subject to a penalty tax of $250 (amount of distribution shortfall less $500 multiplied by 50 percent penalty).

Beneficiary Distribution Options
There are a number of distribution options available to a designated IRA beneficiary, generally dependent on whether the deceased IRA owner's sole primary beneficiary is a spouse and whether the deceased IRA owner has reached 70½, the age for RMDs. Remember, a living IRA owner is not required to take an RMD until the IRA owner reaches the age of 70½.

Distribution Option if the IRA Beneficiary Is a Spouse and the IRA Owner Was under the Age of 70½ When He or She Died

If an IRA owner dies before he or she reaches the age of 70½ and designates a spouse as the primary and sole beneficiary, the spouse IRA beneficiary has the following options:

1. **Transfer.** A surviving spouse who is the sole beneficiary of a deceased spouse's IRA and has an "unlimited right to withdraw" from it may, at any time after the owner's death, elect to treat the IRA as though he or she were its owner rather than its beneficiary. The election may only be made if the spouse is the only beneficiary of the IRA. In other words, the deceased IRA owner's IRA may be transferred to the surviving spouse's IRA. Essentially, the surviving spouse may roll over the deceased IRA owner's IRA into his or her own.

2. **Life-expectancy rule.** Minimum distributions to an electing surviving spouse are determined under the rules for the deceased IRA owner, not the rules for beneficiaries, except that the election may not cause there to be a minimum distribution for the year of the owner's death if the owner died before his or her required beginning date. For example, if a surviving spouse is seventy-five years old when a sixty-four-year-old IRA owner dies, no distribution is required for the year of death, even if the spouse makes the election, even though the spouse's required beginning date occurred before that year. An electing spouse is treated as IRA owner "for all purposes under the IRC," including the premature-withdrawal penalty. In other words, a surviving spouse can wait until the year the deceased spouse would have turned 70½ to begin receiving required distributions. This deferral option is only available to a surviving spouse IRA beneficiary. The surviving spouse can choose the option even if she is over the age of 70½ as long as the account remains in the deceased IRA owner's name.

If a surviving spouse elects to use the Life Expectancy Payment methods to take IRA distributions, the surviving spouse would have to do the following:

a. Ascertain the IRA value. The surviving spouse must determine the IRA value of the deceased IRA owner's balance as of December 31 of the year before the IRA owner would have turned 70½ to calculate the first required distribution.
b. Calculate the applicable distribution period. Using the surviving spouse's age in the year the deceased IRA owner would have turned 70½, the surviving spouse must look up the appropriate life-expectancy factor as provided by the IRS—also called the applicable distribution period.
c. Calculate the required distribution. The surviving spouse would need to calculate the first required distribution, which is calculated by dividing the account balance by the applicable distribution period. That amount must be distributed by December 31 of the year in which the deceased IRA owner would have turned 70½.

Example 1

Joe was born June 10, 1939, and died on July 1, 2007, at age 68—before reaching his RBD. His wife, Jane, is the sole beneficiary of his IRA. Jane will elect to use the life-expectancy rule to determine required distributions. Jane will be able to defer distributions until the year 2010, the year Joe would have turned 70½. To compute the required distribution, Jane would have to use the account balance as of December 31, 2009, the year before Joe would have turned 70½.

Example 2

If Jim was the sole primary beneficiary of his wife's IRA when she died during 2007 at age 68, distributions to him must begin by the end of the calendar year during which his wife would have reached age 70½. If that year is 2009 and Jim is 65 on his birthday during 2009, the applicable distribution period for the year is twenty-one, which is his life expectancy as of that birthday, and the minimum distribution for the year is the account balance as of the end of 2008, divided by twenty-one.

3. **Five-Year Rule.** If the surviving spouse elects to use the five-year method, all of the deceased IRA holder's IRA assets must be distributed within five years of the IRA holder's death. In actuality, the surviving spouse has a little more than five years to withdraw the IRA assets. This is because the official distribution deadline is December 31 of the year continuing the fifth anniversary of the IRA holder's death. For example, if the IRA holder dies on April 12, 2009, the deceased IRA holder's IRA assets would not need to be completely distributed until December 31, 2014—five years and almost nine months.

    a. How much must be distributed over the five-year period?

    The five-year rule option only requires that all assets be distributed from the IRA account by December 31 of the year of the fifth anniversary of the IRA holder's death, but it places no limitations on the amount of each annual payment. What this means is that the IRA beneficiary can receive the entire amount as a lump sum immediately after the IRA holder's death, in equal monthly installments or even nothing at all until December 31 of the fifth and final year.

When Is Using the Five-Year Rule Mandatory for an IRA Beneficiary?

The five-year rule option is mandatory for an IRA beneficiary when both of the following occur:

1. The IRA holder dies before the age of 70½.
2. The deceased IRA holder's IRA did not designate a beneficiary as of September 30 of the year of his or her death.

What Distribution Is Required When the Surviving Spouse Beneficiary Dies?

If a surviving spouse beneficiary inherits an IRA and begins taking required distributions on December 31 of the year after the deceased IRA holder's death but dies before all assets of the retirement account are distributed, the surviving spouse's beneficiary must take distributions in the following form:

- In the year of the surviving spouse's death, the spouse's beneficiary will divide the account balance as of December 31 of the year before the surviving spouse's death by the applicable distribution period (ADP) for the surviving spouse in the year of the spouse's death.
- For the second year and beyond, the surviving spouse's beneficiary will reduce the ADP determined in the above paragraph by one and divide it into the account balance as of the previous December 31. This computation continues using this method until the entire IRA account has a zero balance.

Distribution Option if the IRA Beneficiary Is a Nonspouse and the IRA Owner was under the Age of 70½ When He or She Died

If an IRA holders dies and designates a nonspouse a beneficiary as the primary beneficiary of his or her IRA, the nonspouse beneficiary will typically have only one option for taking IRA distributions—the life-expectancy rules.

The Life-Expectancy Rules

The IRS allows a nonspouse beneficiary to use the life-expectancy rules to calculate the IRA required distributions after the deceased IRA holder's death. The IRA distributions must begin to be taken no later than December 31 of the year after the death of the deceased IRA holder's death. There are no additional opportunities for delaying IRA distributions for nonspouse beneficiaries.

If distributions are made under the life-expectancy rule to a designated nonspouse beneficiary, the ADP for the calendar year immediately after the year of the IRA owner's death is the beneficiary's remaining life expectancy as of his or her birthday during that year, and the applicable period is reduced by one for each subsequent distribution calendar year. Unlike in the case of a spouse beneficiary, which is required to use the life expectancy of the deceased IRA owner for purposes of calculating the annual required distribution amount, a nonspouse beneficiary is required to use his or her life expectancy when calculating the annual required distribution amounts. For example, if Mary is designated as sole beneficiary of an IRA of her mother, who dies during 2007, her first distribution calendar year is 2008. If she becomes sixty years old during that year, the applicable distribution period would be based on the life expectancy of a sixty-year-old.

Five-Year Rule

The five-year rule applies to a nonspouse beneficiary if allowed by the IRA's terms or at the election of the deceased IRA owner or beneficiary.

Can a Nonspouse IRA Beneficiary Do a Roth IRA Conversion?

No. If a nonspouse IRA beneficiary inherits an IRA, the nonspouse IRA beneficiary does not have the option to convert the traditional inherited IRA to a Roth IRA.

Distribution Option if the IRA Beneficiary Is a Nonindividual (i.e., a Qualified Trust) and the IRA Owner Was under the Age of 70½ When He or She Died

In general, if a nonindividual, such as a trust, is designated as the beneficiary of an IRA and the IRA owner was under the age of 70½ when he or she died, the "qualified" trust would have the option to distribute the funds over a five-year period or based on the life expectancy of the oldest beneficiary of the "qualified" trust.

What Is the Advantage of Designating a Trust as IRA Beneficiary?

There are a number of advantages to naming a trust as beneficiary of an IRA. The most common purpose is for estate-tax purposes. The use of a trust for estate-planning purposes is a common method used to minimize estate taxes and maximize the amount that can be transferred to family members tax free.

The trust- and estate-tax rules are quite complex and beyond the scope of this book, but below is a brief overview of how the estate-tax rules work.

Maximizing Your Estate Tax "Exclusion Amount"

Upon death, federal law allows each individual to transfer a certain amount, known as the "exclusion amount" of his or her assets tax free. The "exclusion amount" for 2016 is $5.450 million or $10.90 million per couple. What this means is that an individual can transfer $5.450 million to his or her heirs over a lifetime without the transfer being subject to estate tax. In addition, an individual may transfer an unlimited amount upon his or her death to a surviving spouse tax free. Without proper estate planning, an individual may squander some or all of the "exclusion amount."

For example, a husband and wife have a combined net worth of less than $11 million. If the husband dies in 2016 and leaves all his assets to his wife, never using his $5 million exclusion amount, the wife would receive all the funds tax free since all funds transferred to a surviving spouse are tax free; however, when the surviving spouse dies, she would only be able to use her exclusion amount to pass her assets to her children, which would likely be insufficient to protect all assets from estate tax. In other words, if the husband had given his $5 million to the children when he died instead of to his spouse, his entire estate could have been transferred tax free, and the surviving spouse could have used his or her exclusion amount to shelter the assets from tax that would pass to the children upon her subsequent death. Now, some might say, "Wait a minute. Do I really want to leave so much money to my children without any restrictions?" This is where the idea of using a trust has so much value. By designating a trust as the IRA beneficiary, when the husband dies, he can direct his $5 million exclusion amount to the trust, which can designate his wife as the trust beneficiary and then the children upon her death. Because the assets of the trust do not belong to the wife technically, upon her death the trust's assets can be passed to the children tax free, allowing the wife to give additional amounts. Thus, by using the trust, the husband would be able to use his exclusion to pass his assets to his spouse and upon her death to his children tax free as well as freeing up his wife's exclusion to transfer additional funds to her children in satisfaction of her "exclusion amount."

Maintaining Control after Death

In certain situations, the IRA holder may wish to maintain some control and impose some oversight about how distributable IRA funds may be spent by a beneficiary of a "qualified trust." For example, if (i) the IRA holder has a special-needs child who relies on government benefits, (ii) the beneficiary is a minor, or (iii) the beneficiary has financial difficulties or has substance-abuse problems, using a trust can provide the IRA holder with the assurance that an appointed trustee will have control in terms of the amount of trust funds that are being distributed.

What Happens to the RMDs if an IRA Owner Does Not Have a Designated Beneficiary?

If an IRA owner does not have a designated beneficiary for his or her IRA, then the distribution options are limited. In essence, if the beneficiary of the deceased IRA owner's IRA is not designated, and if the IRA owner dies before his or her required beginning distribution date, the five-year distribution rule would apply, and the entire IRA account must be distributed by December 31 of the year containing the fifth anniversary of the IRA owner's death.

If there is no designated IRA beneficiary, the life-expectancy rule is not an option, and the IRA beneficiary as per the deceased IRA holder's will or pursuant to probate must use the five-year rule.

What Happens to the RMD if an IRA Owner Dies and Has Multiple IRAs with Different Beneficiaries?

If an IRA owner dies and has multiple IRAs with different beneficiaries, then each IRA is treated separately for purposes of the required distribution rules. In other words, the determination of which distribution rules would apply would be separate for each IRA.

What Happens if an IRA Owner Dies and Has Multiple Beneficiaries for One IRA?

There are specific distribution rules that would apply in determining the required IRA distributions in the case of an IRA owner who dies with an IRA, which has multiple beneficiaries.

The date for determining the beneficiaries of an IRA is September 30 of the year following the IRA holder's death. If, on that date, all the beneficiaries of the deceased IRA owner's IRA are designated beneficiaries, then the beneficiaries have until December 31 to divide the account so that each beneficiary gets his or her separate share. If the IRA is split in a timely manner, then the required distribution rules would apply separately to each share of the split IRA.

In a case in which you have multiple beneficiaries for a deceased IRA owner's IRA, all beneficiaries are treated as nonspouse beneficiaries even if one of them is your spouse. As a result, the most limiting rules—those that will generally produce the most accelerated distribution payment schedule—will apply to all beneficiaries. For example, if a deceased IRA owner names her spouse and children, the beneficiaries must choose from the options available to the surviving spouse's children because children have more restricted distribution options than spouses.

The Life-Expectancy Rules

The life-expectancy-distribution rule generally applies when there are multiple IRA beneficiaries on a single IRA. However, the least favorable distribution period is the one the IRA beneficiaries are required to use. The IRA must be distributed over the single life expectancy of the oldest beneficiary. This will ultimately create the largest possible annual distribution and as a result will reduce the size of the IRA the quickest (exactly what the government wants). The oldest beneficiary's life expectancy is determined based on his or her age in the first distribution year. Once the distribution amount is determined, it is allocated among the IRA beneficiaries pro rata based on their IRA interests.

For example, Joe who is forty-five years old dies in 2014 and names his mother and his two children as equal beneficiaries of his IRA. The beneficiaries will use the life-expectancy method for determining the distribution amounts. Since Joe's mother is the oldest beneficiary, Joe's IRA must be distributed over her life expectancy.

Five-Year Rule

If, by the IRA's terms, or at the election of the deceased IRA owner or beneficiary, the five-year distribution option were selected, the five-year distribution option would apply to all beneficiaries. Even if the life expectancy option would be available to the spouse, the spouse would nevertheless be prohibited from using the life-expectancy option if the spouse is one of the multiple beneficiaries since the five-year option would be the least favorable distribution period.

How Is the IRA Transferred to the Beneficiaries?

When transferring the deceased IRA owner's account to the beneficiaries, the IRA assets must be transferred directly from the current custodian of the IRA to the beneficiary's new IRA custodian. The beneficiary must not have control of any of the IRA funds at any time.

In the case of a nonspouse beneficiary, the account must remain in the name of the deceased IRA holder. Thus, in the case of a nonspouse beneficiary, the IRA must remain in the name of the deceased IRA owner. However, if the spouse is one of the beneficiaries, the spouse would be able to roll his or her share into an existing or new IRA in the spouse's name.

Whose Name Should Go on the Account?

In the case of a nonspouse beneficiary, the IRS requires that the new account be in the name of the deceased IRA holder's name. (If a spouse is named as the beneficiary, then the spouse may roll over the deceased spouse's IRA into an IRA in the name of the spouse.) Typically, many custodians will modify the name of the account by including the name of the deceased IRA owner and the beneficiary. For example, Dave Smith died, leaving his IRA to his two children, John and Steve. The children elect to split the IRA into two separate IRAs so that each can manage his own account. The IRA custodian set up the two new IRA accounts in Dave's name and transferred half of Dave's original IRA into each one. The title on John's account would be something like: Dave Smith, Deceased, for the benefit of (or FBO) John Smith. The other account is titled Dave Smith, Deceased, for the benefit of (or FBO) Steve Smith.

How Is This Reported to the IRS?

IRA custodians are required to comply with a number of reporting requirements after an IRA holder dies. Generally the IRA custodian must file Form 5498 for each beneficiary. The IRS would use this information to determine the source of the IRA funds and determine the liability for required distributions, if any. The form must be filed by the IRA custodian each year until the account has a zero balance.

Distribution Option if the IRA Beneficiary Is a Spouse and the IRA Owner Was over the Age of 70½ When He or She Died
If an IRA owner dies after he or she reaches the age of 70½ and designates a spouse as the primary and sole beneficiary, the spouse IRA beneficiary has the following options.

Life-Expectancy Rule
Minimum distributions to an elected surviving spouse are determined under the rules for the deceased IRA owner, not the rules for beneficiaries, except that the election may not cause there to be a minimum distribution for the year of the owner's death if the owner died before his or her required beginning date. The minimum required distributions for the year of the deceased spouse's death will be calculated in the same way as what would have applied had the deceased spouse been alive. The surviving spouse will use the Uniform Lifetime Table issued by the IRS each year and find the ADP for the deceased spouse based on his or her age in the year of his or her death. Then the surviving spouse would divide the deceased spouse's IRA balance as of December 31 of the previous year by the ADP.

    Note: If the surviving spouse is more than ten years younger than the deceased spouse and if the deceased spouse was using the Joint and Last Survivor Table for purposes of determining the annual required IRA distributions, the surviving spouse would use the same table to find the ADP in the year of the deceased spouse's death.

I Thought a Surviving Spouse Can Treat the Deceased Spouse's IRA as His or Her Own?
Correct. A surviving spouse beneficiary has the option of treating a deceased spouse's IRA as his or her own. However, if the deceased spouse died after the age of 70½, the surviving spouse must take the required distribution for the year of the surviving spouse's death before the surviving spouse can make the account his or her own. It is important to remember that once the deceased spouse's IRA has been transferred into the surviving spouse's name, all the required distribution rules apply as though the surviving spouse were the original owner.

What Happens for Required Distributions in Year Two if the Surviving Spouse Is Younger than the Deceased Spouse?
If the surviving spouse is younger than the deceased spouse, beginning in the second year, he or she is required to take minimum required distributions (assuming the spouse does not roll over the IRA into his or her name); the surviving spouse will use his or her own age to determine the ADP each year.

What Happens for Required Distributions in Year Two if the Surviving Spouse Is Older than the Deceased Spouse?
If the surviving spouse is older than the deceased spouse, the surviving spouse will calculate the required distribution amount using the greater of

- the deceased spouse's life expectancy at the time of his or her death, reduced by one each subsequent year or
- the surviving spouse's life expectancy, redetermined each year using his or her age, looking up the ADP in the Single Life Table.

Since the surviving spouse is permitted to elect to use the largest ADP (the most favorable to the surviving spouse), typically the surviving spouse will start out using the deceased spouse's life expectancy and then switch to his or her own once the ADP surpasses the deceased spouse's life expectancy.

ROLLOVER OPTION FOR SPOUSE

A surviving spouse has the option of rolling over a deceased spouse's IRA into his or her own IRA or can leave the IRA in the name of the deceased spouse. In general, a surviving spouse has several ways of making a deceased spouse's IRA his or her own:

- Rolling over the IRA into a new or existing IRA in the name of the surviving spouse

- Failing to take postdeath required minimum distributions in a timely manner
- Contributing an additional amount to the deceased spouse's IRA

What Do Most Surviving Spouses Do?

Most surviving spouses elect to roll over a deceased spouse's IRA into his or her own. At the time the rollover is complete, the deceased spouse's IRA will belong to the surviving spouse in every respect. This means that the surviving spouse can name a new IRA beneficiary and that the surviving spouse's age—not the deceased IRA owner's—will determine whether required minimum distributions must be taken.

Example 1

Jane, a surviving spouse, was 65 years old when her husband Steve, who was 74, died. Jane elects to roll Steve's IRA into her own. Since Jane was under 70½ at the time of Steve's death, Steve's required minimum distributions may be stopped until Jane reaches the age of 70½. Then Jane must begin taking required distributions using the Uniform Lifetime Table to determine her ADP.

Example 2

Tina, a surviving spouse, was 75 when her husband Dave, who was 77, died. After Dave's death, Tina rolled Dave's IRA over into her own. Since Tina was over the age of 70½ when Dave died, Tina is required to take a distribution in the year of Dave's death, and then she must take a distribution on her own behalf since Dave's IRA is now in her name.

Remember, if the deceased spouse was over the age of 70½ at the date of his or her death, the surviving spouse is required to take the required minimum distribution for the deceased spouse for the year of the deceased spouse's death before the surviving spouse can complete the IRA rollover to his or her name.

Is There a Deadline for Doing the Rollover?

The IRC imposes no deadline for a surviving spouse to convert a deceased spouse's IRA into his or her own account. The election can generally be made anytime, months or years after the deceased spouse's death, as long as the surviving spouse continues to take the required minimum distributions.

If the surviving spouse is over the age of 59½, then waiting to do the rollover has no benefit since the spouse can technically take distributions from his or her own IRA without penalty. However, if the surviving spouse is under the age of 59½, by rolling over the IRA of a deceased spouse who was over the age of 70½ at the time of his or her death, into his or her own IRA may not be advantageous if the surviving spouse wishes to access those funds without penalty. Remember, if the surviving spouse is under the age of 59½, once the IRA is rolled over from the deceased spouse's to the surviving spouse's account, it becomes the spouse's IRA in every respect.

Can a Surviving Spouse Convert a Deceased Spouse's IRA into a Roth IRA?

If the deceased spouse had a traditional IRA, in order to convert the traditional IRA to a Roth IRA, the surviving spouse would first have to roll over the deceased spouse's IRA to a traditional IRA in the surviving spouse's name. Once the assets are in the surviving spouse's IRA, the surviving spouse may convert the account to a Roth IRA.

DISTRIBUTION OPTION IF THE IRA BENEFICIARY IS A NONSPOUSE AND THE IRA OWNER WAS OVER THE AGE OF 70½ WHEN HE OR SHE DIED

The IRS allows a nonspouse beneficiary to use the life-expectancy rules to calculate the IRA required distributions after the deceased IRA holder's death. The IRA distributions must begin to be taken no later than December 31 of the year after the death of the deceased IRA holder's death. There are no additional opportunities for delaying IRA distributions for nonspouse beneficiaries.

In the Year of Death

In the year of the death of the deceased IRA owner, if the deceased IRA owner had not yet taken the required minimum distributions for the year, the nonspouse IRA beneficiary is required to take the minimum distribution before the end of the year. The IRA beneficiary will use the Uniform Lifetime Table based on the age of the deceased IRA owner. If the deceased IRA owner had already taken the required minimum distribution for that year, then the nonspouse beneficiary is not required to take another distribution that year.

Second Year and After

Starting in the year after the IRA owner's death, minimum required distributions are determined based on whether the nonspouse beneficiary is older or younger than the deceased IRA owner.

Younger Nonspouse Beneficiary

In the case in which the nonspouse beneficiary is younger than the deceased IRA owner, the nonspouse beneficiary would calculate the required distributions for the second year and beyond using the beneficiary's single life expectancy as provided by the IRS in the year after the deceased IRA owner's death. In subsequent years, the nonspouse beneficiary will reduce the ADP by one each year.

Older Nonspouse Beneficiary

In the case in which the nonspouse beneficiary is older than the deceased IRA owner, the nonspouse beneficiary would calculate the required distributions using the deceased IRA owner's single life expectancy in the year of the deceased IRA owner's death, reduced by one. In subsequent years, the nonspouse beneficiary will reduce the ADP by one each year.

For example, Jim turned 70½ in 2004 and began taking required distributions from his IRA at that time. Jim's designated beneficiary was his sister Tracy, who turned 72 in 2004. Jim had been using the Uniform Lifetime Table, as provided by the IRS, for purposes of determining the required minimum distributions. Jim died in 2007 after taking his required minimum distributions for the year. In 2008, the year after his death, Tracy is required to take a distribution based on Jim's single life expectancy. Tracy would have to determine her life expectancy in 2007, the year of Jim's death, and reduce it by one.

Can a Nonspouse Beneficiary Do a Rollover?

No. A nonspouse beneficiary is not permitted to roll over a deceased IRA owner's IRA into the nonspouse beneficiary's own IRA. Any attempted rollover would be treated as a taxable distribution.

Can a Nonspouse Beneficiary Convert the Deceased IRA Owner's Traditional IRA to a Roth IRA?

No. If a nonspouse beneficiary inherits an IRA, the nonspouse beneficiary is not permitted to convert the traditional inherited IRA into a Roth IRA.

What Happens if the Deceased IRA Owner Designates Multiple Nonspouse Beneficiaries?

If the deceased IRA owner designates more than one nonspouse beneficiary for a single IRA, then the required minimum distributions will be calculated as though the nonspouse beneficiary with the shortest life expectancy (oldest beneficiary) was the sole beneficiary. The one exception to this rule is that if the nonspouse beneficiary with the shortest life expectancy (the oldest beneficiary) is older than the deceased IRA owner at the date of his or her death, the designated nonspouse beneficiaries will be required to use the deceased IRA owner's single life expectancy to calculate the required minimum distributions after his or her death.

DISTRIBUTION OPTION IF THE IRA BENEFICIARY IS A NONINDIVIDUAL (I.E., A QUALIFIED TRUST) AND THE IRA OWNER WAS UNDER THE AGE OF 70½ WHEN HE OR SHE DIED

In general, if you name a trust as a beneficiary of your IRA, and if the trust is treated as a "qualified trust" by meeting certain requirements, you would look through the trust to determine the beneficiary. The trust beneficiary would be treated as a designated beneficiary for purposes of computing required minimum distributions.

What Happens if the Trust Has Multiple Beneficiaries?

If a trust has multiple beneficiaries, the multiple beneficiaries would be required to take minimum required distributions based on a single life expectancy using the life expectancy of the oldest beneficiary.

Selecting a trust as beneficiary of an IRA may provide certain estate-planning benefits; however, it may also cause certain beneficiaries of the trust to take greater required minimum distributions than they would have been required to take if a trust was not used and, instead, the IRA holder designated such person(s) as beneficiaries of the IRA.

The following is a chart that summarizes the Required Minimum Distributions.

IRA Required Minimum Distribution Worksheet

Use this worksheet to figure this year's required withdraw for your traditional IRA UNLESS your spouse[1] is the sole beneficiary of your IRA and he or she is more than 10 years younger than you.

Deadline for receiving required minimum distribution:
- Year you turn age 70 ½ - by April 1 of the following year
- All subsequent years - by December 31 of that year

1. IRA balance[2] on December 31 of the previous year. $_____

2. Distribution period from the table below for your age on your   _____
   birthday this year.

3. Line 1 divided by number entered on line 2. This is your required $_____
   minimum distribution for this year from this IRA.

4. Repeat steps 1 through 3 for each of your IRAs.

Table III (Uniform Lifetime)

Age	Distribution Period	Age	Distribution Period	Age	Distribution Period	Age	Distribution Period
70	27.4	82	17.1	94	9.1	106	4.2
71	26.5	83	16.3	95	8.6	107	3.9
72	25.6	84	15.5	96	8.1	108	3.7
73	24.7	85	14.8	97	7.6	109	3.4
74	23.8	86	14.1	98	7.1	110	3.1
75	22.9	87	13.4	99	6.7	111	2.9
76	22.0	88	12.7	100	6.3	112	2.6
77	21.2	89	12.0	101	5.9	113	2.4
78	20.3	90	11.4	102	5.5	114	2.1
79	19.5	91	10.8	103	5.2	115 and over	1.9
80	18.7	92	10.2	104	4.9		
81	17.9	93	9.6	105	4.5		

Once you determine a separate required minimum distribution from each of your traditional IRAs, you can total these minimum amounts and take them from any one or more of your traditional IRAs.

For additional information, see:

- Publication 590-B, *Distributions from Individual Retirement Arrangements (IRAs)*
- Retirement Topics -- Required Minimum Distributions

[1] Generally, your marital status is determined as of January 1 of each year. If your spouse is the beneficiary of your IRA on January 1, he or she remains a beneficiary only for purposes of calculating the required minimum distribution for that IRA even if you get divorced or your spouse dies during the year.

[2] You must increase your IRA balance by any outstanding rollover and recharacterized Roth IRA conversions that were not in any traditional IRA on December 31 of the previous year.

OPTIONS IF THE IRA OWNER DIES AFTER THE AGE OF 70½

"Wow. That was tons of info. Do you have any of this in writing you can send me?" Amy asked.

"No problem. I know it seemed over the top, but it is really important to understand all the rules surrounding a traditional IRA, especially how distributions work because that is one of the main differences between a traditional IRA and a Roth IRA. Now that we have gone through the traditional IRA in great detail, let's turn to the Roth IRA, which I know is something you are a huge fan of," John said.

THE ROTH IRA

The Roth IRA was originally called an "IRA Plus"; the idea was proposed by Senator Bob Packwood of Oregon and Senator William Roth of Delaware in 1989. The Packwood-Roth plan would have allowed individuals to invest up to $2,000 in an account with no immediate tax deductions, but the earnings could later be withdrawn tax free at retirement.[23]

The Roth IRA was established by the Taxpayer Relief Act of 1997 (Public Law 105-34) and named for its chief legislative sponsor, Senator William Roth of Delaware. When the landmark legislation was passed as part of the Taxpayer Relief Act of 1997, Senator Roth and his colleagues did not quite know what they had created and how much of an impact it would ultimately have on Americans and their ability to have a financially secure retirement. In an interview Senator Roth gave to Dr. Gibind Daryanni, he often compared the Roth IRA as a way to realize the American Dream. He told his interviewer, "If you work hard and save hard, you can have a good retirement income that allows you to leave something to your children." Like most American and even other citizens around the world, parents want to provide their children with a better life than the one they had, and the Roth IRA is an excellent tool to do just that.[24]

---

23 https://en.wikipedia.org/wiki/Roth_IRA.

24 http://www.rothira.com/blog/what-senator-william-roth-envisioned-for-the-roth-ira.

Since 1997, the Roth IRA has not only grown in stature and popularity, but it has become one of the cornerstones of many Americans' retirement portfolios. Originally, American taxpayers were only allowed to contribute up to $2,000 of their after-tax earned income to a Roth IRA, and there was not a catch-up contribution allowed for citizens over the age of fifty yet. It took several years for the contribution limits to increase to the current amounts of $5,000 per taxpayer or $6,000 if you are making a catch-up contribution if you are over fifty years of age. Also, originally the Roth IRA had a contribution limit of $150,000 per year for couples and $95,000 for individual taxpayers.

The big advantage of a Roth IRA is that if you qualify to make contributions, all distributions from the Roth IRA are tax free—even the investment returns—as long as the distributions meet certain requirements. In addition, unlike traditional IRAs, you may contribute to a Roth IRA for as long as you continue to have earned income (in the case of a traditional IRA, you can't make contributions after you reach age 70½). The rules for the Roth IRA are found in the IRC under Section 408A.

WHAT IS A ROTH IRA?

A Roth IRA is an IRA that the owner designates as a Roth IRA. A Roth IRA is generally subject to the rules for traditional IRAs. For example, traditional and Roth IRAs and their owners are identically affected by the rules treating an IRA as distributing its assets if the IRA engages in a prohibited transaction or the owner borrows against it. The reporting requirements for IRAs also apply to Roth IRAs. However, several rules, described below, apply uniquely to Roth IRAs.

The most attractive feature of the Roth IRA is that even though contributions are not deductible, all distributions, including the earnings and appreciation on all Roth contributions, are tax free if certain conditions are met.

ROTH IRA CHARACTERISTICS

The following is an overview of the tax characteristics of the Roth IRA.

- Contributions are not tax deductible.
  Unlike a traditional IRA, an individual is not permitted to take an income tax deduction for their Roth IRA contributions. All Roth IRA contributions are made with after-tax dollars. This means that the amount of the contribution is treated as basis in the IRA.
- Earnings are tax deferred.
  Earnings and gains from a Roth IRA are tax deferred and may be tax exempt if certain conditions are met (a "qualified distribution"). This means that all income and gains generated by a Roth IRA investment are not subject to income tax.
- Tax-free earnings.
  The attraction of the Roth IRA is based on the fact that qualified distributions of Roth earnings are tax free. As long as certain conditions are met and the distribution is a qualified distribution, the Roth IRA owner will never pay tax on any Roth distributions received.

ROTH IRA CONTRIBUTIONS

An individual may make several types of contributions, including regular, spousal, conversion, and catch-up contributions.

Regular Contributions

In the case of a Roth IRA, there are no maximum-age restrictions for making Roth IRA contributions; however, there are income restrictions that must be met.

No Maximum- or Minimum-Age Restriction

Unlike traditional IRAs, there is no maximum-age restriction for making Roth IRA contributions. As long as the individual satisfies the required-income guidelines, he or she may make Roth IRA contributions even after the age of 70½. In addition, federal law does not impose minimum-age restrictions for making Roth IRA contributions. However, typically, most financial institutions will verify the appropriate state laws relating to minors signing contracts.

WHAT IS THE ELIGIBLE COMPENSATION REQUIREMENT?

Earned Income. As with a traditional IRA, an individual must generally have earned income from personal services rendered in order to be eligible to make Roth IRA contributions.

WHAT IS COMPENSATION?

Compensation includes wages, salaries, tips, professional fees, bonuses, and other amounts received for providing personal services. It also includes commissions, self-employment income, nontaxable combat pay, military differential pay, and taxable alimony and separate maintenance payments.

WHAT ARE THE INCOME LIMITS FOR MAKING ROTH IRA CONTRIBUTIONS?

Unlike in traditional IRAs, to be eligible to contribute to a Roth IRA, an individual or married couple must have a modified adjusted gross income (MAGI) below a certain income limit as prescribed by the IRS. If the individual or married couple has MAGI equal to or greater than the applicable income-threshold limit, the individual is not eligible to make Roth IRA contributions. If an individual has income less than the applicable income threshold but more than the specified minimum threshold, the amount of Roth IRA contributions the individual is eligible to make is phased out.

For the tax year 2016, the applicable Roth IRA contribution income-threshold levels are as follows:

- For a "single filer," the Roth IRA contribution MAGI limit is $117,000–$132,000.
- For a "married couple filing a joint federal income-tax return," the Roth IRA contribution MAGI limit is $184,000–$194,000.
- For "married individuals living together but filing separate federal income-tax returns," the contribution phase-out range is $0–$10,000.

HOW DO YOU CALCULATE THE MAGI?

An individual is not permitted to make a Roth IRA contribution if the individual's MAGI exceeds a certain income threshold as provided by the IRS each year. When calculating an individual's MAGI, the following adjustments must be made to the individual's adjusted gross income (AGI) as shown on the federal income-tax return. The AGI is a number used to determine how much of your income is taxable. AGI is your gross income minus deductions. Deductions include retirement-account contributions, health-insurance contributions (for self-employed persons), trade or business expenses, depreciation on rental property, losses from sales of property, alimony payments, medical savings-account contributions, moving expenses, and charitable-cash contributions. The AGI does not include standard or itemized deductions or personal exemptions.

- Subtract any converted Roth IRA amount.
- Subtract any Roth IRA rollovers from a qualified plan.
- Subtract any minimum required distributions from an IRA.
- Add traditional IRA deductions.
- Add student-loan interest deductions.
- Add tuition and fees deductions.
- Add domestic-production activities deductions.
- Add foreign-earned income exclusion.
- Add foreign housing exclusion or deduction.
- Add exclusion of qualified bond interest shown on Form 8815.
- Add exclusion of employer-provided adoption benefits shown on Form 8839.

What Happens if an Individual's MAGI Is Above the Roth IRA Income Threshold?

If an individual's MAGI is above the Roth IRA contribution MAGI limit, the individual's Roth IRA contribution limit is gradually reduced.

ROTH IRA CONTRIBUTIONS

A regular contribution to a Roth IRA is generally limited to the lesser of the annual contribution limit or 100 percent of the individual's compensation. The Roth IRA contribution limit is the same as the traditional IRA limit. For the year 2016, the annual Roth IRA contribution limit for an individual under the age of fifty is $5,500 and $6,500 for an individual over the age of fifty. An individual making Roth IRA contributions must reduce those contributions by the amount of any contributions made to a traditional IRA. In other words, the annual IRA contribution limit for 2016 ($5,500 or $6,500) applies to all IRAs and cannot be applied separately to one or more traditional IRAs or Roth IRAs. For example, if Jim had a traditional and Roth IRA and was under the age of fifty, Jim could *not* make a $5,500 contribution to both his traditional IRA and Roth IRA. Jim would be limited to making a $5,500 contribution to his traditional IRA, Roth IRA, or some sort of combination contribution made to both his traditional and Roth IRA as long as the combined contribution does not exceed $5,500 for 2016.

HOW DO I CALCULATE THE ROTH IRA CONTRIBUTION REDUCTION?

For 2016, if the amount you can contribute must be reduced, you can figure your reduced contribution limit according to this formula:

1. Start with your modified AGI.
2. Subtract from the amount in (1):
    a. $194,000 if filing a joint return or qualifying widow(er);
    b. $0 if married filing a separate return, and you lived with your spouse at any time during the year; or
    c. $117,000 for all other individuals.
3. Divide the result in (2) by $15,000 ($10,000 if filing a joint return, qualifying widow(er), or married filing a separate return and you lived with your spouse at any time during the year).
4. Multiply the maximum contribution limit (before reduction by this adjustment and before reduction for any contributions to traditional IRAs) by the result in (3).

5. Subtract the result in (4) from the maximum contribution limit before this reduction. The result is your reduced contribution limit.

"Here's an example from IRS Publication 590 on how this works," John said.

Example
Joe, a forty-five-year-old, single individual with taxable compensation of $113,000, wants to make the maximum allowable contribution to his Roth IRA for 2013. Joe's modified AGI for 2013 is $113,000. Joe has not contributed to any traditional IRA, so the maximum contribution limit before the modified AGI reduction is $5,500.

YOUR FILING STATUS IS:	And Your Modified AGI Is...	Then You Can Contribute...
Married filing jointly or **qualifying widow(er)**	< $184,000	up to the limit
	≥ $184,000 but < $194,000	a reduced amount
	≥ $194,000	zero
Married filing separately, and you lived with your spouse at any time during the year	< $10,000	a reduced amount
	≥ $10,000	zero
Single, head of household, or married filing separately, and you did not live with your spouse at any time during the year	< $117,000	up to the limit
	≥ $117,000 but < $132,000	a reduced amount
	≥ $132,000	zero

"So, are you saying that if I earn more than $193,000 on my joint return, I can't do a Roth IRA?" Amy asked.

"Yes and no," John answered. "One way for high earners to contribute to a Roth IRA is something called the 'backdoor' Roth IRA. The 'backdoor'

Roth IRA approach allows a high-income earner (someone who makes over $194,000 in 2016) to make an after-tax IRA contribution, which has no income threshold, and then immediately convert the after-tax IRA to a Roth IRA. As of 2010, there is no longer any income-level restriction for making Roth IRA conversions; hence a high-income earner can do a conversion of the after-tax IRA funds to a Roth IRA immediately upon making the contribution. However, a tax could be due on the conversion under the pro rata rules if the IRA holder has other traditional IRAs that have not been taxed. In general, the taxes owed on the conversion will depend on the ratio of IRA assets that have been taxed to those that have not, making the 'backdoor' IRA unattractive for some."

"When are Roth IRA contributions due?" Amy asked.

"You can make contributions for 2016 by the due date (not including extensions) for filing your 2016 tax return. This means that most people can make contributions for 2016 by April 15, 2017."

"The only thing I worry about, though, is what if I contribute too much to my Roth IRA since these Roth calculation limits are so complicated?"

"A six percent excise tax applies to any excess contribution to a Roth IRA. But don't worry; there is a way to correct any excess contributions made. Any contribution that is withdrawn on or before the due date (including extensions) for filing your tax return for the year is treated as an amount not contributed. This treatment only applies if any earnings on the contributions are also withdrawn. The earnings are considered earned and received in the year the excess contribution was made."

"OK, that's a relief," Amy said.

"If you filed your 2014 tax return in a timely way," John continued, "without withdrawing a contribution that you made in 2014, you can still have the contribution returned to you within six months of the due date of your 2014 tax return, excluding extensions. If you do, file an amended return with 'Filed pursuant to section 301.9100-2' written at the top. Report any related earnings on the amended return and include an explanation of the withdrawal. And make any other necessary changes on the amended return."

How Do the Catch-up Contribution Rules Work for Roth IRAs?

Like with a traditional IRA, an individual who turns fifty before the end of the taxable year may be eligible to make Roth IRA catch-up contributions. The maximum amount that an individual over the age of fifty may contribute annually as a catch-up contribution is $1,000 for 2016. An individual must reduce a Roth IRA contribution by any catch-up contribution made to a traditional IRA.

Can I Make Roth IRA Contributions if I Have No Eligible Compensation but My Spouse Does?

As with a traditional IRA contribution, an individual with no eligible compensation but who is married may generally make a Roth IRA contribution based on his or her spouse's compensation. This is often referred to as a "spousal contribution."

What Are the Rules for Making a Roth IRA Spousal Contribution?

1. No age requirement. There is no maximum-age restriction for making a spousal Roth IRA contribution. In other words, spousal Roth IRA contributions may be made even after the spouse with no compensation reaches the age of 70½.
2. Eligible compensation. Like with a regular IRA contribution, a spouse must have earned income from personal services.
3. Joint tax return. In order to be eligible for a spousal contribution, the married couple must file a joint federal income-tax return.
4. Spousal-contribution limit. The maximum combined spousal-contribution limit is the lesser of the annual contribution limit (including catch-up contributions if applicable) per married couple, or 100 percent of the married couple's combined compensation (reduced by

any traditional IRA contributions). For example, if both spouses are under the age of fifty, the maximum combined spousal-contribution limit is $5,500 per spouse or a combined $11,000 annual contribution limit for 2016. As I discussed earlier, the maximum annual contribution amount is decreased for married couples with MAGI in the phase-out range of $184,000 to $194,000 for the year 2016.

WHEN ARE ROTH IRA CONTRIBUTIONS DUE?

An individual must make regular or spousal Roth IRA contributions to either a traditional or Roth IRA by the individual's due date of his or her federal income-tax return (not including extensions) for the tax year. April 15 is the due date for IRA contributions for most individuals who file a federal income-tax return.

CAN I MAKE IRA CONTRIBUTIONS AFTER JANUARY 1 FOR THE PREVIOUS YEAR?

As long as the IRA contributions for the previous year are made between January 1 and April 15.

Note: If April 15 falls on a Saturday, Sunday, or legal holiday, the individual will generally have until the next business day to make the IRA contribution. If April 15 falls on a weekend or legal holiday, the IRS will typically announce the federal income-tax return and IRA contribution due date at the beginning of the year. These types of contributions are generally referred to as carryback contributions. The IRA owner must generally make a written, irrevocable election designating an IRA contribution as a carryback IRA contribution.

WHAT IF I MAIL THE CONTRIBUTION CHECK ON APRIL 15? WHEN IS IT TREATED AS RECEIVED BY THE CUSTODIAN?

If an IRA contribution is mailed to the financial institution (IRA custodian), it is treated as timely contributed if it is postmarked by the due date for making IRA contributions (i.e., April 15).

WHAT IF I CONTRIBUTE TOO MUCH?

A 6 percent excise tax applies to any excess contribution to a Roth IRA.

What Happens if I Correct this Mistake Prior to Filing My Tax Return?

Any excess Roth IRA contribution that is withdrawn on or before the due date (including extensions) for filing your tax return for the year is treated as an amount not contributed. This rule only applies if any earnings (i.e., income or gains) from the contributions are also withdrawn.

Can I Apply the Excess Contributions to the Following Year?

If an individual makes Roth IRA contributions in excess of the annual limit (for 2016, $5,500 if the individual is under the age of fifty and $6,500 if the individual is over the age of fifty), he or she can apply the excess Roth IRA contribution made to a subsequent year as long as the contribution made in the subsequent year is less than the annual contribution limit for that year.

ROTH IRA DISTRIBUTIONS

"The difference between a traditional IRA and a Roth IRA is most evident in the treatment of distributions. Don't worry; we will go through the Roth IRA distribution rules in greater detail down the road," John said.

As a brief reminder, in the case of a traditional IRA, an IRA distribution is taxed as ordinary income unless it is rolled over into another retirement plan. If the individual is under the age of 59½ when the distribution is made, a 10 percent excise tax would apply to the distribution in addition to the ordinary income tax due on the value of the distribution. If the individual is over the age of 70½ at the time the distribution is taken, then no excise tax applies; however, the individual is required to pay ordinary income tax on the amount of the traditional IRA distribution. Remember also that an individual over the age of 70½ is required to take minimum annual distributions based on a percentage of the individual's total IRA value at the end of the year. Each year the IRS releases a table that determines the amount of the required minimum distribution.

DETERMINING THE TAX STATUS OF ROTH IRA DISTRIBUTIONS: THE ORDERING RULES

In order to determine which contributions, rollovers, or earnings are distributed from a Roth IRA, the IRS has established a set of ordering rules. Under the ordering rules, the first Roth IRA assets distributed are considered to be a return of the amounts contributed to the Roth IRA. Once the total Roth IRA contributions that have been made have been completely distributed, the ordering rules require that the next assets to be distributed are rollover or conversion amounts (excluding designed Roth IRA account rollovers), if any. Once all those types of assets have been distributed, any further Roth IRA distributions would come from any earnings accumulated by the Roth IRA investments.

AREN'T ALL ROTH IRA DISTRIBUTIONS TAX FREE? SHOULD I CARE ABOUT THE ORDERING RULES?

Yes and no. If an individual is over the age of 59½ and the Roth IRA account has been established for at least five years, then any distributions from a Roth IRA would be tax free (qualified distributions). However, in the case of a nonqualified distribution (discussed below in more detail), the ordering of the distributions is significant because of the different tax and penalty consequences that could apply based on the type of asset distributed (i.e., Roth IRA contribution, which is always nontaxable versus Roth IRA earnings, which may be taxable).

WHAT IS A QUALIFIED ROTH IRA DISTRIBUTION?

A qualified distribution from a Roth IRA is not subject to tax or penalty when made. To have a qualified distribution, the Roth IRA owner must have satisfied a "five-year waiting period" (starting with the first taxable year in which the Roth IRA owner made a contribution to any Roth IRA) and must meet any one of the following requirements:

- reached the age of 59½;
- qualify as disabled;
- qualify as a first-time homebuyer ($10,000 limitation); or
- death.

HOW IS THE FIVE-YEAR WAITING PERIOD CALCULATED?

In order for a Roth IRA distribution to be a qualified distribution, one of the requirements is that the Roth IRA owner must have satisfied a five-year waiting period (starting with the first taxable year in which the Roth IRA owner made a contribution to any Roth IRA). For purposes of calculating the five-year rule, all Roth IRA accounts are treated as one account. Therefore, as long as an individual has made a contribution to a Roth IRA, the five-year waiting period would begin running at that point.

For example, Joe established a Roth IRA in 2007 at age fifty-five and made a contribution of $1,000. In 2013, at age sixty-one, Joe decided to establish another Roth IRA. Because Joe established a Roth IRA account more than five years ago, Joe has already satisfied the five-year rule and would thus be able to take distributions of after-tax contributions and investment income and gains from either Roth IRA tax free, even the recent Roth IRA that was opened less than five years ago.

Helpful Tip

Even if you do not currently have any interest in opening a Roth IRA, you may at some point, so if you are under 59½, you may want to establish a Roth IRA with just a minimal amount, even one dollar, just to start the five-year waiting period. This way, if you ever want to make Roth IRA contributions in the future, you would have already likely satisfied the five-year waiting period, and as long as you are over 59½, you would be able to take distributions of after-tax contributions, and investment income and gains from your Roth IRA(s) tax free. Note: There are separate five-year waiting periods in the case of Roth IRA conversions.

DISTRIBUTION OF AFTER-TAX CONTRIBUTIONS

In the case of a Roth IRA, the amount you contribute is never subject to tax when it comes out. Even if you take it a day after you contribute it and are under 59½, the amount you contributed to your Roth IRA is never subject to tax. The reason for this is simple—you already paid tax on that amount, so the IRS isn't going to tax it again. Remember, in the case of a traditional IRA, the amount you contribute is pretax—meaning you have not paid tax on that amount and, in fact, you have likely received a tax-deduction for the contribution amount, which is why the contribution amount will be subject to tax upon withdrawal.

Because all Roth contributions are never subject to tax upon withdrawal, any distribution taken from a Roth IRA is considered to be a return of your Roth IRA contributions until all Roth IRA contributions you have made over the years have been withdrawn. This rule applies to all Roth IRA contributions you have made, even if you have more than one Roth IRA. This means that all Roth IRA contributions are withdrawn tax free before Roth IRA earnings are recovered. Therefore, once you make a Roth IRA contribution, you will always be able to withdraw that money tax free. For this reason, some people use the Roth IRA as an emergency fund. If they ever get into a financial jam and need money, they will always have the ability to withdraw the Roth IRA contributions tax free and without penalty, which would not be the case if a traditional IRA contribution was made.

For example, Joe began making Roth IRA contributions of $5,000 each year beginning in 2006. By the beginning of 2011, Joe's Roth IRA had grown to $35,000. Of that amount, $25,000 was from Joe's annual contributions and $10,000 was from investment gains. In March 2011, Joe was in a difficult financial position and needed additional funds to help pay some personal bills. Joe decided to withdraw $25,000 from his Roth IRA. The $25,000 is not subject to tax because Joe's distribution is deemed to be a return of his contributions. However, if Joe decided to withdraw $30,000, the first $25,000 would be tax free because it is a return of his contributions. The excess $5,000 would be subject to income tax and a 10 percent excise tax if Joe was under the age of 59½ and the Roth IRA had been open for less than five years.

WHAT HAPPENS IF YOU DIE BEFORE THE FIVE-YEAR WAITING PERIOD IS UP?

If a Roth IRA owner dies before satisfying the five-year waiting period, the Roth IRA owner's beneficiary is required to wait until the Roth IRA owner would have satisfied it for the distribution to be qualified.

WHAT IS A NONQUALIFIED DISTRIBUTION?

Any distribution from a Roth IRA that is not treated as a "qualified" distribution is by default treated as a "nonqualified" distribution—in other words, if the five-year waiting period has not been satisfied or if one of the qualifying events has *not* occurred:

- reach the age 59½;
- qualify as disabled;
- qualify as a first-time home buyer (up to a lifetime $10,000 limitation); or
- death.

HOW ARE NONQUALIFIED DISTRIBUTIONS TREATED?

A nonqualified distribution is treated much like a traditional IRA distribution. The Roth IRA contributions you made will always come out tax free, but the earnings generated by your Roth IRA will be subject to income tax.

ROTH IRA DISTRIBUTION ORDERING RULES

In order to determine which Roth IRA distributions are taxable, it is important to determine which part of the distribution is attributable to Roth IRA contributions and which part is attributable to Roth IRA earnings. It would be nice if you could pick and choose which amount can come out of your Roth IRA first, but unfortunately the IRS has established ordering rules for how to take Roth IRA distributions.

1. Roth IRA Contributions

As discussed earlier, the contributions you made to your Roth IRA are distributed first. The amount you contributed to your Roth IRA (contributory basis) is always withdrawn tax free and penalty free, irrespective of whether the distribution is treated as a qualified or nonqualified distribution.

2. Conversion and Retirement Plan Rollover Assets

Once all Roth IRA contributions have been distributed, then any conversion and retirement plan rollover assets are distributed first by year with the taxable accounts that were subject to tax upon conversion (i.e., traditional IRA), and then the nontaxable accounts (i.e., nondeductible traditional IRA) for that year distributed second. For example, if a Roth IRA owner did a conversion and rollover in 2013 and 2014, her 2013 conversion rollover assets are distributed before her 2014 Roth IRA conversion/rollover assets. As long as the Roth rollover amount is treated as a qualified distribution, it will not be subject to tax upon withdrawal. In addition, a nonqualified distribution of nontaxable conversion or rollover assets (nondeductible traditional IRA) is not taxable, nor is it subject to a 10 percent early-distribution penalty. However, a nonqualified distribution of taxable conversion of retirement rollover assets (i.e., traditional IRA) being distributed within five years of being converted to a Roth IRA is not subject to tax but would be subject to a 10 percent early-distribution tax. The reason for this is that since you have already paid tax on the conversion, the IRS felt it would not be fair to double tax that amount but still wanted to impose a penalty for the early withdrawal.

3. Roth IRA Earnings

If a Roth IRA owner takes a nonqualified distribution, any portion of the distribution that represents earnings or appreciation of the Roth IRA contributions for the year is subject to ordinary income tax and a 10 percent early-distribution penalty, unless he or she qualifies for a penalty exception (i.e., reached the age of 59½, death, or disability). For example, Ben, who is 52 years old, began making Roth IRA contributions of $4,000 each year beginning in 2011. By the beginning of 2014, Ben's Roth IRA had grown to $26,000. Of that amount, $16,000 was from Ben's annual contributions and $10,000 was from earnings or investment gains. In February 2015, Ben was in a difficult financial position and needed additional funds to help pay some personal bills. Ben decided to withdraw his entire Roth IRA amount: $26,000. The $16,000 would not be subject to tax because Ben's distribution is deemed to be a return of his contributions. However, the $10,000 of earnings, or investment appreciation, would be subject to income tax and a 10 percent early-distribution penalty since Ben was under the age of 59½ and the Roth IRA was open for less than five years. In contrast, if at the time of the distribution, the Roth IRA had been established for longer than five years and Ben had been over the age of 59, then the entire $25,000 distribution, even the investment earnings, could have been withdrawn tax free.

As you can see, the timing for taking a Roth IRA distribution can have significant tax implications. For example, if you take a Roth IRA distribution after you turn 59½ and the Roth IRA account has been established for longer than five years, then the entire distribution is tax free. In contrast, if you took a Roth IRA distribution prior to turning 59½ or before the account has been open for more than five years, you would be subject to ordinary income tax and even an early distribution tax on any earnings or appreciation.

Remember, in order to satisfy the Roth IRA qualified-distribution rules, the Roth IRA holder must be over the age of 59½ *and* the Roth IRA account must have been open for at least five years.

Alternatively, if you converted a traditional IRA to a Roth IRA and then took a distribution before the Roth IRA had been open for five years, a 10 percent early-distribution penalty would be triggered. Hence, the origin and timing of a Roth asset has a dramatic impact on the potential tax treatment of a Roth IRA distribution. That being said, if you can hold off taking Roth IRA distributions for at least five years from the establishment of the Roth IRA and after you have reached the age of 59½, you will not have to pay tax on any Roth distribution, regardless of whether it is a contribution, conversion/rollover, or investment earnings.

The following is a summary of the Roth IRA ordering-distribution rules and the tax and penalty that may apply.

Order of Roth IRA Assets for Distribution	"Qualified" Distribution	"Nonqualified" Distribution
Amount contributed to Roth IRA	Not subject to tax or penalty	Not subject to tax or penalty
Amounts converted to a Roth IRA that were subject to tax	Not subject to tax or penalty	Not subject to tax but subject to a 10% early distribution penalty
Amounts converted to a Roth IRA that were not subject to tax	Not subject to tax or penalty	Not subject to tax or penalty
Roth IRA earnings and investments gains	Not subject to tax or penalty	Subject to tax and 10% early distribution penalty

No Required Minimum Distributions

Unlike a traditional IRA, a Roth IRA owner is never required to take a Roth IRA distribution. In other words, the required minimum distribution rules do not apply to Roth IRA owners. This is one of the main differences between a traditional IRA and a Roth IRA. With a traditional IRA, the IRA owner is required to begin taking required minimum distributions when he or she reaches the age of 70½, whereas, in the case of a Roth IRA, the owner is never required to take a distribution—allowing the Roth IRA owner to accumulate retirement funds tax free and then pass those funds on to another generation. The reason is likely due to the IRS's belief that since the Roth IRA was structured to provide for tax-free distributions, there was no real need to require distributions since the account was growing tax free anyway and there was no opportunity for the IRS to collect any tax revenue.

Does My Roth IRA Beneficiary Need to Take Distributions after I Die?

As with a traditional IRA, the answer depends on whether a spouse has been designated as a beneficiary of your Roth IRA. The options available to a designated beneficiary of a Roth IRA generally follow the options available to a beneficiary of a traditional IRA when the traditional IRA owner dies before the age of 70½. Unlike a traditional IRA, however, a Roth IRA owner is not required to take Roth IRA distributions, but certain Roth IRA beneficiaries may be required to take distributions.

WHAT HAPPENS IF THE ROTH IRA BENEFICIARY IS A SPOUSE?

In the case of a spouse who is designated as the beneficiary of his or her spouse's Roth IRA, the spouse beneficiary has several options when it comes to Roth IRA distributions. The options include the

- five-year rule;
- life-expectancy payments;
- transfer to own spouse's Roth IRA; and
- distribute and roll over.

Under all these options, the spouse would be able to take Roth IRA distributions tax free as long as the distribution would be treated as "qualified" under the Roth IRA rules. The spouse would not be required to take RMDs for the Roth IRA.

WHAT HAPPENS IF THE ROTH IRA BENEFICIARY IS A NONSPOUSE?

A nonspouse beneficiary of the Roth IRA holder is subject to the RMD rules. Like with a traditional IRA, a nonspouse beneficiary of a Roth IRA may apply the five-year rule or life-expectancy rule for determining when Roth IRA distributions must be taken. As long as the Roth distributions are "qualified," there will be no tax due on the distribution when taken by the nonspouse beneficiary.

HOW ARE ROTH IRA DISTRIBUTIONS REPORTED TO THE IRS?

The IRS is able to monitor whether a Roth IRA distribution is subject to tax or penalty by requiring IRA custodians (financial organizations) and Roth IRA owners to report when Roth IRA assets are withdrawn. The IRS achieves this by generally comparing Form 1099-R with what the Roth IRA owner reports on his or her federal income-tax return.

DIFFERENCES BETWEEN A TRADITIONAL IRA AND A ROTH IRA

"I am sure that most of what I just described about the traditional and Roth IRA seems a bit confusing and is starting to make your head spin. Don't worry; you are not alone. For that reason I want you to have this chart that summarizes the main differences between a traditional and Roth IRA." John handed Amy the following chart.

Traditional IRA	Roth IRA
Tax-deductible contributions.	Contributions are not tax deductible. Contributions made to a Roth IRA are from after-tax dollars.
Distributions may be taken by age 59½ and are mandatory by 70½.	No mandatory distribution age. With a Roth IRA, you are not required to take distributions ever.
Taxes are paid on amount of distributions (10 percent excise tax may apply if withdrawn prior to age 59½).	No taxes on distributions if rules and regulations are followed.
Available to everyone; no income restrictions with earned income.	• For 2016, subject to adjustments each year, Single filers, Head of Household, or Married Filing Separately (and you did not live with your spouse during the year) with modified adjusted gross income up to $132,000 can make a full contribution. Contributions are phased out starting at $117,000, and you cannot make a contribution if your adjusted gross income is in excess of $132,000. • Joint filers with modified adjusted gross income up to $194,000 can make a full contribution. Once again, this contribution is phased out starting at $184,000, and you cannot make a contribution if your adjusted gross income is in excess of $194,000.

Funds can be used to purchase a variety of investments (stocks, real estate, precious metals, notes, etc.).	Funds can be used to purchase a variety of investments (stocks, real estate, precious metals, notes, etc.).
IRA investments grow tax free until distribution (tax deferral)	All earnings and principal are 100 percent tax free if rules and regulations are followed. No tax on distributions, so maximum tax-deferral.
Income/gains from IRA investments are tax free.	Income/gains from IRA investments are tax free.
Purchasing a real-estate property and then taking possession of the property after 59½ would be subject to tax.	Purchasing a domestic or foreign real-estate property and then taking possession after 59½ would be tax free.

FINANCIAL INSTITUTION REPORTING REQUIREMENTS FOR ROTH IRA DISTRIBUTIONS

The Roth IRA custodian (financial institution) is required to report Roth IRA distributions using Form 1099-R. The gross distribution amount is reported in Box 1. This should include any federal income tax withheld. Box 2A, taxable amount, is left blank. For Box 2B, "Taxable amount not determined" must be checked. Box 7 is where it would be indicated whether the distribution was qualified or nonqualified. Code Q would be included if the distribution were qualified, and code J would be used if the distribution were nonqualified.

ROTH IRA OWNER'S REPORTING REQUIREMENTS

The Roth IRA owner is required to compute the taxable amount of a Roth IRA distribution. Form 1099-R instructions direct the Roth IRA owner to the instructions to Form 1040 and to Form 8606 for additional information on calculating the taxable amount of a Roth distribution.

In any year that the Roth IRA owner takes a nonqualified distribution from a Roth IRA, the Roth IRA owner must file Form 8606 with the IRS to report the distribution.

In any year that the Roth IRA owner takes a qualified distribution, the Roth IRA owner is not required to file Form 8606 with the IRS. Instead, a Roth IRA owner who takes a qualified distribution will report the distribution directly on IRS Form 1040.

"That was really helpful. I knew a lot about the Roth IRA, especially about making Roth IRA contributions, but was not one hundred percent clear on all the Roth IRA distribution rules," Amy said.

"OK, great. I knew you would find this helpful especially because you are building up quite a large Roth IRA considering your young age," John said. "I now want to discuss two types of IRAs that must be established by a business, the SEP IRA and SIMPLE IRA. As you know, the pretax and Roth IRA may be established by an individual and not a business. However, since you have a new business that is doing quite well, I wanted to start discussing some retirement-plan options for your small business."

"OK, that sounds great. I assume, once you discuss the SEP and SIMPLE IRA, you will get into the Solo 401(k) plan," Amy said.

"Yes, for sure," John responded.

"Great, because I have been reading up on the Solo 401(k) plan, and it seems to be a really great fit for me," Amy said.

"I agree with you, and by learning about the SEP and SIMPLE IRA, I think you will be able to better understand the advantages a Solo 401(k) plan offers," John said.

WHAT IS A SEP IRA?

A Simplified Employee Pension (SEP) plan provides business owners with a simplified method to contribute toward their employees' retirement as well as their own retirement savings. A SEP is essentially an employer-sponsored profit-sharing plan. Contributions are made to an individual retirement account or annuity (IRA) set up for each plan participant (a SEP IRA). The main difference between a SEP IRA, a traditional IRA, and Roth IRA is that a SEP IRA must be established by a business whereas a traditional IRA and Roth IRA are established by individuals. In other words, an individual who is not an owner of a business cannot establish a SEP IRA.

A SEP IRA account is a traditional IRA and follows the same investment, distribution, and rollover rules as traditional IRAs.

Employees must be included in the SEP plan if they have

- reached age twenty-one;
- received at least $550 in compensation from your business for the year; and
- worked for your business in at least three of the last five years.

The three-of-five eligibility rule means you must include any employee in your plan who has worked for you in any three of the last five years (as long as the employee has satisfied the other plan-eligibility requirements). This is the most restrictive eligibility requirement allowable. You can choose to use less restrictive participation rules in your plan, such as allowing employees to participate immediately after they start work or after a shorter period of employment. If you use the three-of-five rule, you must count any work, no matter how little, in each of the previous five years. Use plan years (often the calendar year), not years based on the date the employee started working for you.

John said, "Using the three of five rule is a nifty way for business owners to make SEP IRA contributions for themselves without having to make contributions for their employees. However, once the three-five rule is met, the employer is required to provide all eligible employees with equal-percentage profit-sharing contributions."

"So the three-five rule could help the business owner out for a couple of years, but after that, the employer is required to provide all eligible employees with a SEP IRA contribution using the same percentage it used for the business owner?" asked Amy.

"That is correct," John said.

"How do the contributions work?" Amy asked.

"The contributions you make to each employee's SEP IRA each year cannot exceed the lesser of

- twenty-five percent of compensation (twenty percent in the case of a sole proprietorship of single-member LLC) or

- fifty-three thousand dollars for 2016.

"There are *no* catch-up contributions for a SEP IRA as there are for a 401(k) plan."

These limits apply to contributions you make for your employees to all defined contribution plans, which includes SEPs. Compensation up to $265,000 in 2016 of an employee's compensation may be considered for contribution purposes. Also, contributions must be made in cash, and you cannot contribute property.

WHAT IS A SIMPLE IRA?

A SIMPLE (savings incentive match plan for employees) IRA plan allows employees and employers to contribute to traditional IRAs set up for employees. Like a SEP IRA, a SIMPLE IRA can only be established by a business. Employees may choose to make salary-reduction contributions, and the employer is required to make either matching or nonelective contributions. Contributions are made to an individual retirement account or annuity (IRA) set up for each employee (a SIMPLE IRA).

A SIMPLE IRA plan account is an IRA and follows the same investment, distribution, and rollover rules as a traditional IRA.

Any employer (including self-employed individuals, tax-exempt organizations, and governmental entities) that had no more than one hundred employees with $5,000 or more in compensation during the preceding calendar year (the "hundred-employee limitation") can establish a SIMPLE IRA plan. You can set up a SIMPLE IRA plan effective any date between January 1 and October 1 provided you (or any predecessor employer) didn't previously maintain a SIMPLE IRA plan. If you're a new employer that came into existence after October 1 of the year, you can establish the SIMPLE IRA plan as soon as administratively feasible after your business came into existence.

All employees who received at least $5,000 in compensation from you during any two preceding calendar years (whether or not consecutive) and who are reasonably expected to receive at least $5,000 in compensation during the calendar year are eligible to participate in the SIMPLE IRA plan for the calendar year.

Each eligible employee may make a salary-reduction contribution, and the employer must make either a matching contribution or nonelective contribution.

An employee may defer up to $12,500 in 2016 (subject to cost-of-living adjustments for later years).

Employees aged fifty or over can make a catch-up contribution of up to $3,000 in 2016 (subject to cost-of-living adjustments for later years).

With respect to employer contributions, the employer is generally required to either

- match each employee's salary-reduction contribution on a dollar-for-dollar basis up to 3 percent of the employee's compensation (not limited by the annual compensation limit) or
- make nonelective contributions of 2 percent of the employee's compensation up to the annual limit of $265,000 for 2016, subject to cost-of-living adjustments in later years).

If you choose to make nonelective contributions, you must make them for all eligible employees whether or not they make salary-reduction contributions.

With respect to the 3 percent match, you may elect to reduce the 3 percent matching contributions for a calendar year, but only if

- the limit isn't reduced below 1 percent;
- the limit isn't reduced for more than two years out of the five-year period that ends with (and includes) the year for which the election is effective; and
- you notify employees of the reduced limit within a reasonable time before the sixty-day election period during which employees can enter into salary-reduction agreements.

Generally, the same tax results apply to distributions from a SIMPLE IRA as to distributions from a regular IRA with one notable exception. During the two-year period, you may transfer an amount in a SIMPLE IRA to another SIMPLE IRA in a tax-free trustee-to-trustee transfer. If, during this two-year period, an amount is paid from a SIMPLE IRA directly to another IRA that is not a SIMPLE IRA, then the payment is treated as a distribution from the SIMPLE IRA and a contribution to the other IRA that doesn't qualify as a rollover contribution. After the expiration of the two-year period, you may transfer an amount in a SIMPLE IRA to any IRA or 401(k) plan without tax. In addition, a SIMPLE IRA has an exclusive-plan rule, which does not allow a business to adopt both a SIMPLE IRA and a Solo 401(k) plan in the same taxable year, whereas, a business can adopt both a SEP IRA and a 401(k) plan.

"I hope this meeting wasn't too painful for you," John joked.

"Not too bad," Amy responded.

"Good. I was going to dive into the Solo 401(k) plan, but I just think it would be too much information for now. What I am thinking is that the next time we meet, we discuss the advantages of tax deferral and tax-free investing, and then we can move on to discussing the self-directed IRA and Solo 401(k) plan. I just think it will be easier to focus on IRAs first to get a good handle on how they work and operate, including tax advantages and investments opportunities, and then move on the Solo 401(k) plan," John said.

"Before we adjourn for today, I just wanted to mention something called the Saver's credit. The Saver's credit may not work for you because I believe your income is above $60,000; however, I wanted to mention it because it is worth knowing about and may prove helpful to your sister or friends. For someone who is a low-to-moderate income worker, you can take steps now to save two ways for the same amount. With the saver's credit, you can save for your retirement and save on your taxes with a special tax credit. The saver's credit helps offset part of the first $2,000 you voluntarily save for your retirement. The saver's credit can increase your refund or reduce the tax you owe. The maximum credit is $1,000 or $2,000 for married couples. In essence, the saver's credit is a nice way to help incentivize Americans to save for retirement by offering a tax credit for making up to $2,000 in retirement-account contributions. This includes amounts you contribute to IRAs, 401(k) plans, and similar workplace plans. The one issue is that it really only helps couples that make less than $60,000 annually. It would be great if Congress increased the annual-income limitation so that more American families could take advantage of the saver's credit. For example, one is eligible for the credit if (i) aged eighteen or older, (ii) not a full-time student, and (iii) not claimed as a dependent on another person's return. The amount of the credit is 50 percent, 20 percent, or 10 percent of your retirement plan or IRA contributions up to $2,000 ($4,000 if married filing jointly), depending on your adjusted gross income (reported on your Form 1040 or 1040A). In general, a couple filing jointly will get a credit of 50 percent of their retirement account contributions if they earn not more than $36,500. However, a couple filing jointly will only get a credit of 10 percent of their retirement-account contribution if they earn between $39,501 and $61,000 for 2016. All in all the saver's credit is a great start to help make retirement savings attractive for some, but it is not enough in order to make a real impact for many Americans, including yourself, Am." Johns said.

"OK, this has been so awesome and so incredibly helpful. Same place next week? I will buy the cappuccinos and muffins," Amy said.

"It's a deal," John responded.

4

Power of Tax-Free Investing

Amy arrived early the following week for her meeting with John and waited in line to get the cappuccinos and muffins. She took a seat at their usual table toward the back of the coffee shop. John arrived soon after.

"Today should be much easier to digest than our last meeting when we dove into all the features of the various IRAs in excruciating detail. Again, I am sorry I had to put you through that, but I really think it will prove useful to you down the road," John said.

"I actually found the information you presented quite useful, especially since I am a huge Roth IRA believer and didn't really know much about the traditional IRA, SEP IRA, and SIMPLE IRA," Amy said.

"That is good to hear. I think you will enjoy today's discussion and feel pretty comfortable with the content since it is one of the main reasons why you have established a Roth IRA—tax deferral and tax-free investing."

What Is Tax Deferral?

Tax deferral literally means that you are putting off paying tax. The most common types of tax-deferred investments include those in IRAs or qualified retirement plans (i.e., 401(k)s). Tax deferral means that all income, gains, and earnings, such as interest, dividends, rental income, royalties, or capital gains will accumulate tax free until the investor or IRA owner withdraws the funds and takes possession of them. As long as the funds remain in the retirement account, the funds will grow tax free. This allows your retirement funds to grow at a much faster pace than if the funds were held personally, allowing you to build for your retirement more quickly. And when you withdraw your IRA funds in the form of a distribution after you retire, you will likely be in a lower tax bracket and be able to keep more of what you accumulated. So, using a traditional IRA as a retirement-savings vehicle, not only are you not paying taxes on the money you invested, you could be paying them at a lower rate when you finally do "take home" your money.

As long as the funds remain in the account, they grow without taxes eroding their value. This enables assets to accumulate at a faster rate, giving you an edge when saving for the long term.

WHAT ARE THE ADVANTAGES OF TAX DEFERRAL?

By using an IRA to make investments, the IRA owner is able to defer taxes on any investment returns, thus, allowing the IRA owner to benefit in three ways. The first benefit is tax-free growth: instead of paying tax on the returns of an investment, tax is paid only at a later date, leaving the investment to grow tax free without interruption. The second benefit of tax deferral is that IRA investments are usually made when the IRA owner is in his or her highest income-earning years and is thus subject to tax at a higher tax rate. The third benefit is the ability to defer taxes on investments in the face of increased federal income-tax rates. With tax rates at a historic low (the highest income-tax bracket in 1986 was 50 percent and in 2000 was 39.6 percent), the likelihood of higher federal income-tax rates in the near future are significant, especially with the financial strain the baby-boomer generation is expected to have on the federal budget. Thus, the ability to defer tax on investments until the IRA owner is 70½ and likelier to be in a lower income-tax bracket makes an IRA a highly attractive investment vehicle.

TAX DEFERRAL BY THE NUMBERS

The following examples illustrate the powerful advantage of tax-deferred contributions and compounding through a traditional IRA versus making contributions to a taxable account.

Example 1

Joe is forty years old and makes a $5,000 contribution to an IRA. Assume Joe is in a 30 percent federal income-tax bracket. Joe invests his IRA funds and receives a 6 percent average annual return. When Joe retires at age seventy, his $5,000 contribution would be worth $21,609.71. If Joe had invested the $5,000 personally, the account would only be worth $14,033.97.

Example 2

Jane is thirty-five years old and makes a $5,000 contribution to an IRA. Jane makes a $5,000 contribution to her IRA each year until she reaches the age of seventy. Assume Jane is in a 30 percent federal income-tax bracket. Further assume that Jane was able to generate a 7 percent average annual return on her investment. When Jane retires at the age of seventy, her IRA account would be worth $792,950.21. If Jane made these $5,000 contributions though a taxable account, the account would only be worth $490,707.49.

Tax Advantages of Using an IRA

There are always great tax advantages to saving for retirement, but this is especially easy to do with an IRA. Not only are you reducing your immediate tax burden by making tax-deferred contributions to the plan, but also all the income and gains generated by your IRA are generally directed back to your plan tax deferred or tax free in the case of an after-tax (Roth) account.

All of this means that you can build more wealth at a faster rate. The advantages of saving money for retirement are not as well understood as they should be. In particular, tax deferrals are wildly underappreciated.

The concept of tax deferral is premised on the notion that all income and gains generated by a pretax retirement account investment flow back into the retirement account tax free. So, instead of paying tax on the returns of a self-directed IRA investment such as real estate, tax is paid only at a later date, leaving the investment to grow unhindered. For example, if an IRA invested $100,000 in 2013 and the account earned $15,000 in 2013, the investor would not owe tax on that $15,000 in 2013. Instead, the IRA holder would be required to pay the taxes when he or she withdraws the money from the IRA, which could be many years later. Assuming the IRA holder mentioned above is in a 30 percent federal income-tax bracket, she avoided paying $5,000 in federal income taxes on the $15,000 earned on the IRA investment in 2013. That would have left $10,000 in the account, which would only produce an $800 return assuming an 8 percent rate of return. Whereas, at an 8 percent annual return, the IRA earnings actually go on to produce $1,200 in total if we go back to the original account balance of $15,000. The beauty of tax deferral is that the deferral compounds each year.

Even more eye-popping, take the example of Ben. Ben is thirty years old when he decides to start an IRA. He has a current retirement-account balance of zero at that time. Assuming Ben decides to make annual IRA contributions of just $3,500 each year until he reaches the retirement age of seventy, and that he is able to generate an average annualized rate of return of 9 percent with a prevailing tax rate of twenty-five percent, then, at age seventy, Ben will have $1,289,022 of tax-deferred income in his IRA. In contrast, if that money had been invested outside of a retirement account as personal funds, the same assumptions would have produced just $699,475.

In other words, using an IRA allows Ben to accumulate an additional $589,547 of wealth. While Ben is not rich, he is able to put about $67 a week away for his retirement account every year. This small amount of money will turn into more than a million dollars for Ben by the time he retires.

"We'll start with a popular theme we've already touched on—the concept of tax deferral or tax-free savings in the case of a Roth IRA. Tax deferral is great, and using a pretax IRA is a great retirement-planning tool, but the Roth IRA offers tax-free growth, which has made the Roth account the last, best legal tax shelter out there. Let me explain why," John said.

TAX-FREE SAVINGS OF A ROTH IRA

"Americans love to spend and hate to save," John began.

"That's for sure," Amy agreed. "I read recently that Americans have one of the lowest savings rates for developed countries. We're the ultimate consumers."

"That definitely plays a role," John said. "However, I believe that education—or its lack thereof—is a big factor. Most people don't understand the basic concepts of retirement planning and how crucial it is, largely because it is not taught in our high schools or even our colleges and universities."

"Ideally, before they reach the age of thirty," Amy said, "so they can start supercharging their retirement savings."

"Exactly," John said. "For example, if young workers began funding an individual retirement account with $3,000 per year at age twenty and continued on through to age sixty-five, they will wind up with $2.5 million at retirement (assuming they earn the long-run annual compound growth rate in stocks, which was 9.88 percent from 1926 to 2011). Not a bad result for investing only $3,000 a year. Imagine if they learned that in school like we learn about history or sociology."

"I know," Amy said. "The entire country would be better off."

"With a traditional IRA, you gain all the advantages of tax deferral and tax-free gains. All income and gains generated by your IRA investment will flow back to your IRA tax free. By using a traditional IRA to make investments, as the IRA owner you will be able to defer taxes on any investment returns, thus, allowing you to benefit from tax-free growth. Instead of paying tax on the IRA returns of an investment, tax is paid only at a later date when a distribution is taken, leaving the investment to grow tax free without interruption."

"It's incredibly powerful," Amy said.

"OK, let's start with the basics. Tax deferral literally means that you are putting off paying tax. The most common types of tax-deferred investments include those in IRAs or qualified retirement plans (i.e., 401(k)). Tax deferral means that all income, gains, and earnings, such as interest, dividends, rental income, royalties or capital gains will accumulate tax free until the investor or IRA owner withdraws the funds and takes possession of them. As long as the funds remain in the retirement account, the funds will grow tax free. This allows your retirement funds to grow at a much faster pace than if the funds were held personally—allowing you to build for your retirement more quickly. And when you withdraw your IRA funds in the form of a distribution after you retire, you will likely be in a lower tax bracket and thus be able to keep more of what you accumulated. So, with using a traditional IRA as a retirement-savings vehicle, not only are you not paying taxes on the money you invested, you could be paying them at a lower rate when you finally do 'take home' your money."

"I just love that concept," Amy said.

"As long as the funds remain in the account, they grow without taxes eroding their value. This enables assets to accumulate at a faster pace, giving you an edge when saving for the long term. And when you withdraw funds after you retire, you'll likely be in a lower tax bracket and be able to keep more of what you've accumulated."

"What are the advantages of tax deferral?" Amy asked.

"By using an IRA to make investments," John said, "the IRA owner is able to defer taxes on any investment returns. This benefits the IRA owner in three ways. The first benefit is tax-free growth. Instead of paying tax on the returns of an investment, tax is paid only at a later date, leaving the investment to grow tax free without interruption. The second benefit is that IRA investments are usually made when the IRA owner is in his or her highest income-earning years and is thus subject to tax at a higher tax rate. The third benefit is the ability to defer taxes on investments in the face of increased federal income-tax rates."

"And tax rates are at historic lows right now," Amy said. "So the likelihood of higher federal income-tax rates in the near future are significant, especially with the financial strain the baby-boomer generation is going to have on the federal budget."

"Very true," John agreed. "So the ability to defer tax on investments until the IRA owner is 70½ and likelier to be in a lower income-tax bracket makes an IRA or 401(k) plan a highly attractive investment vehicle."

"And the returns keep growing too, right?" Amy said.

"Yes," John said. "Tax-deferred investments not only help investors avoid cash outflows for taxes in the immediate future, but they can help them generate higher returns, too. That's because the money that would normally be used for tax payments is instead allowed to remain in the account and earn a return. For example, if the IRA investor we talked about before is in a thirty-three percent tax bracket, he or she would have had to pay $3,333 in income taxes on the $10,000 earned on the IRA in 2011. That would have left $6,667 in the account. At a ten percent annual return, those earnings would go on to produce $667 in 2012. However, because IRAs are tax deferred, the investor is able to earn a return on the full $10,000 rather than the $6,667 she would have had if she had to pay taxes that year. At a ten percent annual return, she'd earn $1,000 in 2012. As you can see, the advantage of tax deferral compounds with each year."

"Do you have any other examples of the benefits of tax deferral?" Amy asked.

"You bet," John said. "Here are a few that illustrate the powerful advantage of tax-deferred contributions and compounding through a traditional IRA versus taxable-making contributions to a taxable account."

Example 1

Joe is forty years old and makes a $5,000 contribution to an IRA. Joe is in a 30 percent federal income-tax bracket. Joe invests his IRA funds and receives a 6 percent annual return. When Joe retires at age seventy, his $5,000 contribution would be worth $21,609.71. If Joe invested the $5,000 personally, the account would only be worth $14,033.97.

Example 2

Jane is thirty-five years old and makes a $5,000 contribution to an IRA. Assume that Jane makes a $5,000 contribution to her IRA each year until she reaches the age of seventy. Jane is in a 30 percent federal income-tax bracket. Further assume that Jane was able to generate a 7 percent annual return on her investment. When Jane retires at the age of seventy, her IRA account would be worth $792,950.21. If Jane had made these $5,000 contributions through a taxable account, the account would have only been worth $490,707.49.

Example 3

Ben is twenty-eight years old and has been working for a few years. Ben is in a 25 percent federal income-tax bracket. Ben has been doing well at work and believes he can make a $2,500 annual IRA contribution. Ben spoke to his CPA about this, and his CPA ran some numbers and came back with some incredible numbers. Assuming Ben can generate a rate of return of 7 percent annually and he makes $2,500 contributions to the IRA until he reaches the age of seventy, he would have almost $617,000 in his IRA. Ben's CPA then mentioned that if he was able to increase his contributions to $3,500 each year and was able to generate a 7 percent return, Ben would have almost $864,000 versus $734,160 if non-IRA funds were used. Ben thought that was a pretty impressive number for just putting away $3,500 a year in his IRA.

Example 4

Amy is twenty-five years old and just started her first job. Amy is in the 25 percent federal income-tax bracket and was told about the IRA benefits. Amy thought that she would be able to make a $1,500 annual contribution. Amy's CPA ran some numbers and mentioned that if she was able to generate an 8 percent rate of return and kept making IRA contributions until she reached the age of seventy, she would have a whopping $626,239 versus $469,604 if non-IRA funds were used.

"Those are great," Amy said, "and very helpful."

"It makes it clear that one of the key principles of tax deferral is starting early. The earlier you start making tax deferrals the better off you will be."

"You keep mentioning seven and eight percent annual returns. Looking at 2015 and 2016, that seems kind of unrealistic." Amy said.

"That is a fair point, but when you are saving for retirement you are generally looking at many years and even if you have one or two years where your returns are not great, history has shown us that over thirty or forty years, a prudent equity investor should be able to average close to eight percent. We know this because the average annual return for the S&P 500 since its inception in 1928 through 2014 is approximately ten percent."

Tax Advantages of Using a Roth IRA

It always comes down to the taxes. With a Roth IRA, as long as you have some patience and can wait until you are over 59½ and have had the Roth IRA open at least five years, all Roth IRA contributions, income, and appreciation will be tax free. That means no federal or state income tax, ever, upon withdrawal and not simply tax-deferred growth but tax-free growth. "As a tax attorney, I have to say, things don't get much better than that," John said.

In order to get a better handle on the potential advantages of making after-tax Roth contributions, it is helpful to run several possible scenarios:

Starting balance: $0
Annual contribution: $1,500
Current age: 35
Age of retirement: 70
Expected rate of return: 8 percent
Marginal tax rate: 25 percent
Total amount of contributions: $52,000

At age 70, with a Roth IRA, the individual would have $279,153 tax free, tax savings of $177,181.

Starting balance: $0
Annual contribution: $5,500
Current age: 30
Age of retirement: 65
Expected rate of return: 9.77 percent
Marginal tax rate: 25 percent
Total amount of contributions: $192,000

At age 65 with a Roth IRA, the individual would have $1,552,705.118 tax free, tax savings of $876,642.

Now, assuming the individual wanted to retire at age 70:

Starting balance: $0
Annual contribution: $5,500
Current age: 30
Age of retirement: 70
Expected rate of return: 9.77 percent
Marginal tax rate: 25 percent
Total amount of contributions: $200,000

At age 70 with a Roth IRA, the individual would have $2,510,367 tax free, tax savings of $1,282,637.

Starting balance: $0
Annual contribution: $3,500
Current age: 38
Age of retirement: 70
Expected rate of return: 8 percent
Marginal tax rate: 25 percent
Total amount of contributions: $112,000

At age 70 with a Roth IRA, the individual would have $507,327 tax-free, tax savings of $337,201.

As a recap, the foundation of retirement investing is based on the concept of tax deferral. Tax deferral means that you can postpone taxes on any earnings you make on the money in your tax-deferred accounts. That means your money is growing each year without having to remove any funds to pay tax. For example, if you contributed $2,000 to a traditional IRA each year for ten years and averaged a 7 percent annual rate of return, assuming a 25 percent income-tax rate, your traditional IRA would be worth $31,291, whereas if you invested the funds personally, you would have just $23,468. Now, imagine that instead of contributing over ten years, you contributed over thirty years. Assuming the same facts, your traditional IRA would be worth $244,692 versus just $183,519. Pretty impressive numbers for just saving around $5 a day. If a traditional IRA was used, you would eventually have to pay the taxes on the income deferred. But here's the good news. You may be in a lower tax bracket in retirement, so the taxes you pay will be less than if you had paid them during your working years, and you only pay tax on the amount you withdraw from your tax-deferred accounts. The rest of the money in your tax-deferred account continues to grow tax deferred—and compound interest continues to work its magic over time. Of course, you could always open a Roth IRA, assuming you satisfied the income limitations, and all your income and gains would be tax free, assuming you were over the age of 59 ½ when you took a Roth IRA distribution and the Roth IRA had been open at least five years.

The thing with tax deferral is that, generally, the earlier you start, the greater the tax deferral power will be. This is exactly why today is a perfect time for millennials or generation Xers to start saving for retirement and kick-start their tax-deferral clock. Of course, it is never too late to start saving for retirement, but millennials are at the perfect age to take advantage of the amazing power of tax deferral. Much has been made of the enormous impact that student loans and a soft job market have had on millennials and how it has hurt their ability to save for retirement. For example, as of April 2015, national student debt total has reached $1.2 trillion and of the consumers who are currently in the repayment stage, their average payment is $279 per consumer.[25] This is all true, but the power of tax deferral can help you retire in style by just saving $5 a day—that's one less Grande Cappuccino at Starbucks each day. Not a huge sacrifice for potentially having hundreds of thousands of dollars when you retire. I know not all millennials or generation Xers can save thousands of dollars a month, but I really believe almost everyone can save $1 or $2 a day by just making some small changes in their lifestyles and spending habits. The key is starting early, which gives the millennials a huge advantage over generation X and the baby boomers. Take a look.

Let's assume that Dylan is twenty-five years old and saves $5 a day or $1,825 a year, which he contributes to a Roth IRA. Let's also assume that Dylan is able to save $1,825 a year until he reaches the age of seventy. Not a very unrealistic assumption. Let's also assume that Dylan is able to average 7 percent annually on his investments, which is actually below the average S&P 500 return since its inception through 2014, which is close to 10 percent. Let's further assume that the tax rate stayed static at 25 percent. Based on the facts, Dylan would have $557,997 in his Roth IRA at age seventy versus just $419,498 had he made the investments personally.

---

25 http://college.usatoday.com/2015/04/08/national-student-loan-debt-reaches-a-bonkers-1-2-trillion/.

Now, let's take Susan, who is forty-five years old and has not yet started saving for retirement. If she was able to contribute $5,000 a year to a Roth IRA until she reached the age of seventy, then, assuming the same 7 percent rate of return as Dylan and the same 25 percent tax rate, Susan would have $338,382 in her Roth IRA at age seventy but only $253,787 if she had made the investments personally.

As you can see, from a retirement standpoint, Dylan is much better off than Susan because he started contributing at a young age. Dylan's Roth IRA contributions equaled $82,125 whereas Susan's contributions equaled $125,000, yet, because her Roth IRA funds have less tax-deferral power behind it, her Roth IRA was close to $219,000 less than Dylan's. Now, even if Susan earned a 9 percent rate of return on her investments instead of 7 percent, that would only increase Susan's Roth IRA to $461,620, still almost $100,000 less than Dylan's.

The examples above show the enormous retirement benefits of making (Roth) contributions starting at a young age and on a consistent basis. Of course there is no guarantee that you will generate high returns each year, but over a long period of time, history has shown us that targeting a 7 or 8 percent average return is not unrealistic. That being said, there is certainly nothing wrong with having a million dollars or so in a pretax retirement account; although, if your federal and state income-tax rate was at 50 percent when you retired, that million-dollar-plus retirement account would still be nice but definitely not as nice as being able to live off the money tax free without ever having to pay tax on the money again. Taking this a step further, one can argue, that with a 50 percent tax rate, having $1 million in a Roth IRA plan is like having $1.5 million in a pretax account. Numbers never lie—the hard part is turning down an accountant who is pushing for you to make the pretax contribution, so it reduces your current income tax and makes him or her look better in your eyes. You need to think long term by focusing on the advantages of tapping a tax-free account when you retire, especially if taxes will be higher than they are now.

"That was really helpful. I feel so good that I started making Roth contributions at such an early age. My decision came down to the benefits of tax-free growth, which in my mind made the Roth IRA so attractive. If my sister or one of my friends asked whether they should use a traditional IRA or Roth IRA, do you have any tips on how I should answer?" Amy said.

"I do. It's a great question, but here are some thoughts." John said.

SHOULD I MAKE ROTH OR PRETAX CONTRIBUTIONS?

Often tax professionals and financial advisers are asked whether it makes sense to make a Roth after-tax contribution or a pretax contribution. The upside with Roth contributions is that your Roth withdrawals in retirement (including any earnings and gains on your Roth contributions) are completely federal income-tax free if you meet certain requirements.

When deciding whether you should make Roth contributions, pretax contributions, or a combination of the two, here are some important considerations.

If you feel your tax rate in retirement will be higher than it is today, Roth contributions may make sense for you. If you expect your tax rate to be lower in retirement than during your working years, you may benefit more from making before-tax contributions and paying taxes when you withdraw your money. It is hard to imagine now, but we are currently in a historically low tax-rate environment. For most of the century, including some boom times, top-bracket income-tax rates were much higher than they are today. In fact, during the 1950s and early 1960s, the top-bracket income-tax rate was over 90 percent. In light of our growing deficit, social-security shortfall, and heavy government spending, it is not far off to suggest that income-tax rates will be higher when you retire than they are now. Of course, no one knows what will happen tomorrow when it comes to Congress and taxes, and especially not in twenty or thirty years, so an educated guess is all one can make.

How confident are you in your expected returns? If you are very confident that your investments and/or cash flow from your investments are relatively secure and will grow over time, a Roth account would make sense. Bear in mind that many people felt that Enron, Lehman Brothers, and Bear Stearns were safe investments and suitable for Roth funds, and we all know how those companies turned out. In general, Roth IRA investments seem to work well with real-estate-income-producing investments as well as dividend-growth investments in which the cash flows are generally perceived as stable.

The further away your retirement, the greater opportunity for tax-free growth and the more potential you have for tax-free gains. Basically, if you will not be retiring in the near future, Roth contributions may make a good deal of sense, since your account has more time potentially to grow in value. This may make the tax advantages of Roth contributions even more important to you—although Roth dollars can benefit retirement savers of all ages.

Important Considerations in Determining Whether to Make Pretax IRA or After-Tax (Roth) IRA Contributions

Pre-tax Contribution	After-Tax (Roth) contribution
Tax deductible contributions	Contributions are not tax deductible – contributions made to a Roth IRA are from after tax dollars
Distributions may be taken by age 59½. and are mandatory by 70 1/2.	No Mandatory Distribution Age – with a Roth IRA you are not required to ever take distributions
Taxes are paid on amount of distributions (10% excise tax may apply if withdrawn prior to age 59½.)	No taxes on distributions if rules and regulations are followed
Available to everyone; no income restrictions with earned income	• For 2015, subject to adjustments each year, Single filers, Head of Household or Married Filing Separately (and you did not live with your spouse during the year) with modified adjusted gross income up to $131,000 can make a full contribution. Contributions are phased-out starting at $116,000 and you cannot make a contribution if your adjusted gross income is in excess of $131,000. • Joint filers with modified adjusted gross income up to $193,000 can make a full contribution. Once again, this contribution is phased-out starting at $183,000 and you cannot make a contribution if your adjusted gross income is in excess of $193,000.
Funds can be used to purchase a variety of investments (stocks, real estate, precious metals, notes, etc.)	Funds can be used to purchase a variety of investments (stocks, real estate, precious metals, notes, etc.)
IRA investments grow tax-free until distribution (tax deferral)	All earnings and principal are 100% tax free if rules and regulations are followed – No tax on distributions so maximum tax-deferral
Income/gains from IRA investments are tax-free	Income/gains from IRA investments are tax-free
Purchasing a real estate property than taking possession of the property after 59½. would be subject to tax	Purchasing a domestic or foreign real estate property then taking possession after 59/1/2 would be tax-free

"The primary benefit lies in the power of tax-free investing," John said. "One of the main attractions to the Roth IRA is that qualified distributions of Roth earnings are tax free. As long as certain conditions are met and the distribution is a qualified distribution (the Roth IRA holder is over the age of 59½ and any Roth IRA account has been open for at least five years), the Roth IRA holder will never pay tax on any Roth distributions received."

"It's hard to comprehend that putting away just a few thousand dollars a year in a Roth IRA can leave you with millions of dollars tax free," Amy said.

"I know," John said. "But it's as simple as making annual contributions to your Roth IRA and then generating tax-free returns from making real-estate or other investments with your Roth IRA. The earlier you start making contributions to your IRA, the better. Of course, starting at any point is good. Take the example of Ron, who is forty-five years old and began funding a Roth IRA with $5,500 and wanted to know how much he would have at age seventy if he continued to make $5,500 annual contributions and was able to earn an eight percent rate of return. At age seventy, Ron would have $434,249 tax free, which he could then live on or pass to his wife or children tax free."

"That is just incredible. I just can't believe more young people don't take advantage of a Roth IRA. Saving just four dollars a day can mean having a million dollars tax free when you retire. One less Starbucks coffee, Big Mac, burrito, or iTunes download can make the difference. It's really hard to comprehend the enormous power of tax deferral and tax-free investing. The IRS is really giving us the tools to retire rich through a pretax or Roth IRA, but unfortunately many Americans are not taking advantage of it or are just uninformed. It is a shame that colleges or universities don't have some basic course on retirement planning. I went to a top university and actually took a course on the Internet where I literally got ten percent of my grade for sending a professor an email but wasn't able to take a course on a subject that could help me retire rich. Just doesn't make sense," Amy said.

"I couldn't agree more with you. I actually set up a not-for-profit charity called Roth & Roll, whose main goal is to help educate the millennials and generation Xers on the power of the Roth IRA. Saving just $6 a day ($2190 annually) starting at twenty-two and continuing until the age of seventy can generate $1,159,261 tax free, assuming an eight percent rate of return, which is below that of the S&P historical rate of return. People are amazed. They always say, 'How can that be? Why hasn't anyone ever shown me this or told me about the Roth IRA before? I can totally save six dollars a day— that is basically one less Grande Caramel Macchiato a day. Even with all my expenses, such as rent, car payments, entertainment costs, and student loans, I could find a way to put a few dollars away a day especially if it could turn into serious money when I retire.' The next question then becomes, 'What happens if I am able to save more?' When I run the numbers, they are just stunned," John said.

"I think the nonprofit you set up is a great idea. Totally makes sense. The IRS is giving us the tools to retire in style, and so many Americans are just unaware of it. This is especially true of millennials like my sister who really have no clue about saving for retirement and probably have never heard of a Roth IRA. I bet if I showed her some of the examples you just mentioned, she would be totally blown away. I agree with you that the key to a successful retirement plan is starting young, and it all comes down to education and knowledge. The issue is that the millennials and many generation Xers are just not being educated or informed about the huge advantage of starting retirement saving early as well as the power of the Roth IRA. I really hope your charity is able to reach many millennials and generation Xers because it could truly have an enormous impact on how well they live when they retire," Amy said.

"The problem is that many millennials and generation Xers see retirement as off in the distance, which it is; however, the tricky thing is that putting off retirement saving until later in life might prove too little too late. That is why I believe education is so important. If we can show the millennials and generation Xers how important it to start saving for retirement at a young age and the power of the Roth IRA, we can hopefully have a meaningful impact on their future wealth and help them have a more financially secure retirement," John said.

"OK, that would be great. I know my sister and her boyfriend would be better off if they understood the power of tax deferral," Amy said.

"Next week I want to start talking about something called a self-directed IRA, which is a vehicle that allows an IRA holder to make traditional investments, such as stocks and mutual funds but also alternative-asset investments, such as real estate. I know you have close to one hundred thousand dollars in a Roth IRA and over one hundred thousand dollars in a 401(k) plan, so learning about some of the advantages of using a self-directed IRA to make alternative-asset investments may be useful and could actually enhance the value of your IRA," John said.

"OK, that sounds cool. I know I mentioned that I had no idea that the IRS allowed me to buy real estate or other alternative assets with my IRA, but I would certainly be interested in potentially looking at some alternative-asset investment opportunities for my Roth IRA. I have done quite well with the mutual funds I own, but I always read that having a well-balanced and diversified portfolio is healthy," Amy said.

"Well, I am not an investment advisor or financial planner, so I am probably not the right guy to ask about investment matters, but for my retirement accounts, I do have some assets in real estate along with stocks and mutual funds, and it has worked out really well for me. Same place and time next week," John said.

"Yes, for sure," Amy said.

5

THE SELF-DIRECTED ROTH IRA

THIS TIME JOHN arrived early and bought the cappuccinos and muffins. Amy arrived a little late because of the heavy rain and apologized. John was eager to get started and dove right into discussing the idea of the self-directed Roth IRA.

WHAT IS A SELF-DIRECTED ROTH IRA

"There are around forty-seven million IRAs in existence today. Believe it or not, most of those forty-seven million IRAs could be considered self-directed IRAs."

"Wait," Amy said. "Are you saying that most IRA holders are using their IRAs to invest in real estate, precious metals, tax liens, or private businesses?"

"No," John answered. "Even if it's allowed under IRS rules, they're not doing that. But what I am saying is that the majority of all IRA investments are technically self-directed since the IRA holder is typically the one who determines what type of investments will be made with his or her IRA."

"You mean, the way I select the mutual funds or even stocks that my IRA purchases?"

"Exactly. When you decide which investments to make using your IRA, you are technically self-directing your IRA investment. I wish that more people knew, however, that the IRS allows them to do more than simply select mutual funds or stocks to buy when making IRA investments."

"But I'm getting the feeling that not all IRAs, even those that are technically self-directed, would allow me to make real-estate investments."

"That's correct. Whether or not an IRA is a self-directed IRA depends on two factors—control and investment opportunities."

"My Roth IRA is through a local bank, and I am invested in mutual funds, so I doubt they will allow me to buy real estate or make other alternative-asset investments," Amy said.

"Correct again. The 'traditional financial institution' self-directed IRA is by far the most popular type of self-directed IRA. Like your Roth IRA, the majority of all IRAs are held at traditional financial institutions, such as Fidelity, Vanguard, Charles Schwab, Bank of America, Merrill Lynch, and so on. Many traditional financial institutions advertise themselves as offering a self-directed IRA, but what that really means is that you will be limited to purchasing stocks, mutual funds, bonds, and other traditional types of investments that earn the institution commission. In other words, you need the consent of your IRA custodian before making an investment."

"What's an IRA custodian?"

"A custodian is your IRA trustee. Basically, that's the institution that holds your IRA account, in your case your local bank. By law, every retirement account must be held at a custodian or trustee. A trustee may be a bank, trust company, credit union, or a large brokerage firm that is licensed by the IRS. IRS regulations require that either a qualified trustee or custodian hold the IRA assets on behalf of the IRA owner."

"Are there some financial custodians that will allow you to invest in areas you want to invest in?"

"Yes. A true self-directed IRA custodian is known as a passive custodian—and a passive custodian allows the IRA holder to engage in nontraditional investments like real estate. What it generally doesn't do is offer investment advice."

"Can you trust them?" Amy asked.

"Good question. As long as the institution is authorized to establish IRAs and holds the retirement funds at a Federal Deposit Insurance Corporation (FDIC), you have no worries about your money being safe."

"So, to get this straight," Amy said, "when you have a self-directed IRA at a traditional financial institution, you're technically able to self-direct your IRA investments. But you're probably limited to investing in the financial products offered by the financial institution."

"That's right," John answered. "For example, a financial institution such as Vanguard or Fidelity will allow you to select the type of investments for your own IRA, but your choices are generally limited to the financial products they offer—in other words—stocks, mutual funds, and bonds. They won't permit you to make alternative-asset investments such as real estate, precious metals, private business investments, foreign currency, and options."

"Why won't they allow me to purchase real estate with my IRA if it's permitted by the IRS?"

"It's just business. Financial institutions are in business to earn profit and generate strong earnings for shareholders. Like any business, they're motivated to enhance the bottom line. So they require IRA holders to invest in financial products they market and sell. That way they can earn a fee or commission and probably gain use of the funds. In fact, they make money by using the funds they have on deposit for their own investment purposes or to hold as financial reserves."

"In other words, they don't make any money by allowing you to purchase real estate or other alternative-asset investments, so it doesn't make any sense to let you do that."

"Exactly. If they could make money when you bought real estate with your IRA funds, they'd probably allow you to do that. But when an IRA holder buys real estate, the parties that benefit from the investment are the seller of the property, the real estate agent, the title-insurance company, and the closing attorney. On the other hand, if an IRA holder uses IRA assets to purchase mutual funds or stocks, the financial institution selling you those stocks benefits directly from the investment."

"So if they let you shift your IRA assets away from financial products, such as mutual funds, that generate their fees and commissions to nontraditional investments such as real estate, that's going to negatively affect the financial institution's bottom line."

"Right. It'll reduce the financial institutions profits for sure and probably put a strain on their financial reserves. So, most traditional financial institutions just don't allow it."

"Before you get into how you can make self-directed Roth IRA investments, what are some of the benefits of using a self-directed Roth IRA?" Amy asked.

"Good question. Here's my answer."

1. DIVERSIFICATION

With the self-directed IRA or Roth IRA, you can invest in almost any type of investment, including real estate, allowing you to diversify and better protect your retirement portfolio. If the 2008 financial crisis had any positive features, it was that many Americans started asking about alternative investment options for their retirement accounts. Diversification is a strategy to help make sure all your retirement assets aren't concentrated in a certain type of investment or area.

Retirement-account diversification has become a popular concept for many retirement-account holders. It is believed that the financial crisis cost retirees almost 25 percent of their retirement assets, and many are still trying to get back to where they were before the crisis. The sudden and steep stock-market fall, coupled with the lack of faith in Wall Street and the global financial markets, caused many Americans to seek a more balanced and diversified retirement portfolio. This shift brought a sharp increase in the number of Americans looking at a self-directed IRA as the vehicle for attaining a level of account diversification. Accordingly, balance and diversification have become popular hallmarks of a strong investment-retirement portfolio.

Alternative investments such as real estate have always been permitted in IRAs; it even says so right on the IRS website. But few people seemed to know about this option until the last several years. The alternative-asset and self-directed retirement markets were relatively small and unknown prior to 2008. There were a few small groups of early adopters in the retirement world who had heard about the nontraditional-asset option and took advantage of it to buy real estate and other nontraditional assets. These groups were on the cutting edge of investment options and largely did not have an impact on the greater retirement-investment community. The crossover only started after the 2008 financial crisis, when many Americans actively set out to determine whether alternative-investment options were available to them rather than waiting for these options to be advertised or offered.

After the 2008 financial crisis, allocating a portion of an investment portfolio to alternative-asset investments, such as real estate or precious metals, was seen as a way to help diversify a retirement-investment portfolio of stocks and bonds and reduce risk. Alternative-asset investments for retirement accounts were also shown to provide an income stream and hedge against inflation.

Of course, there is no certainty that a diversified investment-retirement portfolio will provide greater benefits to stockholders than a portfolio that is more concentrated in any particular individual real-estate investment sector or location. History still suggests that stocks are a solid investment over the long term. For example, according to historical records, the average annual return for the S&P 500 since its inception in 1928 through 2014 is approximately 10 percent. However, that number can be very misleading. Accurate calculations of average returns, taking all significant factors into account, can be challenging. Nevertheless, having your retirement account properly diversified and not wholly subjected to the ups and downs of Wall Street has become a priority since the 2008 financial crisis and is one of the factors behind the emergence of the self-directed IRA solution.

2. INVEST IN SOMETHING YOU UNDERSTAND

Many Americans became frustrated with the equity markets after the 2008 financial crisis. Thankfully, we have seen the financial markets rebound since then and have even seen some years of over 20 percent growth in the equity markets. Nevertheless, many Americans are still somewhat shell-shocked from the market swings and not 100 percent sure what exactly goes on on Wall Street and how it all works. Real estate, in comparison, is often a more comfortable investment for the lower and middle classes because they grew up exposed to it, whereas the upper classes often learned about Wall Street and other securities during their younger years and college days. Everyone has heard someone talk about the importance of owning a home or the amount of money that can be made by owning real estate—from Donald Trump to reality-TV stars. Real estate is fast becoming mainstream and one of the most trusted asset classes for Americans. It is, of course, not without risk, but many retirement investors feel more comfortable understanding the real-estate market and buying and selling real estate than they do stocks.

3. INFLATION PROTECTION

Rising food and energy prices, coupled with high federal-debt levels and low interest rates, have recently fueled new inflationary fears. As a result, some investors may be looking for ways to protect their portfolios from the ravages of inflation. It is a matter of guesswork to estimate whether these inflation risks are real, but for some retirement investors, protecting retirement assets from inflation is a big concern. Inflation can have a nasty impact on a retirement portfolio because it means a dollar today may not be worth a dollar tomorrow. Inflation also increases the cost of things that are necessary for humans to live and enjoy life, such as food, gas, shelter, clothing, and medical services, decreasing the value of money so that goods and services cost more. For example, if someone has an IRA worth $250,000 at a time of high inflation, that $250,000 will be worth significantly less or have significantly less buying power. This can mean the difference between retiring and working the rest of your life. Buying hard assets is seen as one way of protecting your assets against inflation. Many investors have long recognized that investing in commercial real estate or precious metals can provide a natural protection against inflation, as rents tend to increase when prices do, acting as a hedge against inflation.

4. HARD ASSETS

Many nontraditional assets, such as real estate and precious metals, are tangible hard assets that you can see and touch. With real estate, for example, you can drive by with your family, point out the window, and say, "I own that." For some, that's important psychologically, especially in times of financial instability, inflation, or political or global upheaval.

5. TAX-FREE WEALTH FOR YOUR RETIREMENT

The Roth IRA is truly the best legal tax shelter available, and it is accessible to everyone. Remember, a Roth IRA is an after-tax account in which no tax deduction is received on the contribution, but all income and gains associated with the Roth IRA would be tax free, in general, as long as the Roth IRA has been open at least five years and the Roth IRA holder is at least 59½. Along with the great tax benefits of generating tax-free asset growth and income, especially in light of an expected higher-tax environment in the near future, the Roth IRA can serve as a valuable estate-planning tool by allowing you to pass tax-free wealth to your heirs.

Using retirement funds to make alternative-asset investments is not for everyone. That being said, buying real estate or other alternative assets with retirement funds through a self-directed IRA or Roth IRA is an option that more and more people are starting to consider. According to the data provider, Preqin,[26] the alternative-assets industry's leading source of data and intelligence, the alternative-assets industry added more than $600 billion in assets under management in 2015, and as of January 2015, the assets under management of alternative-asset classes now stand at $6.9 trillion.

Certainly the 2008 financial crisis had a large impact on many Americans looking to alternative assets as a source of diversification. These numbers are even more impressive when you consider that the alternative-asset investment market is not advertised to the average American, especially when it comes to retirement accounts. When is the last time you saw a TV commercial from a major bank or financial institution proclaiming an opportunity to buy real estate or gold through your IRA? Those institutions do not allow their IRA accounts to invest in any alternative-asset class for the simple reason that they don't make money when you purchase real estate or other alternative assets, but they do make money when you buy their financial products. The genie is now out of the bottle, and more and more American retirement investors are starting to learn about the self-directed IRA and Roth IRA and some of the exciting retirement, tax, and investment benefits they present.

---

26 https://www.preqin.com/docs/reports/Preqin-Investor-Outlook-Alternative-Assets-H1-2015.pdf.

"So tell me about the financial institutions that allow me to make nontraditional investments with my IRA funds," Amy said.

"OK," John said. "There are two kinds of those too. Ready?"

CUSTODIAN-CONTROLLED SELF-DIRECTED IRAS WITHOUT CHECKBOOK CONTROL

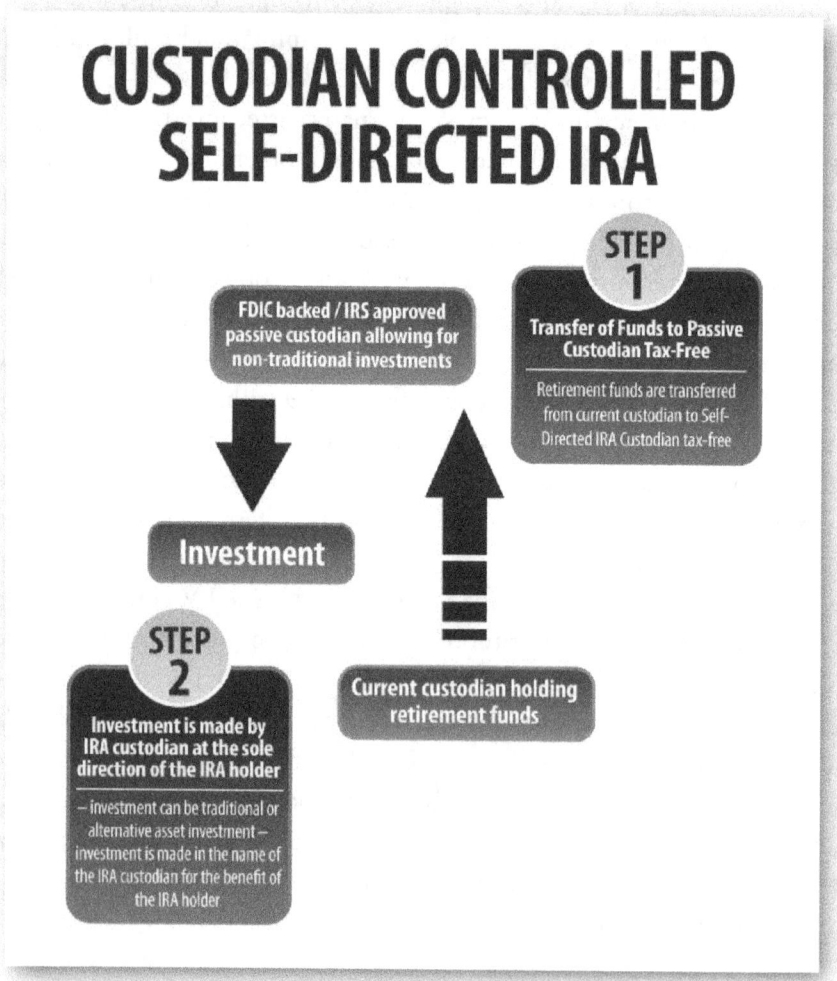

John took another sip of his latte and drew a line on a yellow pad.

"Unlike the traditional financial institutions such as Fidelity, Vanguard, Charles Schwab, or Bank of America, there are a number of financial institutions or IRA custodians that do allow IRA holders to make nontraditional investments with their IRA funds."

"Have I heard of them?"

"Maybe. They include Equity Trust and IRA Financial Trust, for example."

"Sounds sort of familiar. How are they different from the Vanguards?"

"They have a slightly different business model. Unlike a traditional financial institution, which makes the majority of its IRA-related earnings from commissions and fees associated with stocks, mutual funds, bonds, and other equity or debt-type investments, these custodians typically generate their profits through annual account valuation fees and transaction fees."

"OK, so they charge you an annual fee or a fee whenever you do something with your money, or both?"

"Exactly. They generally permit you to make alternative-asset investments such as real estate."

"I still don't like that word 'permit,'" Amy laughed. "It's my money, right?"

"It is," John said, "but even in this type of financial institution, you still don't have 'checkbook control.' In other words, you need custodian consent to enter into and execute any transaction."

"Sounds like a pain."

"Well, it can be. In fact, like any bureaucratic matter, it can be very inefficient. There are typically long delays between asking for consent and getting approval, and on top of that there can be high custodian fees associated with the transaction. So, before engaging in an IRA investment, they require you to get the consent of the custodian. You'll need to provide the custodian with the transaction documents for review as part of their transaction-review process. And even upon approval, your IRA investment would be made in the name of the custodian for the benefit of ("FBO") the IRA holder's IRA. So, for example, ABC Trust Company FBO Amy Jones IRA. This doesn't give the IRA owner any privacy or limited liability protection."

"Sounding less appealing by the minute."

"And the minutes can count, right, when you're trying to pounce on an opportunity."

"And the fees too. I don't like the sound of that."

"You shouldn't. It's common for a moderately active investor with $1 million in assets with a self-directed IRA custodian without checkbook control to end up paying from $500 to $1,500 in aggregate annual fees (including account-value fee, transaction fees, and approval letters)."

"And they can still say no to your investment idea?"

"They sure can. There's no guarantee that the custodian will approve your investment even though the investment would not violate IRS rules. Overall, with a custodian-controlled self-directed IRA, even though you will generally be permitted to make most alternative-asset IRA investments, time delays and high custodian fees are a major downside. For example, if Jim, the guy who sits in the front row of class, wants to use his retirement funds to invest in real estate, let's say he elects to use a custodian-controlled self-directed IRA to make the investment. He selects ABC Trust Company as the IRA custodian. Before making the real-estate investment, Jim would be required to provide all real-estate transaction documents, including the purchase agreement and all ancillary purchase documents to ABC Trust Company for review and signature. Then ABC Trust Company must approve the transaction. If the transaction is approved, Jim needs to wait for ABC Trust Company to sign all documents before proceeding with the real-estate purchase. In other words, even before Jim makes an offer on a piece of real estate, he's required to seek ABC Trust Company's consent as well as receive all required signatures before the offer can be submitted. Then, the funds required to make the purchase would be transferred directly from ABC Trust Company, and Jim would be required to pay an annual account fee based on the annual value of his IRA as well as fees for each IRA transaction."

"So, for Jim to pull that real estate deal off, he's got to hope no one else snaps it up before him, ABC Trust Company has to make the purchase for him, and he's got to pay them fees on top of all the fees and costs of the transaction."

"That's correct."

"I'm assuming there's a better way."

"You're right, there is."

THE SELF-DIRECTED IRA LLC WITH "CHECKBOOK CONTROL"

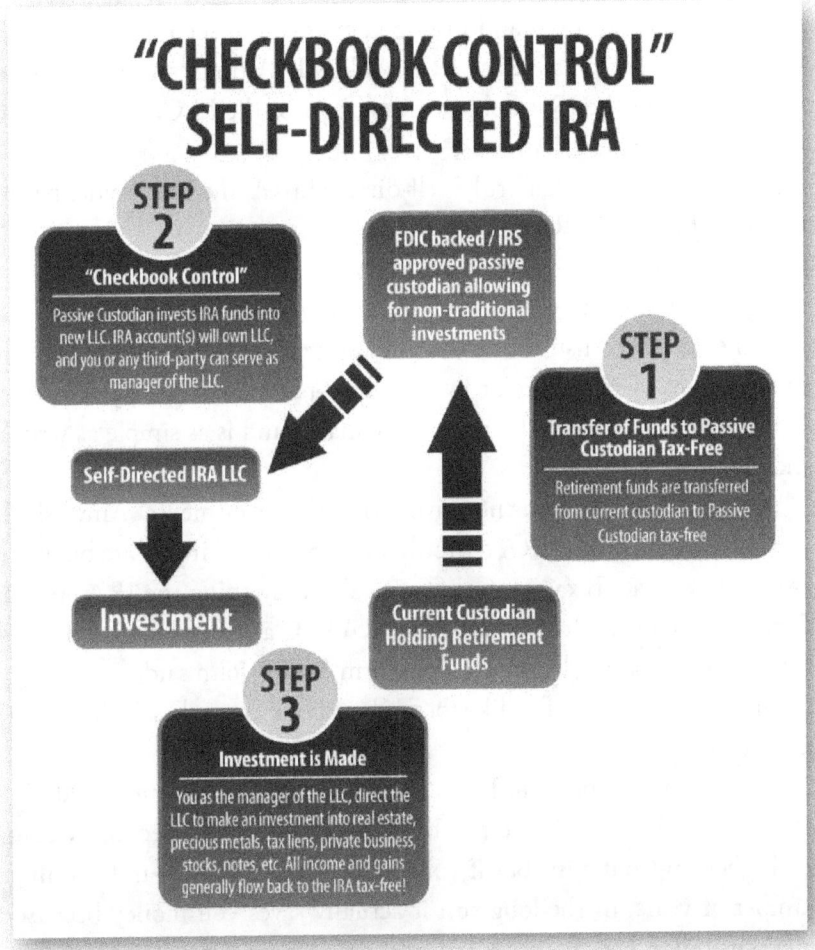

The cappuccinos were finished, and Amy sat back as John told her a very interesting story.

Beginning in the mid-1990s, a new type of self-directed IRA structure started taking shape allowing the IRA holder to make IRA investments directly without seeking the consent of a custodian. Unlike a custodian-controlled self-directed IRA, which requires the IRA holder to seek the consent of the custodian before making investments, with a self-directed IRA LLC with "checkbook control," a limited liability company (LLC) is established that is owned by the IRA account and managed by the IRA account holder. A passive custodian then transfers the IRA holder's IRA funds to the LLC's bank account providing the IRA holder, as manager of the LLC, with checkbook control over his or her IRA funds.

"So," John said, "with a 'truly' self-directed IRA, the IRA holder has total control over his or her IRA funds."

"No need to get custodian consent?"

"Right. You no longer have to get each investment approved by the custodian of the account. Instead, all your investment decisions are made by you, as the manager of the LLC, or by any third-party manager you assign. All LLC investments are made by you as a manager and is as simple as writing a check," John said.

"So the IRA custodian is not involved in the investment?" Amy asked.

"That is correct. The IRA custodian will not know if you are buying real estate in New York, Texas, or California. The only thing the IRA custodian will request from you is the value of the IRA LLC assets, which it will need to report to the IRS annually on the IRS Form 5498," John said.

"OK, so what are the fees like for a "checkbook control" self-directed IRA LLC?" Amy asked.

"That is a good question. I have seen fees that range from $1000–$1500 depending on the state where the LLC is formed. The 'checkbook control' has a higher up-front cost, but if you keep the structure up and running for a number of years, in the long run it actually saves you money because the annual custodian fees are quite low and range from $150 to $300, which is much less than a custodian controlled self-directed IRA," John said.

"Is it popular?"

"The popularity of self-directed IRA LLC with checkbook control is increasing each year. More and more custodians are getting more comfortable with their clients using these types of investment structures for their IRA funds. What do you think?" John asked.

"I think it sounds great, and if I decided to use a self-directed IRA to make investments I would strongly consider the 'checkbook control' self-directed IRA because of the freedom and flexibility it offers," Amy said. "One quick question. Is there a difference between a self-directed IRA and a self-directed Roth IRA in terms of the setup of the structure?"

"No. The only difference is that a self-directed IRA involves a pretax IRA and a self-directed Roth IRA involves a Roth IRA. Whether you elect to use a custodian controlled self-directed IRA or a 'checkbook control' self-directed IRA, the structures are the same; the only difference is the type of IRA that is being used," John said.

"OK, thanks," Amy said.

ROTH IRA TAX STRATEGIES

"What are some examples of tax strategies using a self-directed Roth IRA LLC?" Amy asked.

"Using a self-directed Roth IRA LLC presents a number of exciting tax-planning opportunities. The primary advantage of using a self-directed Roth IRA LLC to make investments is that all income and gains associated with the Roth IRA investment grow tax free and will not be subject to tax upon withdrawal or distribution. This is because unlike traditional IRAs, you are generally not subject to any tax upon taking Roth IRA distributions once you reach the age of 59½ and the Roth IRA has been opened for five years. This presents a number of exciting tax strategies:

- Purchasing a vacation home with Roth IRA funds and moving in tax free at age 59½
- Purchasing a retirement home with Roth IRA funds and moving in tax free at age 59½
- Purchasing an office building with Roth IRA funds and then using the building for your own business after you turn 59½
- Investing in precious metals and then taking possession of the metals once you reach the age of 59½

- Investing in tax deeds and then taking possession of the property personally once you reach the age of 59½
- Investing in a distressed property—generating large gains and then withdrawing the funds tax free for personal use upon reaching the age of 59½
- Investing in an investment fund—generating large gains and then withdrawing the funds tax free for personal use upon reaching the age of 59½"

SELF-DIRECTED ROTH IRA INVESTMENTS

"I assume if you can generate strong returns with your self-directed Roth IRA investments, you can build up a nice tax-free retirement nest egg pretty quickly," Amy said.

"Using a self-directed Roth IRA to purchase real estate or make other alternative-asset investments is the most tax-beneficial way to make such investments. I know you are well versed on the benefits of using a Roth IRA to make investments, which you have done for a number of years with traditional investments, but I think you will find the concept of the self-directed Roth IRA quite interesting. With federal and state income-tax rates expected to increase in the future, gaining the ability to generate tax-free returns from your retirement investments when you retire is the last surviving legal tax shelter. With a self-directed Roth IRA you can make almost any investment tax free, including real estate, tax liens, precious metals, currencies, options, and private business investments, and once you hit the age of 59½ you will be able to live off your Roth assets without ever paying tax. Imagine if someone told you that if you started making Roth IRA contributions in your forties and by just generating a modest rate of return on your real-estate investments, you could have over a million dollars tax free when you retire. Once you have reached the age of 59½ and have had the Roth IRA plan opened for at least five years, all income and gains from your self-directed Roth IRA can be used tax free and penalty free. You can also pass the Roth IRA funds to your spouse or children upon your death, allowing them to use the Roth funds for any purpose without paying tax."

"Sounds great," Amy said. "What are some of the tax advantages of buying real estate or making alternative-asset investments with a self-directed Roth IRA?"

TAX-FREE GROWTH

"The primary benefit lies in the power of tax-free investing," John said. "One of the main attractions to the self-directed Roth IRA is that qualified distributions of Roth earnings are tax free. As long as certain conditions are met and the distribution is a qualified distribution (the Roth IRA holder is over the age of 59½ and any Roth IRA account has been open for at least five years), the Roth IRA holder will never pay tax on any Roth distributions received."

"How about an example to show the power of tax-free investing?" Amy said.

Example 1
Joe, a self-employed consultant began funding a self-directed Roth IRA with $3,000 per year at age twenty and would continue on through age sixty-five. At age sixty-five Joe would wind up with $2.5 million at retirement (assuming they earn the long-run annual compound growth rate in stocks, which was 9.88 percent from 1926 to 2011). Not a bad result for investing only $3,000 a year.

Example 2
Ben, who is thirty years old, began funding a Roth IRA with $4,000 and wanted to know how much he would have at age seventy if he continued to make $4,000 annual contributions and was able to earn at an 8 percent rate of return. Ben did some research and was astonished that at age seventy he would have a whopping $1,119,124 tax free, which he could then live on or pass to his wife or children tax free.

Example 3
Mary, who is thirty-five years old, began funding a Roth IRA with $5,000 and wanted to know how much she would have at age seventy if she continued

to make $5,000 annual contributions and was able to earn at a 10 percent rate of return, which she felt was possible based on her past investment returns. Mary did some research and was astonished that at age seventy she would have a whopping $1,490,634 tax free, which she could then live on or pass to her husband and children tax free.

Example 4

Steve, who is eighteen years old, began funding a Roth IRA with just $1,200 and wanted to know how much he would have at age seventy if he continued to make just a $1,200 annual contribution and was able to earn at an 8 percent rate of return. Steve did some research and was astonished that at age seventy he would have a whopping $870,038 tax free, which he could then live on or pass to his wife or children tax free. By just saving $100 a month, Steve would be able to have close to $900,000 tax free when he retired.

"It's hard to comprehend that putting away just a few thousand dollars a year in a Roth IRA can leave you with millions of dollars tax free," Amy said.

"I know," John said, "But it's as simple as making annual contributions to your self-directed Roth IRA and then generating tax-free returns from making real-estate or other investments with your self-directed Roth IRA. The earlier you start making contributions to your IRA, the better. Of course, starting at any point is good. Take the example of Ron who is forty-five years old and began funding a Roth IRA with $5,500 and wanted to know how much he would have at age seventy if he continued to make $5,500 annual contributions and was able to earn an 8 percent rate of return. At age seventy, Ron would have $434,249 tax free, which he could then live on or pass to his wife or children tax free."

"What about a self-employed person like myself? Is the Roth IRA the best option?" Amy asked.

"If you're self-employed, I certainly recommend the Solo 401(k) plan because of the high-contribution options, especially in the case of Roth contributions. I will get into the Roth Solo 401(k) plan when we meet again, so I don't want to go into too much detail now. A Solo 401(k) plan is a 401(k) qualified retirement plan that is established by any business that has no full-time employees (over one thousand hours) other than the business owner(s) and spouse(s). It is far more robust than a SEP IRA, which is another popular retirement plan for a small business and does not include a Roth feature, because the Solo 401(k) plan has an employee-deferral feature, loan feature of fifty thousand dollars, and high Roth-contribution options."

"Can you touch on how the Roth Solo 401(k) contributions work?" Amy asked.

John nodded. "A Roth Solo 401(k) combines features of the traditional 401(k) with those of the Roth IRA. Like a Solo 401(k) plan, the Roth Solo 401(k) plan is perfect for any self-employed individual or small-business owner with no employees. The Roth Solo 401(k) plan contains the same advantages of a Solo 401(k) plan, but as with a Roth IRA, contributions are made with after-tax dollars. While you don't get an up-front tax deduction, the Roth 401(k) account grows tax free, and withdrawals taken during retirement aren't subject to income tax, provided you're at least 59½ and you've held the account for five years or more. For the 2015 taxable year, an individual under the age of fifty can make an after-tax Roth Solo 401(k) plan contribution of up to eighteen thousand dollars, whereas an individual over the age of fifty can make Roth Solo 401(k) plan contributions of up to twenty-four thousand dollars for the 2016 taxable year. As for the employer profit-sharing contributions, the employer may make contributions equal to twenty-five percent (twenty percent in the case of a sole proprietorship or single-member LLC) of the plan participant's W-2 or self-employment income amount up to fifty-three thousand dollars (fifty-nine thousand dollars for individuals over the age of fifty), including any employee deferrals made by the employee during the year. The employer profit-sharing contributions must be made pretax, but as of 2013, those employer contributions can be converted immediately to Roth as long as the Solo 401(k) plan allows for in-plan Roth conversions. A tax would have to be paid on the Roth conversion amount, but one would technically be able to make Roth contributions of up to fifty-three thousand dollars (fifty-nine thousand dollars if over the age of fifty) for the 2016 taxable year, almost ten times the amount of an IRA."

MAKING INVESTMENTS WITH A SELF-DIRECTED ROTH IRA

"I assume you make self-directed Roth IRA investments the same way you would make investments with a traditional pretax self-directed IRA," Amy said.

"Absolutely," John said. "The only difference lies in the type of IRA being used and the taxation of the income and appreciation. In the case of a pretax IRA, just like a Roth IRA, all income and gains would flow back to the IRA without tax. The difference lies in the distribution rules. In general, with a pretax IRA, distributions prior to the age of 59½ are subject to income tax and a ten percent early-distribution penalty, and distributions after the age of 59½ are just subject to income tax. In contrast, with a Roth IRA, as long as the Roth IRA has been open at least five years and the individual is over the age of 59½, there is generally no tax on any distributions from the Roth IRA. This obviously leads to a number of exciting tax-planning opportunities and strategies."

"Sounds good."

"Let's go into a few of those opportunities in more detail so you understand the finer points," John said.

Real Estate

Real estate has become one of the most popular nontraditional-investment options for IRA and Roth IRA investors. According to McKinsey & Company report, "The Mainstreaming of Alternative Investments: Fueling the Next Wave of Growth in Asset Management," by Onur Erzan, principal, dated June 2012, in the United States, institutional investors expect to have 28 percent of their portfolios allocated to alternative investments by the end of 2013, up from 26 percent in 2010. That quote was taken from a recent *Financial Advisor* magazine article. The same piece also referenced a multiyear McKinsey & Company study that noted year-end 2011 assets under management for global alternatives reached record levels of $6.5 trillion, having grown at a five-year rate of over seven times that of traditional asset classes.

Real estate offers diversification from overexposure to Wall Street for both personal and retirement funds. After the 2008 financial crisis, many retirement investors began to appreciate the importance of having a well-balanced and diversified retirement portfolio that can help protect against another financial crisis. People generally like to invest in something they know and understand. Real estate is reemerging as an asset class that more Americans have confidence and comfort in compared to the vagaries of the stock market. Buying tangible assets, such as real estate, is seen as a solid way of protecting retirement savings from the threat of inflation.

Plus, all income and gains from real estate owned in a self-directed IRA are exempt from tax, making real estate an even more powerful investment. For example, if you purchased a piece of property with your self-directed IRA for $100,000 and you later sold the property for $300,000, the $200,000 of gain appreciation would generally be tax free. Whereas, if you purchased the property using personal funds (nonretirement funds), the gain would be subject to federal income tax and, in most cases, state income tax.

The IRS allows you to use a self-directed Roth IRA to purchase real estate or raw land, as long as your plan does allow for it. Remember, it is up to the IRA custodian whether nontraditional-investment options, such as real estate, are permitted to be made with IRA or Roth IRA funds. In general, most financial institution–established IRAs do not allow for real-estate investments, while a custodian-directed and checkbook control self-directed IRA will allow for the real-estate investment option. If you elect to use a "checkbook control" self-directed Roth IRA LLC, as manager of the self-directed IRA LLC, making a real-estate investment is as simple as writing a check from your self-directed IRA LLC bank account.

Tax Liens and Tax Deeds

Tax-lien and tax-deed investments have become popular investment choices for many self-directed IRA investors. Beginning in 2009, as foreclosures continued to pile up, many properties were saddled with unpaid property taxes. For some investors, this created a great investment opportunity.

Tax collectors in twenty-nine states as well as Washington, DC; Puerto Rico; and the US Virgin Islands use tax-lien sales to force owners to pay unpaid property taxes. The process varies by state, but here's how it generally works: When property owners don't pony up for their property taxes, tax collectors wait the time period required by state law and then put those unpaid property taxes up for auction. The time period varies from just a few months to several years depending on the state.

In most states, the person willing to pay the most cash for the tax lien wins the auction. Some states, however, have a bid-down process, in which investors' bids indicate how much interest they're willing to accept on their investment, and the lowest bidder wins. Whatever method is used, the tax collector takes the payment for the overdue taxes from the winning bidder. In exchange, the purchaser gets a lien on the property. As the winning bidder, you'd get a return on your investment in one of two ways: interest on your bid amount or ownership of the property.

With a tax deed, on the other hand, you will actually own the property in which the owner has been delinquent in paying the property taxes. A tax-deed sale generally involves property being sold by a taxing authority or the court to recover delinquent taxes.

The IRS permits the purchase of tax liens and tax deeds with a self-directed IRA. The advantage of purchasing tax liens or tax deeds with a self-directed IRA is that your profits are tax deferred back into your retirement account until a distribution is taken. In the case of a self-directed Roth IRA, all gains are tax free.

Once again, you have checkbook control and can make purchases on the spot without custodian consent.

Loans and Notes

The IRS permits using IRA or Roth IRA funds to make loans or purchase notes from third parties. By using a self-directed IRA to make loans or purchase notes from third parties, all interest payments received are tax deferred until a distribution is taken. In the case of a self-directed Roth IRA, all gains are tax free. When engaging in private lending transaction or purchasing notes, it is important to make note of the IRS–prohibited transaction and disqualified-person rules, which are found in IRC 4975.

For example, if you used a self-directed Roth IRA to loan money to a friend, all interest received would flow back into your self-directed IRA, whereas if you lent your friend money from personal funds (nonretirement funds), the interest received would be subject to federal and, in most cases, state income tax.

Precious Metals and Coins

You can also use your self-directed assets to make investments in precious metals and certain coins. The advantage of using a self-directed Roth IRA to purchase precious metals and/or coins is that their values generally keep up with, or exceed, inflation rates better than other investments. The IRS under IRC 408(m) provides a detailed overview of the type of metals and coins that can be purchased with retirement funds. We will discuss the types of IRS-approved precious metals when we discuss the prohibited-transaction rules.

Foreign Currencies and Options

There is no IRS prohibition against using retirement funds to purchase foreign currencies or engaging in option trading. Many investors believe that foreign-currency investments offer liquidity advantages compared to the stock market as well as significant investment opportunities. With respect to option trading, there is a belief that it can potentially generate increased cost efficiency, may be less risky than equities, and has the potential to deliver higher-percentage returns.

Again, all foreign-currency gains and income from the lapse or termination of an option are generally tax deferred until a distribution is taken, and in the case of a self-directed Roth IRA, all gains are tax free.

Stocks, Bonds, Mutual Funds, CDs

In addition to nontraditional investments such as real estate, a self-directed IRA or Roth IRA may also purchase stocks, bonds, mutual funds, and CDs. According to the Investment Company Institute report titled, "The IRA Investor Profile: The Traditional IRA Investors' Activity, 2007–2012," dated March 10, 2014, traditional IRA investors' allocation to equity holdings fell, on average, although some of the change merely reflects market movement rather than investors' rebalancing. For example, among consistent traditional IRA investors aged twenty-five to fifty-nine, about three-quarters of their traditional IRA assets were invested in equity holdings—which includes equities, equity funds, and the equity portion of balanced funds—at year-end 2007, and about two-thirds of their traditional IRA assets were invested in equity holdings at year-end 2012. Accordingly, it's easy to conclude that stocks, mutual funds, ETFs, and other equities are by far the most popular investment for retirement accounts.

The advantage of using a self-directed IRA or Roth IRA with checkbook control is that you are not limited to just making these types of investments. You can open a stock-trading account with any financial institution.

No one is arguing against stocks as the best retirement investment. Indeed, history has shown that owning stocks is one of the easiest and most profitable ways to grow your wealth over the long term. From January 1, 1900, through December 31, 2013, for example, the average return of the S&P 500, which tracks the five hundred largest stocks based on market capitalization, was 11.6 percent.

Stocks have proven to be a good investment over time. Could you do better with a different investment? Possibly. The bigger concern, however, is that such heavy exposure to the US equity markets carries some risk. Diversification is a must when it comes to retirement planning.

USING A SELF-DIRECTED ROTH IRA TO INVEST IN A BUSINESS

"Can I use my Roth IRA to invest in my business and shelter all income from tax?" Amy asked.

"Unfortunately, no," John said. "The same prohibited-transaction rules that apply to traditional IRAs also apply to Roth IRAs. We will go into all the IRS–prohibited transaction rules in detail in the future, so don't worry. So, just as you are not permitted to invest your traditional IRA in your own business as it would violate the prohibited-transaction rules under IRC 4975, the same rules would apply to Roth IRAs. Imagine if you can invest your Roth IRA funds in your own business and shelter all the income tax for your business. That would be pretty nice, but unfortunately the IRS doesn't feel the same way. In fact, the IRS has issued a number of letter rulings outlining this exact type of situation, so it is highly risky to try to use a Roth IRA to shelter personal or business income. Not only could it trigger civil penalties, but the IRS could also pursue criminal charges."

"What about investing a Roth IRA in a friend's business? Can I shelter all income from tax?"

"Yes and no," John said. "On the yes side, just like with a traditional IRA, you could use a self-directed Roth IRA to invest in a friend's business or any nondisqualified person's business. However, if the business is being conducted via an LLC or other flow-through entity, a set of tax rules known as the Unrelated Business Taxable Income (UBTI or UBIT) would kick in and could potentially impose close to a forty percent tax on the business income allocated to your Roth IRA. So, it would turn your potentially tax-free investment into a very tax-unfriendly investment. You would need to run the numbers and see how the UBTI or UBIT tax would affect your expected returns and would need to determine whether using personal funds instead of Roth IRA funds would make more sense."

"What exactly is UBTI"? Amy asked.

UBTI

"Let me explain. In general, if you make passive investments with your self-directed IRA, such as stocks, mutual funds, precious metals, foreign currency, and rental real estate, the income generated by the investment will not be subject to any tax. Only if your self-directed IRA makes investments into an active business, such as a retail store, restaurant, real estate—development business, or software company, using a pass-through entity such as an LLC or partnership will your self-directed IRA likely be subject to a tax known as the unrelated business taxable income tax, also known as UBTI or UBIT."

"Can you give me another example?" Amy asked.

"Let's say a self-directed IRA invests in an LLC that operates an active business such as a restaurant or water franchise; the income or gains generated from the investment will generally be subject to the UBTI tax. However, if the self-directed IRA invested in an active business through a C corporation, such as Apple or Google, there would be no UBTI since the C Corporation acts as a blocker blocking the income from flowing through to the self-directed IRA shareholder. A C Corporation is an entity taxed separate from its shareholders (blocker corporation), whereas, an LLC is treated as a partnership or pass-through entity (flow through) for tax purposes. This is why most Americans have never heard of the UBTI rules and why you can invest your IRA into a public company, since almost all public companies traded on the public markets or that make up mutual funds, such as Apple, Google, J.P. Morgan, or GE are C Corporations, will block the application of the UBTI tax since the income from the C Corporation gets trapped at the corporate level and does not flow through to the shareholders. Remember that if an IRA makes a passive investment, such as rental income, dividends, and royalties, such income would not be subject to the UBTI rules pursuant to IRC Section 512."

"I'm still not sure I get it," Amy laughed.

"Here we go," John said. "One of the advantages of using retirement funds through your self-directed IRA to make investments is that, in most cases, all income and gains from the investments flow back to your IRA LLC tax free. This is because an IRA is exempt from tax, pursuant to IRC Section 408. Pursuant to IRC Section 512, most of the popular forms of income generated by a retirement income will be exempt from tax. This is why most American investors look at you funny when you start telling them about the Unrelated Business Taxable Income rules, also known as UBTI or UBIT, which triggers a tax on certain categories of retirement-account income."

"I know; I never hear about it," Amy said. "OK, makes sense"

"The good thing about the UBTI rules is that they won't apply to over ninety percent of American retirement investors because most types of income and gains generated by a retirement account are exempt from the UBTI rules. The IRC exempts dividends, interest, capital gains, royalties, and rental income from being subject to the UBTI-tax rules. Even so, the UBTI rules are new and somewhat intimidating to most people when learning about them for the first time. For example, buying public stocks and mutual funds with a self-directed IRA will not trigger the UBTI; neither would receiving a dividend from a public stock or interest from a bond or even rental income from an investment property. In the case of a self-directed IRA, the UBTI tax is essentially triggered in three main types of investments:

1. Investing in an active trade or business via a pass-through entity, such as an LLC
2. Using margin when buying stock
3. Using a nonrecourse loan to buy real estate

"Before I go through the three ways the UBTI tax can be triggered when using a self-directed IRA, I think it is helpful to examine why the UBTI tax came into law," John stated.

"What's the back story on that?" Amy asked.

"It's pretty interesting," John said. "Back in the 1950s Congress was concerned that for-profit companies would set up a charity and run their business through a charity and escape taxation forever, thus, providing them with an unfair advantage because of their tax-exempt status. With that in mind, they created the UBTI rules under IRC 512. These rules can be found under IRC Sections 511–514 and have become known as the Unrelated Business Taxable Income rules or UBTI or UBIT. If the UBTI rules are triggered, the income generated from those activities will generally be subject to a tax of approximately thirty-five percent. Of note, a self-directed IRA investing in an active trade or business using a C Corporation, which consists of almost all public-stock companies and mutual funds, will not trigger the UBTI tax. The reason is that a C Corporation is not a pass-through entity, and so the C Corporation essentially 'blocks' the income from traveling to the shareholders, thus blocking the active trade or business income from flowing to the IRA. You can think of a C Corporation as a box and an LLC or partnership as a funnel, which I think helps to understand why the UBTI tax would not apply to a retirement account owning shares in a C Corporation."

"What is Unrelated Business Taxable Income?" Amy asked.

"UBTI is defined as 'gross income derived by any organization from any unrelated trade or business regularly carried on by it, reduced by deductions directly connected with the business.' The UBTI rules only apply to exempt organizations such as charities, IRAs, and 401(k) Plans. With the enactment of ERISA in 1974, IRAs and 401(k) plans, which are considered tax-exempt parties pursuant to IRC Sections 408 and 401, respectively, became subject to the UBTI rules. As a result, if an IRA or 401(k) plan invests in an active business through an LLC or partnership, the income generated by the IRA or 401(k) from the active business investment will be subject to the UBTI rules."

"OK," Amy said.

"In the case of a self-directed IRA or Roth IRA, a transaction would not trigger the UBTI or UBIT rules if the transaction is not considered a trade or business that is regularly carried on. This typically involves passive types of activities that generate capital gains, interest, rental income, royalties, and dividends, the categories of income exempt according to IRC Section 512, which are also the most popular investments for retirement accounts. However, if the tax-exempt organization (your retirement account) engages in an active trade or business that is regularly carried on, such as a restaurant, store, or manufacturing business, the IRS will tax the income."

"What's the UBTI tax rate?" Amy asked.

"IRC 511 taxes 'unrelated business taxable income' at the rates applicable to corporations or trusts, depending on the organization's legal characteristics. In general, a self-directed IRA subject to UBTI is taxed at the trust-tax rate because an IRA is considered a trust. For 2016, a retirement account subject to UBTI can be subject to a tax of close to forty percent."

Amy looked up. "Pretty steep."

"Yes. In fact, they're higher than most individual's income-tax rates as well as the corporation income-tax rate. This is one of the main reasons why the UBTI-tax rules are so important to understand and avoid if possible. In essence, the UBTI tax is imposed on the retirement-account investment and actually creates a double-tax regime since the UBTI tax will apply in the year the income or gain is realized and then also when the plan participant takes a distribution or is required to take a distribution after the age of 70½ (in the case of a pretax IRA). This is just another reason why it is important to be aware of the UBTI-tax rules and their potential application to retirement-account investments.

"So, the question is what level of business activity must you cross before triggering the UBTI or UBIT tax? Unfortunately, there is no clear test as to how much business activity one must engage in a given year in order to trigger the UBTI or UBIT tax. In general, the IRS has a number of factors it will examine to determine whether one has engaged in a high enough volume or transactions, to trigger the UBTI tax. First, the IRS will examine the frequency of the transactions: how many business transactions are done in a year? Second, the IRS will examine the intent of the person: was the person intending to engage in an active trade or business? Third, the IRS will also look at the scope of other activities of the retirement account to determine whether the activity is part of a business activity or an investment. Fourth, the IRS will look at the personal business activities of the IRA investor to help determine whether the IRA investment is part of an overall business model. So, for example, several real-estate flips by Donald Trump's self-directed IRA could look more like a business than if they were made by a teacher or accountant."

"I am sorry I am asking so many questions, but if I ended up using a self-directed Roth IRA to buy real estate, I could see myself doing multiple small real-estate deals in a year and need to know that the transactions would not trigger the UBTI-tax rules. So just to be clear, the determination of whether an activity is an active trade or business and will, thus, trigger the UBTI or UBIT tax, which is taxed at a rate of approximately thirty-five percent, depends on the facts and circumstances," Amy said.

"Yes," John agreed. "Clearly if you have a store or restaurant, or manufacturing plant you are undoubtedly in business. But for some start-ups or real-estate transactions, there can be a question as to whether the activity is a simple investment or hobby or if the activity rises to the level of a trade or business. Thankfully, the IRS has issued some guidance as to whether an activity is a hobby or investment."

John opened the Internet browser on his smartphone and pulled up the IRS page. He started reading to Amy:

In order to make this determination of whether an activity is a business or hobby, taxpayers should consider the following factors:

- Does the time and effort put into the activity indicate an intention to make a profit?
- Does the taxpayer depend on income from the activity?
- If there are losses, are they due to circumstances beyond the taxpayer's control or did they occur in the start-up phase of the business?

- Has the taxpayer changed methods of operation to improve profitability?
- Does the taxpayer or his or her advisors have the knowledge needed to carry on the activity as a successful business?
- Has the taxpayer made a profit in similar activities in the past?
- Does the activity make a profit in some years?
- Can the taxpayer expect to make a profit in the future from the appreciation of assets used in the activity?

"OK, this is really helpful," Amy said. "I can see how doing multiple real-estate transactions can potentially be an issue."

"Yes, you are one hundred percent right; the determination of whether a set of real-estate activities are treated as an investment or a business and, thus, subject to the UBTI taxing regime could be somewhat tricky. Pretty important stuff considering that retirement accounts don't pay tax on investments but investing in an active business through a pass-through entity would be subject to the UBTI tax," stated John.

"OK, I think I am starting to understand the UBTI rules and their potential impact on retirement-account investments. As long as a retirement account did not use margin, a nonrecourse loan, or invest in an active trade or business through a pass-through entity, such as an LLC, the UBTI rules would not apply," Amy said.

"Exactly," John said.

"One last question. Can I take a loan from a self-directed IRA or Roth IRA?" Amy asked.

"Unfortunately not," John said. "You cannot borrow any funds from an IRA without triggering an IRS-prohibited transaction. However, if you are a participant in an employer 401(k) plan or are self-employed and can adopt a Solo 401(k) plan, you are able to borrow the lesser of fifty thousand dollars or fifty percent of their 401(k) plan account value and use the loan for any purpose. We will get into the Roth Solo 401(k) plan features, including the loan feature."

"OK, that sounds great. What about something called a ROBS? When I was starting my Internet-marketing business, I was doing research online about business-funding options and came across a number of websites talking about the ROBS solution. I am sorry if it is a bit off topic, but do you mind explaining to me how it works?" Amy asked.

ROBS

"I am happy you brought the ROBS structure up because it is something I did want to chat about at some point. When it comes to using retirement funds to buy or finance a business that you or another disqualified person will be involved in personally, there is only one legal way to do it and that is through the business acquisition solution, also known as a rollover business start-up solution (ROBS). The ROBS solution takes advantage of an exception in the tax code under IRC Section 4975(d) that allows one to use 401(k) plan funds to buy stock in a C corporation, which is known as qualifying employer securities. The exception to the IRS–prohibited transaction rules found in IRC 4975(d)(13) requires that a 401(k) plan buy qualifying employer securities, which is defined as stock of a C corporation. This is the reason one cannot use a self-directed IRA LLC to invest in a business the IRA holder or a disqualified person will be personally involved in or why a 401(k) plan cannot invest in an LLC in which the plan participant or disqualified person will be involved without triggering the prohibited-transaction rules. Hence, in order to use retirement funds to invest in a business in which a disqualified person will be personally involved, one needs a C corporation to operate a business and adopt a 401(k) plan."

"How does the ROBS arrangement work?" Amy asked.

"The ROBS arrangement typically involves rolling over a prior IRA or 401(k) plan account into a newly established 401(k) plan, which either an already existing or newly established C corporation business sponsored, and then investing the rollover 401(k) plan funds in the stock of the C corporation. The funds are then deposited in the C corporation bank account and are available for use for business purposes."

"So what is the difference between using a self-directed versus ROBS structure to buy a business?" Amy asked.

"In a lot of respects, using a self-directed IRA LLC or a 401(k) plan to purchase stock in a corporation would seem to be subject to the same rules.

However, as described above, using 401(k) plan funds and not IRA funds allows one to take advantage of the prohibited-transaction exemption under IRC 4975(d)(13) for qualifying employer securities. In essence, if one used an IRA to buy an interest in a new business that he or she was personally involved in, that transaction would likely violate the IRS–prohibited transaction rules and would not satisfy the exception in the tax code under IRC 4975(d) since the exception would only apply if a 401(k) plan and C corporation is used and the 401(k) plan purchased stock in the adopting employer C corporation stock."

"That's helpful," Amy said.

"The recent US Tax Court case *T.L. Ellis*, TC Memo. 2013-245, Dec. 59,674(M) highlights the risk and limitations involved when using a self-directed IRA to purchase business assets. In the Ellis case, the taxpayer used IRA funds to invest in a corporation that ultimately purchased business assets. Because Mr. Ellis used an IRA and not a 401(k) plan to purchase the C corporation stock, Mr. Ellis was not able to earn a salary or personally guarantee a business loan, which ultimately was the cause of the IRS–prohibited transaction rule violation."

"OK," Amy said.

"The limitation of using a self-directed IRA LLC to buy a business is that the individual retirement-account business owner would not be able to be actively involved in the business, earn a salary, or even personally guarantee a business loan, whereas, if the business owner used a ROBS strategy, that individual would be able to be actively involved in the business and earn a salary without triggering the IRS–prohibited transaction rules."

"Can I use my Roth IRA in the ROBS transaction?" Amy asked.

"Unfortunately, no. The IRS rollover rules do not permit a Roth IRA to be rolled into a 401(k) qualified retirement plan. However, your pretax 401(k) funds are eligible to be rolled into a 401(k) plan so they can be used in a ROBS transaction. In addition, you can always convert pretax 401(k) funds in a Roth 401(k) account that would hold the corporate stock," John said.

"OK, if I remember right, that is why I didn't really consider the ROBS transaction as a business-funding option because I was not able to use my Roth IRA funds," Amy said.

ANY DOWNSIDE TO USING THE ROBS SOLUTION?

"The ROBS solution sounds pretty good; what are some of the downsides?" Amy asked.

"In my opinion, there are basically four disadvantages of establishing a ROBS," John said.

1.   The C Corporation Requirement

Although there are advantages to establishing a C corporation, such as owner's liability protection from the actions of the company, there are several disadvantages as well.

A. Double Taxation: Corporations, unlike other companies that are considered sole proprietorships and partnerships, file their own taxes separately from their owners at their own tax rates. After the company's profits are taxed at the corporate level, they are then distributed to the shareholders who have to report the amount received on their individual tax returns. The corporate-tax rate is generally 15 percent for corporate profits under $50,000 and 35 percent for profits above $50,000. This isn't the case for subchapter S corporations or LLCs, in which the profits bypass being taxed at the corporate level and are distributed and taxed at the shareholder's level. That is called pass-through taxation. For example, if we assume a 20 percent income-tax rate for both corporations and individuals and a C corporation earned $100 of profits, the C corporation would be required to pay tax of $20 (20 percent of $100) and then the shareholder would be required to pay tax of $16 (20 percent of $80) on any dividend issued by the C corporation to the shareholder, whereas, in the case of an LLC or S corporation, there is no entity-level tax, so the $100 would flow directly to the shareholder or LLC member and a tax of only $20 would be imposed at the shareholder level. Comparing this with the C corporation example, by using a pass-through entity such as an S corporation or LLC, the individual would save $16 in our example (total tax of $36 with a C corporation versus $20 in the case of an LLC or S corporation).

"OK, that's good to know," Amy said.

"Unfortunately, the IRS rules require a C corporation be used when a retirement account holder wishes to use retirement funds to invest in a business he or another disqualified person will be involved in personally since the exception under IRC 4975(d)(13) requires the purchase of 'qualifying employer securities,' which is defined as C Corporation stock. The issue of double taxation is certainly one disadvantage of the ROBS solution, but it is generally perceived as better than paying tax and potentially a ten percent early-distribution penalty on a distribution from your retirement account."

2. Regulations and Formalities

Subchapter C corporations generally involve more corporate formalities than LLCs, for example. In general, C corporations have to report annually to the states in which they're incorporated, and the states in which they do a lot of business, on an annual basis. Also, C corporations must observe certain formalities to be considered corporations. This includes holding regular board and shareholder meetings and issuing stock. Also, the names of corporate officers are made public, which is not required by businesses formed under different organizational structures.

3. 401(k) Plan Administration

Even though 401(k) plan administration costs have come down significantly over the years, there is still a cost of offering a 401(k) plan to employees. In addition to having to make a 3 percent safe-harbor contribution, which I will discuss shortly, 401(k) plans cost money to administer because there are many compliance issues that have to be monitored, there are many ongoing service and administration functions that have to be provided, and there are a host of education and communication services that are required to be offered to plan participants. It is not uncommon for a small business 401(k) plan to cost anywhere from $750 to $1,500 annually for a third-party administration company to administer as well as file the annual IRS Form 5500.

Matching Contributions

A "safe harbor" 401(k) plan, which is a popular type of 401(k) plan for small businesses, offers employees who participate in the plan a 3 percent matching contribution made by the employer.

Starting in 1999 a new twist on the traditional 401(k) plan became available for plan sponsors, the "Safe Harbor 401(k) Plan." This twist on the traditional 401(k) plan promised to be a simpler plan to administer. If an employer adopted this type of 401(k) plan, there would be no need to worry about complex testing at the end of each year and, in some cases, no need to make top-heavy contributions (since 2002, safe harbor plans satisfy top-heavy requirements). All this in exchange for a commitment to make a minimum level of contributions that many sponsors make anyway. Thus, for example, if the employee earns $40,000 in salary during the year and contributes 3 percent of the salary or $1,200 to the 401(k) plan, the employer would contribute an additional $1,200 (3 percent of the salary) to the individual 401(k) plan account. Taking this a step further, if the business has five employees and each employee makes $40,000 a year, the employer now has to make $6,000 in employer safe harbor–matching contributions. Although the contributions are tax deductible to the employer, it is still additional funds that are being removed from the company and could affect the cash flow of a new small business.

4. Potential IRS Audit

"What about a potential IRS audit?" Amy asked.

"Dating back to 2005 or so, the IRS started focusing some attention on the ROBS solutions and some of the abuses they perceived were occurring."

"And what happened?"

"On October 31, 2008, Michael Julianelle, director, Employee Plans, signed a memorandum approving IRS ROBS examination guidelines. The IRS stated that while this type of structure is legal and not considered an abusive tax-avoidance transaction, the execution of these types of transactions, in many cases, have not been found to be in full compliance with IRS and ERISA rules and procedures. In the memorandum, the IRS highlighted several problem areas and compliance issues they uncovered when they examined a number of ROBS transactions. The problem areas involved lack of plan notification to eligible employees, inadequate stock valuation of corporate stock purchased by the 401(k), lack of plan permanency, and failure to purchase business assets. In sum, the IRS was concerned that people were using their retirement funds to buy a business and either the business was not being purchased and the individual then used the funds for personal purposes, thus avoiding tax and potential penalties, or the business that was purchased closed, and the retirement account liquidated, thus leaving the IRS without the potential to tax the retirement account in the future."

"And how did it turn out?"

"The IRS did not publicly comment on the ROBS solution again until August 27, 2010, almost two years after publishing the memorandum. The IRS held a public phone forum that covered transactions involving using retirement funds to purchase a business. Monika Templeman, director of Employee Plans Examinations and Colleen Patton, area manager of Employee Plans Examinations for the Pacific Coast, spent considerable time discussing the IRS's position on this subject. Monika Templeman began the presentation reaffirming the government's position that a transaction involving the use of retirement funds to purchase a new business is legal and not an abusive tax-avoidance transaction as long as the transaction complies with IRS and ERISA rules and procedures. The IRS reinforced their concerns about the potential for abuse and lack of compliance, focusing again on lack of plan notification to eligible employees, inadequate stock valuation of corporate stock purchased by the 401(k), lack of plan permanency, and failure to purchase business assets. The IRS concluded by stating that a transaction using retirement funds to acquire a business is legal and not prohibited as long as the transaction is structured correctly to comply with IRS and ERISA rules and procedures."

DOES ROBS TRIGGER AN IRS AUDIT?

"So, does the ROBS solution trigger an audit?" Amy asked.

"No one knows what factors trigger an IRS audit, but although legal, the ROBS solution is something the IRS and Department of Labor are looking at. As we learned from October 31, 2008, the IRS has been looking at the ROBS transaction closely for a number of years and even examined a number of well-known promoters in the area. Yet still, they clearly state the ROBS solution is one hundred percent legal if established properly. Again, if your structure is set up properly and the funds are used to buy a business, the 401(k) plan is being offered to all eligible employees, a valuation of the stock purchased is performed, and the plan is compliant with all annual testing and IRS filing requirements, there is nothing to be concerned with if your plan was audited by the IRS or DOL."

"That sounds good," Amy said.

"But I'd say if you want to use retirement funds to invest in a business that you will be personally involved in, the ROBS solution should be your last resort, and the 401(k) plan loan option is something that generally makes more sense if the numbers work. It is also advisable to consult with a tax attorney or CPA before electing to use a ROBS strategy," John said.

"OK, thanks. Sorry again to get off topic, but I was wanting to ask you about the ROBS transaction for some time, and it just popped into my heard," Amy said.

"No problem at all. Let's get back to discussing using a self-directed Roth IRA to make traditional as well as alternative-asset investments," John said.

"OK. Are there any differences in the types of investments I can make with a Roth IRA versus a traditional IRA?" Amy asked.

"No," John said. "You can make the same types of investments as you can make with a traditional IRA. The same restrictions against purchasing life insurance and collectibles still apply to a Roth IRA as well as the prohibited-transaction rules under IRC 4975. The main differences between a pretax traditional IRA and a Roth IRA from an investment perspective is that with a Roth IRA all income and gains generated by the investment can be taken tax free as long as the Roth IRA holder is over the age of 59½ and the Roth IRA has been open at least five years, whereas, in the case of a pretax IRA, income and gains would be subject to tax after the IRA holder reached the age of 59½ and an additional ten percent prepayment penalty would apply for an IRA holder who takes a pretax IRA distribution under the age of 59½."

SELF-DIRECTED ROTH IRA ESTATE-PLANNING OPPORTUNITIES

"I've heard that the Roth IRA also offered some estate-planning opportunities," Amy said. "What about that?"

"In addition to the significant tax benefits in using a self-directed Roth IRA LLC to make investments," John said, "the Roth IRA also offers a number of very exciting estate-planning opportunities."

"Such as?"

"In general," John said, "in addition to tax-free growth and no tax on qualified Roth IRA distributions, a Roth IRA holder would not be subject to the required minimum distribution rules (RMD)."

"What about when it comes to estate taxes?" Amy asked.

"In general, an IRA, whether traditional or Roth, is included in the owner's gross estate," John said. "You can't avoid that. But when a traditional IRA is inherited, the beneficiary must include all distributions in gross income just as the original owner would have. The distributions are taxed at the beneficiary's ordinary income-tax rate. The beneficiary is able to stretch out the distributions over his or her life expectancy, but annual distributions are required and will be taxed. So, when passing a traditional IRA to a spouse or child, the beneficiary is required to pay ordinary income tax on the IRA distribution amount taken, which would reduce the amount of traditional IRA funds available to spend, whereas a Roth IRA that is left to a beneficiary would not be subject to tax when a distribution is taken."

"I know we haven't talked a lot about Roth conversions, and I am sure we will at some point, but are there any estate-planning benefits of converting a traditional IRA to a Roth IRA?" Amy asked.

"First, we will get into the Roth conversion rules in greater detail very shortly. In general, in a conversion of a traditional IRA to a Roth IRA, the IRA converted amount is as though it were taken as a distribution. So, you would be subject to ordinary income taxes on the converted amount. Of course, there's no restriction on the amount of IRA funds that can be converted at one time."

"What are the estate-tax benefits of a Roth IRA conversion?" Amy asked.

"Mostly that the Roth IRA holder's estate is reduced by the income taxes paid on the amount of the Roth IRA conversion. There are several estate-planning benefits to paying tax on the Roth conversion while you are alive."

"How do you turn taxable distributions into tax-free distributions?" Amy asked.

"Doing a Roth IRA conversion is, in effect, paying the taxes on the IRA funds for your heirs. They would have owed the taxes in the future when they were required to take a distribution from the inherited IRA. Instead, the Roth IRA holder would be paying the tax now, out of his or her taxable estate and avoiding estate and gift taxes on that amount. Thereafter, when your beneficiary would take a distribution from the inherited Roth IRA, those Roth IRA distributions would be tax free."

"Can you pay tax and reduce estate taxes?" Amy asked.

"Paying the taxes now reduces the size of your estate and any estate-tax bill. This isn't a factor for estates below the taxable level ($5.45 million for 2016), but it could be important for taxable estates."

"What are the tax benefits for a lifetime?" Amy asked.

"A Roth IRA conversion can provide lifetime income-tax benefits to the Roth IRA holder, and it can also benefit your beneficiaries. When you maintain a traditional IRA, after age 70½ you're required to take minimum annual distributions, which would be subject to income tax. If it turned out that you didn't need this money for spending or living purposes, it simply increases the taxes you would be required to pay. In addition, being required to take a traditional IRA distribution could increase your income enough to push you into a higher tax bracket, reduce itemized deductions, increase taxes on social-security benefits, and have other effects. The older you become, the higher the required distributions and taxes become. With a Roth IRA, you or your beneficiaries could benefit from tax-free appreciation of the Roth IRA assets as well as generating tax-free income to live off of."

"I assume the converted funds would benefit from tax-free growth and tax-free income?" Amy asked.

"Once the traditional IRA has been converted to a Roth IRA, the Roth IRA holder and his or her beneficiaries would be able to benefit from tax-free growth and income generated by the Roth IRA. In other words, the assets of the Roth IRA will be able to grow tax free and all qualified distributions from the Roth IRA would be tax free, allowing the Roth IRA holder or his or her beneficiaries to live off of the Roth IRA funds without ever having to pay tax on the income."

"So it's an opportunity to take advantage of historically low tax rates," Amy said.

"Even though a lot has been made of the increasing Obamacare tax rates, our current income-tax rates are still at historic lows. It is conceivable that income-tax rates will rise in the future, especially with the high levels of debt being used by the government to stimulate the economy. Doing a Roth IRA conversion now versus later could potentially be a tax-savvy decision if the Roth IRA grows at a respectable rate and if tax rates increase. Having a Roth IRA to use or offer to your beneficiaries in a high-tax environment will prove to be extremely tax beneficial."

"Where does the Roth stretch IRA fit into the estate-planning benefits?" Amy asked.

"I'm glad you brought up the Roth stretch IRA because it's actually a really neat estate-planning tool that I almost forgot to mention," John said. "Unlike the original Roth IRA owner, a nonspousal beneficiary of a Roth IRA is required to take minimum distributions over his or her life expectancy. Remember, a spousal beneficiary of a Roth IRA is not required to take a Roth IRA distribution."

"Great," Amy said.

"In the case of a nonspousal Roth IRA beneficiary," John continued, "when the beneficiary is relatively young, there is the potential for the distributions to be less than the annual earnings of the Roth IRA, so the Roth IRA grows while the distributions are being taken. Of course, the beneficiary can take more than the minimum, even the entire Roth IRA, at any time tax free. In other words, using a self-directed Roth stretch IRA will allow an individual to transfer tax-free assets to children or other beneficiaries and allow those individuals to benefit from tax-free income while the Roth IRA continues to grow tax free. The Roth stretch IRA strategy generally works best when the beneficiary is young so that Roth IRA distributions can be taken over a longer period of time, allowing the Roth IRA to continue to grow tax free."

"You know I really like the Roth IRA concept a lot," Amy said. "I know you talked about this before, but by way of summary, if my sister or a friend should ask, how do you decide between the traditional IRA and Roth IRA?" Amy asked.

"Unfortunately there is no right or wrong answer when it comes to deciding whether you should make contributions to a self-directed IRA or self-directed Roth IRA. The decision generally depends on a variety of factors, which are generally fact and circumstance based.

- If you expect your retirement tax rate to be equal or higher than it is today, a self-directed Roth IRA should yield the greatest benefit.
- If you expect your retirement tax rate to be much lower than it is today, you may want to choose making contributions to a self-directed traditional IRA.
- If you expect your investment to generate strong returns, then a self-directed Roth IRA could be an option.
- The younger one is, the more attractive a self-directed Roth IRA is because your Roth IRA will have more time to grow without paying any tax."

ROTH IRA PROPOSED LEGISLATION

"I've read that President Obama has proposed certain new rules with respect to IRAs and specifically Roth IRAs," Amy said. "What about that?"

"There've been some proposals floated by President Obama over the past few years concerning limiting the value of IRAs, even eliminating the pretax IRA, as well as eradicating the backdoor Roth IRA strategy. Most of these proposals were in the president's budgets in 2014, 2015, and 2016 and have not gone anywhere. The president has floated a number of proposals limiting the ability for one to accumulate retirement funds, especially after-tax Roth IRA funds. There are a few IRA proposals the president has floated over the last few years since 2014:

- Required minimum distributions, or RMDs, from Roth IRAs once savers turn 70½—similar to the distributions that people must make from traditional IRAs and other retirement accounts.

- Individuals with less than $100,000 in their combined retirement accounts would no longer have to take required minimum distributions.
- Ending the stretch IRA. That proposal would require nonspouse beneficiaries of deceased IRA owners and retirement-plan participants to take inherited distributions over no more than five years instead of being allowed to stretch out the distributions over their lifetimes.
- Limit the size of IRA accounts to $3.4 million.
- Require the original Roth IRA owner to take distributions after 70½.
- Create a twenty-eight percent maximum tax benefit for contributions to retirement accounts."

"What is the myRA I have heard so much about lately?" Amy asked.

"The myRA is a pilot program and a new type of savings account for Americans who don't have access to an employer-sponsored retirement-savings plan. Workers who sign up will be able to have a portion of their paycheck directly deposited into their myRA automatically every payday. But unlike private Roth IRAs, myRAs will be invested solely in government bonds and will be backed by the US government—meaning you can never lose your original investment. Plus, there will be no fees to eat into your annual returns."

"What do you think of it?" Amy asked.

"The myRA is a nice idea to help people who don't have access to a retirement plan at work save money for their retirement," John said. "I am never against retirement savings. The investments will be safe and secure because the funds will be invested in Treasury securities, which means they will be backed by the full faith and credit of the United States. myRAs feature government-backed principal protection, so the account balance will never decrease in value and will earn the same interest rate that is available to federal employees for their retirement savings."

"Is there any downside?" Amy asked.

"The downside is that the myRA requires your funds to be invested in Treasury securities and will earn the same rate as the Thrift Savings Plan's Government Securities Investment Fund that's offered to federal workers. That fund earned less than two percent in 2013, although it earned around five percent before the financial crisis. Not a great return when you look at what your funds can generate by simply buying an S&P mutual fund. In addition, myRA accounts cannot exceed a maximum balance of fifteen thousand dollars. At that point (or when an account has been open for thirty years), it must be rolled over into a private-sector Roth IRA, where the money can continue to grow tax free."

"So it's a nice idea but…" Amy said.

"Exactly," John said. "The 'but' is that an individual can generally do a lot better just by making a contribution to a pretax or Roth IRA, which is available to any individual with earned income, and in the IRA you are not limited to Treasury securities and can better diversify your retirement portfolio. Also, you would not be capped at fifteen thousand dollars, which is not very significant in terms of retirement savings anyway."

"Just to be crystal clear," John continued, "none of these proposals are law, and none of them apply today. The president and his team stated that one of the reasons behind the IRA proposals is to simplify tax law when it comes to retirement accounts. I am not sold on this answer. I think the real impetus behind the president's numerous proposals to curtail the growth of retirement accounts is to limit the ability of the wealthy to generate and maintain wealth in a tax-friendly manner, which seems to go against some of his social policies. Again, this is just my opinion, but I can't see why, if people are able to save and can save a lot of money for their retirement, that is a negative thing."

"Why would the IRS want to get rid of the pretax IRA and force people to set up Roth IRAs?" Amy asked. "That doesn't seem like it would help the IRS down the road.

"You are right; it is very shortsighted on the part of the IRS since the Roth IRA offers the ability to generate huge tax-free retirement accounts that will not generate any future tax revenues from the IRS. However, in the short term, a pretax IRA reduces the amount of tax the IRS collects because it provides tax deductions, which in turn reduces the amount of income tax an individual taxpayer pays to the Treasury, whereas a Roth IRA is an after-tax account, so there is no tax deduction when making the Roth IRA contribution. I actually asked a contact I have at the IRS the same question you asked me, and her answer was that getting rid of the pretax IRA is not a good long-term solution, but due to budget constraints, the IRS is more interested in generating current tax revenues than worrying about future tax revenues. She also mentioned that the IRS looks at seven-year budget cycles and eliminating the pretax IRA would provide a big boost in tax revenues to the IRS in the short term. Just to be clear, this proposal is not close to happening, and it probably never will," John said.

"I have heard rumors about capping the total value of a Roth IRA at a few million. What's the deal with that?" Amy asked.

"In the 2014 budget, the Obama administration reiterated several reforms that have been suggested in the past, including a potential "cap" of $3.4 million on retirement accounts beyond which no further contributions would be allowed. The language in the budget spoke to limiting the value of retirement accounts because, under the current rules, some wealthy individuals are able to accumulate many millions of dollars in these accounts, substantially more than is needed to fund reasonable levels of retirement saving. The proposed rule would not actually force money out of retirement plans over the cap; it would merely prevent new contributions *to* the plan. *The bottom line* is that at this point, the proposal is just that—a proposal, and not something that would generate a huge tax revenue windfall to the Treasury, as it is estimated to raise *only* $9.3 billion of tax revenue over the next decade, in part because the available estimates suggest that fewer than one percent of people even have enough in retirement accounts to be subject to the rule," John said.

"OK, I wish I had the problem of having a three–million-dollar retirement account," Amy joked.

"Me too," John said. "I know I briefly mentioned the Roth IRA conversion option, and this is probably a good time to discuss it in more detail. Because you have pretax 401(k) funds from your former employer plan and are certainly well aware of the advantages of a Roth IRA, the Roth IRA conversion option is something you may ultimately find quite appealing."

"Sounds good. I am ready," Amy said.

IRA ROTH CONVERSION OPTION

"Beginning in 2010," John said, "the modified adjusted gross income (AGI) and filing status requirements for converting a traditional IRA to a Roth IRA were eliminated. This means that no matter what your income level is, you can do a Roth conversion any time. Prior to 2010, if your income level was above a certain threshold, you were not eligible to do a Roth conversion."

"Interesting. I had no idea. What about the tax ramifications of a Roth conversion?" Amy asked.

"When you do a Roth IRA conversion, you must pay tax on the amount converted but no ten percent early-distribution penalty. Tax is due when you file your income-tax return for the year the conversion was taken, and the amount converted is added to your income to determine your applicable income-tax rate. So, if you elected to do a Roth IRA conversion in January 2014, you would not have to pay tax on the amount converted until April 15, 2015. You can convert pretax IRA funds in cash or in-kind, such as stocks or real estate, but you will be required to pay tax on the fair market value of the asset and not what you paid for the asset," John said.

"What's the reason behind the Roth IRA conversion rule change?" Amy asked.

"Really it goes back to the 2008 financial crisis," John said, "which significantly reduced the government's revenues. In response, the IRS loosened its Roth IRA conversion rules and actually encouraged people to make Roth IRA conversions in order to generate immediate tax revenue for the Treasury even if it would ultimately cost them tax dollars in the future," John said.

"OK, so just to be clear. Anyone can do a Roth conversion after 2010, and only tax on the amount of cash or the fair market value of the asset being converted in-kind is due. The ten percent early-distribution penalty does not apply to Roth conversions no matter the age of the IRA holder. Tax is due when the individual income-tax return (IRS Form 1040) is due," Amy said.

"Yes, you are a good listener. In fact, I probably should have mentioned this, but when you do a Roth IRA conversion, there is no withholding tax, and the full amount of the conversion will be moved to the Roth IRA account."

"I assume I could do a tax-free rollover of my pretax 401(k) plan funds to a traditional IRA at any bank and then do a Roth conversion of those funds and pay tax on the amount converted?" Amy asked.

"Yes, exactly," John responded.

THINGS TO CONSIDER WHEN CONTEMPLATING A ROTH IRA CONVERSION

"What should you think about when deciding whether to convert your traditional IRA to a self-directed Roth IRA LLC?" Amy asked.

"The most important question is: do you have the ability to pay income taxes on the money you convert from your traditional IRA?" John said. "Based on your income-tax bracket, does it make sense to pay the entire tax due in 2015? If you expect your rate to go up, converting may be for you. If you think it will go down, then the opposite holds true. Do you anticipate withdrawing Roth IRA funds for personal use within five years of conversion? If so, you may face taxes and penalties if you withdraw within five years of a conversion. Converting a traditional IRA to a Roth self-directed Roth IRA LLC has a number of tax advantages and can offer you multiple retirement and estate-planning benefits."

ROTH IRA DISCOUNT VALUATION STRATEGY

"I've heard of some people trying to get a discount on the value of pretax assets, such as with private LLC interests being converted to a Roth IRA," Amy said. "How risky is that?"

"As I just mentioned, the amount of taxable income on a Roth conversion is based on the fair market value of the IRA assets subject to the conversion," John answered. "So, the lower the fair market value of the IRA assets, the lower the taxes that will be due on the Roth conversion. In general, according to case law, the standard of fair market value is an objective test using hypothetical buyers and sellers. Furthermore, in determining the valuation of an LLC, the assets to be valued must be the interests in the entity. Certain retirement-tax professionals and valuation experts have helped clients in specific situations take a discount when determining the fair market value of the IRA assets subject to the Roth conversion, thus reducing the amount of tax one would have to pay on the conversion."

"How does that work?" Amy asked.

"The Roth conversion valuation discount strategy is based on techniques used in the context of family limited partnerships looking to take gift-tax discounts of certain assets for estate-planning purposes. The valuation discounts applicable to an LLC with IRA assets typically fall into two categories: (1) a discount for lack of control and (2) a discount for lack of marketability. I have had a number of clients use this discount valuation strategy for their Roth IRA, and they were able to take a discount of anywhere from fifteen percent to thirty-five percent on the value of the IRA assets subject to the Roth conversion. I do not recommend this and really don't think it makes much sense, especially if you only have a few hundred thousand dollars in funds being converted. For example if you have $200,000 and want to try to get a twenty percent discount valuation on the funds being converted, that means that you would be paying tax on $160,000 and not $200,000. If you assume a thirty percent income-tax rate, that is only a savings of $12,000 (sixty-thousand-dollar tax on $200,000 vs. a forty-eight-thousand-dollar tax on $160,000)."

"Is that really worth it?" Amy asked.

John nodded. "You have to ask yourself whether it's worth potentially triggering an IRS audit for such small tax savings. And the IRS does not have to accept your appraisal of discounted position, so the onus is on you as the taxpayer to provide the discounted valuation."

"How has that played out?" Amy asked.

"I've had clients that had a traditional IRA and wanted to convert to a self-directed Roth IRA LLC to purchase raw land, real estate, precious metals, or invest in an investment fund and used a type of Roth conversion valuation discount strategy to save thousands in taxes."

"But using a Roth discount strategy for taking a Roth conversion is highly risky and not recommended," Amy said.

"Right," John said. "Remember, you're playing with the IRS's tax money, and unless you are really confident in your discounted position in connection with the Roth IRA conversion, I would stay away from this strategy."

"As you know, I really love the Roth IRA and will strongly consider converting my former employer 401(k) plan to a Roth IRA either this year or next," Amy said.

"OK," John said. "I think that could be a wise move, especially because you are relatively young, and you do have the capacity to pay the tax on the conversion. One thing to consider when doing a Roth conversion is that you are paying the tax up front, so if your investment does not work out (remember Enron), you have just paid tax for money you will never see, which is a double whammy. All in all, the Roth IRA is a really great solution for accumulating tax-free wealth while at the same time building a strong estate-planning platform for your family."

"That sounds great," Amy said.

"Since we have been spending so much time discussing the IRA and Roth IRA, I think it's a good idea, the next time we meet, to turn our attention to the Roth Solo 401(k) plan, which could end up being a great retirement-plan option for your business," John said.

"Sounds great. Looking forward to it," Amy said.

6

The Roth Solo 401(k) Plan

THE NEXT WEEK Amy and John arrived at the coffee bar at around the same time. Since they both had had big lunches, they decided to skip the muffins and just grab two cappuccinos.

"Our first few times together, we discussed the different types of IRA retirement accounts with a special focus on the Roth IRA," John said. "I hope you have found our conversations helpful and are now in a better position to help spread the word to all your friends about the huge benefits of a Roth IRA."

"I have really enjoyed learning all about the IRA and Roth IRA and will certainly try my best to spread the word to all my friends about the importance of starting early and how saving just a few dollars a day can turn into a million dollars upon retirement. I also found our last meeting on the self-directed Roth IRA very interesting and exciting because I really had no idea that retirement funds could be used to buy real estate or invest in other alternative assets," Amy said.

"That is really nice to hear. I think you will find learning about the Roth Solo 401(k) just as interesting, and I have a feeling it may end up being a perfect fit for your new business," John said.

"OK, let's get started," Amy said.

"A Solo 401(k) is perfect for sole proprietors, small-business owners, and independent contractors such as consultants. It is unique and very popular because it was designed by Congress and the IRS explicitly for small owner–only businesses—basically, any business with no employees other than the owner(s). That business can be established as a sole proprietorship, LLC, corporation, or partnership," John said.

"That seems perfect for my business since I am the sole owner of the LLC and have no employees other than myself. Looks like I am eligible," Amy said.

"Your business would be eligible to adopt the Solo 401(k) plan. That is why I am starting to think this will be right retirement plan for you," John said.

"Is the Solo 401(k) plan new? I had never heard about it until you mentioned it to me a few weeks back," Amy said.

"That's a good question. If you haven't heard of the Solo 401(k) before or you don't know very much about it, you are not alone. Most people haven't, even though the option has been available since the 401(k) was created. In fact, many sophisticated and well-educated investors, including many tax attorneys and CPAs, are not familiar with the advantages of the Solo 401(k) and therefore overlook it as a superior means of growing and leveraging retirement savings. Those experts are often unaware that retirement assets can be invested outside of traditional financial markets, including in real estate, precious metals, and foreign currency, and via loans. Are you surprised? I have a law degree and a master's degree in taxation, and have worked at several of the largest law firms in the world, and I only learned about these alternative-investment options through research for a client. When I began to talk to colleagues about the features of a Solo 401(k), I discovered I was not alone in my ignorance. A prestigious tax lawyer and graduate of Yale Law School I worked with a few years ago, for instance, was incredulous when I told him about the Solo 401(k)'s full range of advantages. I showed him the language in the IRC and the IRS publications that support it, and he was astonished to realize it was all true.

I advise tens of thousands of retirement-account holders. A very significant percentage of them are eligible to adopt a Solo 401(k). When I tell them about its advantages, the most frequent questions I get are: Is this legal? Why haven't I heard about it before? It is legal. The IRS created it and wrote it in the IRC, and the US Congress signed it into law," John explained.

"Just curious. Do you know how many self-employed people are out there today?" Amy asked.

"It's difficult to determine exactly how many people in America qualify for the Solo 401(k). The Bureau of Labor Statistics states that there were around 14.4 million self-employed as of January 2014. But then there are also a lot of people who are partially self-employed, yet fall in the category of working for a company or organization because they essentially have a 'day job.' The Freelancers Union claims that there are 42 million independent workers in the United States or around a third of the overall workforce. The Census Bureau counts 20 million nonemployer businesses,"[27] John said.

"Is the term Solo 401(k) plan actually mentioned in the IRC?" Amy asked.

"The Solo 401(k) is not a term of art, and you will not find it named as such in the IRC. To confuse matters even more, there are a number of other terms commonly used by tax professionals to describe the same tool: individual 401(k), one-participant 401(k), self-employed 401(k), self-directed 401(k), and uni 401(k). In fact, you can call it pretty much whatever you want because it is not, as I mentioned, defined specifically in the IRC. I like the term "Solo" because it carries the sense of independence and self-reliance that I find characteristic of the people who are able to take advantage of it the most."

"So let's cut to the chase; what makes the Solo 401(k) so popular with the self-employed and small-business owner with no employees, and why would it be a great fit for my business?" Amy asked.

"There are actually five primary reasons. First, the Solo 401(k) allows you to save *a lot* more money for retirement every year than a traditional IRA, SEP IRA, or SIMPLE IRA (the most common retirement plans for the self-employed). Second, the Solo 401(k) allows you more flexibility for accessing your retirement savings and applying them to investments or other opportunities that you may find interesting or important. Third, the Solo 401(k) plan offers a loan feature that allows a plan participant to borrow up to the lesser of fifty thousand dollars of fifty percent of their account value, whichever is less

---

27 Justin Fox, "Where Are All the Self-Employed Workers," February 7, 2014, http://blogs. hbr.org/2014/02/where-are-all-the-self-employed-workers/.

and use the funds for any purpose. Fourth, of likely interest to you, Amy, the Solo 401(k) plan includes a Roth component that allows you to make Roth-type employee-deferral contributions (for 2015 and 2016, eighteen thousand dollars or twenty-four thousand dollars if over the age of fifty) as well as to convert employer profit-sharing contributions to Roth. Fifth, the Solo 401(k) is a good match for people who are self-employed, who are business own-ers with no full-time employees, or who earn some portion of their income through self-employment. In my experience, the number of people who are self-employed or partially self-employed is growing very quickly these days. In fact, a large number of Americans who have some sort of self-employment income are not even aware of it. I have also known many others who wish they could pursue a dream, hobby, or interest more passionately but are held back by worries that such an activity will detract from their efforts to earn as much as possible in their 'day job.' Knowing that self-employment income of any kind can be leveraged through a Solo 401(k) to build retirement savings faster often gives these people a greater sense of freedom and the confidence to 'go for it,'" John said.

"Are all Solo 401(k) plans the same? In other words, can I just go to a local bank and open up a Solo 401(k) plan?" Amy asked.

"Yes and no. Most institutions will offer you the option of establish-ing a Solo 401(k) plan, but beware; not all Solo 401(k) plans are the same. Most people believe that all Solo 401(k) plans, whether attained for free at a financial institution or provided by a specialized plan provider are the same. But the nuances that differentiate the various plan options are important to understand. In general, there are three ways to establish and use a Solo 401(k) plan for retirement and investment purposes."

1. FINANCIAL INSTITUTION–SPONSORED SOLO PLAN

This is the most common way to establish a Solo 401(k) plan. Most of the major financial institutions and US banks—Vanguard, Charles Schwab, E*Trade, Bank of America, and CIT—provide basic Solo 401(k) plan docu-ments and investment opportunities, typically for no fee. The catch is that the Solo 401(k) plan documents you adopt are very basic and generally limit your options to making pretax employee deferrals and pretax profit-sharing contributions (no Roth-type contributions), while also limiting your 401(k) plan investment options to the financial product offering sold by that financial institution.

In essence, the plan will let you make basic pretax employee-deferral and profit-sharing contributions but will generally restrict your investment options to stocks, mutual funds, ETFs, and other traditional financial products sold by the financial institution. In other words, this type of Solo 401(k) does not permit a loan feature or the ability to make Roth-type contributions or the option to make nontraditional investments, such as real estate and precious metals. The advantage of adopting a Solo 401(k) plan from a major financial institution or bank can be found in the price and simplicity of such a transaction.

2. CUSTODIAN-DIRECTED SELF-DIRECTED SOLO 401(K) PLAN

This option generally offers Solo 401(k) plan participants the ability to make traditional investments, including stock, as well as IRS-approved nontraditional or alternate investments such as real estate, precious metals, private lending, and private business investments through a trust company. The custodian-directed self-directed Solo 401(k) plan option is generally attractive to retirement investors looking to make nontraditional investments with their Solo 401(k) plan while having a third party administering the plan.

These custodians or trust companies do not offer investment advice and are essentially in business to allow you to make IRS-approved nontraditional investments. Unlike a traditional financial institution such as Bank of America or Vanguard, which make money by selling financial products, these passive custodians and trust companies make their money by opening self-directed accounts and charging an annual fee. In some cases, the fees are based on account value and/or the number of transactions done in the account in a given year.

Most of the institutions that allow Solo 401(k) plans to make nontraditional investments are established as trust companies and simply let you use their plan documents and accounts to make the investments. Your Solo 401(k) plan assets are generally held at an FDIC institution associated with the trust company and all investments must go through the custodian, which is why it is referred to as a custodian-directed plan. In practice, this means that you need to go through the custodian and have the custodian send the funds.

In most cases, that custodian must also sign the necessary transaction documents to enable you to make a Solo 401(k) plan investment, including real estate. In some situations, you are permitted as trustee of the plan to sign the transaction documents, including the purchase agreement, but the issuing of check payments or wires for the purchase or for ongoing expenses, such as taxes or repairs, need to go through the custodian because the custodian controls the funds. The custodian-directed self-directed Solo 401(k) plan option has many attractive features, such as the ability to make nontraditional investments, but it also has some limitations, including annual fees and potential time delays that can result from having to go through the trust company to make transactions.

3. OPEN-ARCHITECTURE SELF-DIRECTED SOLO 401(K) PLAN

The open-architecture Solo 401(k) plan is quickly becoming the most popular self-directed option for the self-employed. The beauty of the open-architecture Solo 401(k) plan is that it can generally be opened at most local banks, and it allows the business owner to serve as trustee of the plan with total control over the investments made. Self-directed Solo 401(k) plans are generally provided by specialized plan–provider companies, which are able to customize the plan based on the individual's retirement and investment goals. Most of the companies that offer self-directed open-architecture Solo 401(k) plan documents are not typical financial institutions that sell financial products or house the Solo 401(k) plan account. These plan document–provider companies essentially make money by selling the plan documents and offering advisory services regarding the features of the plan.

Major financial institutions generally do not include the self-directed features in their Solo 401(k) plan documents because that does not serve their financial interests. That has not stopped a number of specialized self-directed retirement facilitators from emerging as firms that specialize in helping to set up self-directed retirement solutions. This includes the self-directed Solo 401(k) plan, which has become more popular because of growing demand for the diversification of nontraditional investments, such as real estate.

The open-architecture self-directed Solo 401(k) plan has started to overtake the custodian-directed Solo 401(k) plan as the most popular self-directed Solo 401(k) plan option for a number of reasons:

- The plan can be opened at most local banks, which gives the plan participant more control and comfort than having the funds sit with a trustee in another state or at an unfamiliar bank.
- Once the documents have been purchased, there are typically very small annual compliance fees, since a Solo 401(k) plan has very little administrative requirements and generally none if the plan's assets are under $250,000.
- You will have "checkbook control," which means that as the trustee, you can make investments from your Solo 401(k) account by simply writing a check or executing a wire.
- You can also customize the plan documents to include all available options allowable by the IRS.

"Interesting. Initially I would have thought that I would have gravitated toward the free Solo 401(k) plan at a traditional financial institution, but I do love the Roth and loan features, which would make using a custodian-directed or open-architecture Solo 401(k) plan pretty attractive. In addition, after hearing about the opportunities to make alternative-asset investments with retirement accounts, I would probably want my Solo 401(k) plan to have that option, which would likely make the financial institution–established Solo 401(k) plan unappealing and lead me to choosing between the custodian-directed and open-architecture Solo 401(k) plan," Amy said.

"OK, that makes sense. Now let's quickly discuss who is eligible to establish a Solo 401(k) plan. In your case determining eligibility is quite simple since you are clearly in business and have no full-time employees, but there are many situations when evaluating eligibility is a bit trickier."

WHO'S ELIGIBLE TO USE A SOLO 401(K)?

"There are two specific eligibility requirements for the Solo 401(k):

1. The presence of self-employment activity
2. The absence of full-time employees

"As with anything drafted by the IRS, in between these dry declarations there is a world of variety and possibility," John began. "Who is a self-employed person? The obvious answer is that he or she works for herself. Think of a self-employed contractor, an independent consultant, a primary-care physician, or a freelance graphic designer. I have come to believe that the variety of ways a person can make a living is nearly limitless. Notice that there is no stipulation that such a person has to own his or her own business or be incorporated in any way. Some people take the formal approach when they work independently by creating a corporation, LLC, or partnership, and some people don't, which means they have a sole proprietorship. In general, any person who is self-employed or performing some activity that generates self-employment income not through an entity is automatically treated as a sole proprietorship.

"Regardless, the Solo 401(k) is still a fit so long as the person doesn't have any full-time employees, defined as people who work over one thousand hours for themselves annually. This means the independent contractor can still hire electricians, laborers, or architects to do a housing job but can't employ such people full time. Or the graphic designer can pay an editor or a web designer or a videographer as an independent contractor, for example, but not as full-time employees. However, the spouse of a small-business owner is not counted as a full-time employee even if the spouse's full-time income comes from the business. This is because spouses are not considered employees for ERISA purposes when it comes to determining 401(k) plan eligibility. Additionally, people under twenty-one are also not considered full-time employees, so you can feel free to put your children to work in the family business.

"Finally, there's nothing in the eligibility requirements of the Solo 401(k) that stipulates how much of your income must come from self-employment activity. In other words, you do not have to be just a contractor or a primary-care physician or a graphic designer. You can, in fact, be an endless variety of other things in addition. For instance, you can be a radio talk–show host who also sells real estate or a physician who works for a hospital and who also provides medical consultations for a local sports team. You might be a graphic designer for a major advertising firm who also does graphic-design work on a freelance basis or the manager of a flower shop who also sells antiques on eBay. Whatever portion of your income arises through self-employment activity can be used to build savings through a Solo 401(k). In essence, as long as there is the anticipation or expectation of earned income, the activity can be treated as a self-employment activity.

"This is the real magic of the Solo 401(k). Rather than discouraging us from earning income in ways that are outside traditional lines, the Solo 401(k) allows us to leverage those interests and activities to save a significantly higher portion of our money for retirement and at the same time reduce a large percentage of the tax due on the income earned through the activity," John said.

"OK, that was clear. I know my business can establish a Solo 401(k) plan because I am the sole owner and have no full-time employees, but my husband cannot because he receives a W-2 from the dental practice and has no side income. However, interestingly, my mother would seemingly be eligible to adopt a Solo 401(k) plan because she earns income from tutoring highs-school kids in math year round," Amy said.

"That sums it up really well. I want to now briefly get into some of the main advantages of using a Solo 401(k) plan. I am not going to spend an enormous amount of time on all the ins and outs of the Solo 401(k) plan because there is a wonderful book by Adam Bergman, Esq. available on Amazon.com called, *Going Solo—America's Best Kept retirement Secret for the Self-Employed*, which covers the Solo 401(k) plan in great detail. If you were interested in learning more about the Solo 401(k) plan, I would certainly recommend it. But, here is a short overview of the primary benefits of adopting a Solo 401(k) plan, which should be sufficient to help you judge whether it is the right retirement plan for you."

HIGH CONTRIBUTION LIMITS

While an IRA only allows a $5,500 contribution limit (with a $1,000 additional "catch-up" contribution for those over age fifty) for 2015 and 2016, the Solo 401(k) annual contribution limit is $53,000 for 2015 and 2016, with an additional $6,000 catch-up contribution for those over fifty. In addition, if your spouse generates compensation from the business, he or she can also make high contributions to the plan.

Under the 2015 and 2016 Solo 401(k) contribution rules, a plan participant under the age of fifty can make a maximum employee-deferral contribution in the amount of $18,000. That amount can be made pretax or after-tax (Roth). On the profit-sharing side, the business can make a 25 percent (20 percent in the case of a sole proprietorship or single-member LLC) profit-sharing contribution up to a combined maximum, including the employee deferral, of $53,000, an increase of $1,000 from 2014.

For plan participants over the age of fifty, an individual can make a maximum employee-deferral contribution in the amount of $24,000. That amount can be made pretax or after-tax (Roth). On the profit-sharing side, the business can make a 25 percent (20 percent in the case of a sole proprietorship or single-member LLC) profit-sharing contribution up to a combined maximum, including the employee deferral, of $59,000, an increase of $1,500 from 2014.

LOAN FEATURE

While an IRA offers no participant-loan feature, if the Solo 401(k) plan your business adopts includes a loan option, then that Solo 401(k) allows participants to borrow up to $50,000 or 50 percent of their account value (whichever is less) for any purpose at a low interest rate (the lowest interest rate is Prime, which was 3.5 percent as of January 1, 2016). This offers a Solo 401(k) plan participant the ability to access up to $50,000 for use for any purpose, including paying personal debt.

A WORLD OF INVESTMENT OPPORTUNITIES

Depending on the type of Solo 401(k) plan your business adopts, you could have the option to invest in almost any type of investment opportunity that you discover, including real estate (rentals, foreclosures, raw land, and tax liens), private businesses, precious metals, hard money, and peer-to-peer lending, as well as stock and mutual funds. Your only limit is your imagination. The income and gains from these investments will flow back into your Solo 401(k) plan without tax. Making an investment with your Solo 401(k) plan is as simple as writing a check. As trustee of the Solo 401(k) plan, you will have total control over your retirement assets to make real estate and other investments tax free and without custodian consent.

THE FLEXIBILITY TO SELF-DIRECT YOUR RETIREMENT FUNDS

With a Solo 401(k) plan, you can serve as trustee of the plan, giving you "checkbook control" over its funds. To this end, making an investment with your Solo 401(k) plan is as easy as writing a check. Another significant benefit of the Solo 401(k) plan is that it does not require the participant to hire a bank or trust company to serve as trustee. This flexibility allows the participant to serve in the trustee role. This means that all assets of the 401(k) trust are under the sole authority of the Solo 401(k) participant. A Solo 401(k) plan allows you to eliminate the expense and delays associated with an IRA custodian, enabling you to act quickly when the right investment opportunity presents itself. Also, because the Solo 401(k) plan trust account can be opened at any local bank or credit union (Chase, Wells Fargo, or Citibank, for example), you will not be required to pay custodian fees for the account as you would in the case of an IRA.

FLEXIBLE CONTRIBUTION OPTIONS

Contributions to a Solo 401(k) plan are completely discretionary. You always have the option to try to contribute as much as legally possible, but you also have the option of reducing or even suspending plan contributions if necessary. In other words, you have the ability to make contributions to your Solo 401(k) plan (up to an aggregate amount of $53,000 if you are under the age of fifty), but you are not required to do so.

ROTH-TYPE CONTRIBUTIONS

"I know you are a big fan of the Roth, as I am, so Roth-type contributions will probably be an important feature of the Solo 401(k) plan for you,; John said.

"I will focus on the Roth aspect of the Solo 401(k) plan in detail in a few minutes. Remember, with IRAs, those who earn high incomes are disallowed from contributing to a Roth IRA or converting their IRA to a Roth IRA. Depending on the type of Solo 401(k) plan your business adopts, your plan could contain a built-in Roth subaccount, which can be contributed to without any income restrictions. The Roth Solo 401(k) plan is not a different type of 401(k) plan but is simply referring to a plan that includes a Roth deferral option. With a Roth Solo 401(k) subaccount, you can make after-tax Roth-type contributions while having the ability to make significantly greater contributions than with an IRA: up to $53,000 or $59,000 if over the age of 59½," John said.

COST-EFFECTIVE ADMINISTRATION

"In general, the Solo 401(k) plan is easy to operate. There is usually no annual filing requirement unless your plan exceeds $250,000 in assets, in which case you will need to file a short information return with the IRS (Form 5500-EZ)," John said

OFFSET THE COST OF YOUR PLAN WITH A TAX DEDUCTION

According to John, "by paying for your Solo 401(k) with business funds, you are eligible to claim a deduction for the cost of the plan, including annual maintenance fees. The deduction for the cost associated with the Solo 401(k) plan and ongoing maintenance will help reduce your business's income-tax liability, which will in turn offset the cost of adopting a self-directed Solo 401(k) plan. The retirement-tax professionals at the IRA Financial Group will help you take advantage of the available business-tax deduction for adopting a Solo 401(k) plan."

NO TAX ON NONRECOURSE LEVERAGE FOR REAL-ESTATE ACQUISITION

"I know you mentioned that you would consider buying real estate with retirement funds. Well, if you needed extra financing for your real-estate transaction, the Solo 401(k) plan offers a huge tax advantage over using a self-directed IRA or Roth IRA. I am not sure if you remember our discussion on the prohibited-transaction rules, but a retirement account is not allowed to personally guarantee a loan involving the retirement account (recourse loan), so only a loan that is not personally guaranteed by the retirement-account holder or any disqualified person (nonrecourse loan) is permitted. When an IRA buys real estate that is leveraged (nonrecourse loan) with mortgage financing, it creates Unrelated Debt Financed Income (UDFI), a type of Unrelated Business Taxable Income (also known as UBTI, or UBIT) on which taxes must be paid. The UBTI tax is approximately 40 percent for 2016. But with a Solo 401(k) plan, you can use leverage without being subject to the UDFI rules and UBTI tax. This exemption provides significant tax advantages for using a Solo 401(k) plan versus an IRA to purchase real estate." Johns said.

RETIREMENT SAVING CONSOLIDATION THROUGH ROLLOVERS

A Solo 401(k) plan can accept rollovers of funds from another retirement-savings vehicle, such as an IRA, a SEP, or a previous employer's 401(k) plan. Thus, you can directly roll over your IRA or qualified plan funds to your new 401(k) plan for investment or loan purposes. Note that only Roth IRA funds cannot be rolled into a Solo 401(k) plan.

"OK, that was really helpful," Amy said. "The Solo 401(k) plan seems like a great fit for the self-employed or any small business with no full-time employees. Do you mind if I summarize what you just said so I can make sure I understood it all?"

"Of course not," John responded.

"OK, here I go. While an IRA only allows a fifty-five-hundred-dollar contribution limit (with a one-thousand-dollar additional catch-up contribution for those over age fifty) for 2015 and 2016, the Solo 401(k) annual contribution limit is fifty-three thousand dollars for 2015 and 2016 with an additional six-thousand-dollar catch-up contribution for those over age fifty. In addition, if your spouse generates compensation from the business, he or she can also make high contributions to the plan.

"Under the 2015 Solo 401(k) contribution rules, a plan participant under the age of fifty can make a maximum employee-deferral contribution in the amount of eighteen thousand dollars. That amount can be made in pretax or after-tax (Roth). On the profit-sharing side, the business can make a twenty-five percent (twenty percent in the case of a sole proprietorship or single-member LLC) profit-sharing contribution up to a combined maximum, including the employee deferral, of fifty-three thousand dollars."

"For plan participants over the age of fifty, an individual can make a maximum employee-deferral contribution in the amount of twenty-four thousand dollars. That amount can be made in pretax or after-tax (Roth). On the profit-sharing side, the business can make a twenty-five percent (twenty percent in the case of a sole proprietorship or single-member LLC) profit-sharing contribution up to a combined maximum, including the employee deferral, of fifty-nine thousand dollars.

"Solo 401(k) plan employee-deferral contributions can be made in pretax or Roth, while employer profit-sharing contributions must be made in pretax but can be converted to Roth in plan.

"The Solo 401(k) is especially appealing to the self-employed and small-business owner with no full-time employees for a number of reasons. First, the contributions you make to the plan are completely up to you. You can contribute up to your limit every year, or you can reduce or even suspend contributions whenever necessary. For a person relying on self-employment income, this can be critical, since some years are certainly better than others in an up-and-down economy.

"In addition, the Solo 401(k) is extremely simple to administer. There is no annual filing requirement when the plan has less than two hundred fifty thousand dollars in assets. If you grow your plan over that amount, you merely need to file IRS Form 5500-EZ (it really is easy), which is a short information return, and you are done.

"Also, depending on the type of Solo 401(k) plan you adopt, your plan would offer a range of investment opportunities, including real estate. And you would be able to use your retirement funds to make almost any type of investments without tax and without needing the consent of a custodian. This includes stocks, bonds, mutual funds, precious metals, and even real estate. As already mentioned, the income and gains generated by your Solo 401(k) assets can flow back to your plan tax free.

"You can even borrow up to fifty thousand dollars or fifty percent of the value of your account (whichever is less) for any purpose, including funding your business, launching or investing in a new business, paying off credit card debt, making personal mortgage payments, or loaning money to friends or family. The loan is tax free and penalty free. It must be repaid over a five-year period with payments that occur at least quarterly, but there are no penalties for early payment if you repay the loan before the five years are up. The interest rate you pay is up to you, though it must be set a reasonable rate, generally considered to be the Prime interest rate as per the *WSJ*.

"As of March 2016, for example, Prime was set at 3.5 percent, so the interest rate on your loan would have been a minimum of 3.5 percent. This is a very attractive rate compared to the interest charged for credit-card debt and would rival anything you could get from your bank as a good customer. You are also permitted to set a higher interest rate, which is a nice way of directing additional funds to the plan in excess of your annual contribution limits," Amy said.

"Wow, you are a great listener and are really picking up this stuff quickly. I am really impressed. As promised, I now want to spend a little bit of time focusing on the Solo 401(k) plan Roth feature."

THE ROTH SOLO 401(K) SECRET

"The Roth Solo 401(k) plan is the ultimate tax-free retirement solution for the self-employed. The Roth Solo 401(k) plan is not a different type of 401(k) plan, but is simply referring to a plan that includes a Roth deferral option," John said.

"So, wait. The Solo 401(k) plan and Roth Solo 401(k) plan are really the same plan, but only with a Solo 401(k) plan can you elect to have a Roth feature apply?" Amy asked.

"Yes, that is pretty much it. Let me explain in a bit more detail. In 2001, Congress passed the Economic Growth and Tax Relief Reconciliation Act (EGTRRA) as part of the so-called 'Bush tax cuts.' This Act, which took effect in 2002, had a tremendous impact on retirement plans in general: increasing limits, making it easier to consolidate plans, and making the plans themselves more flexible, while also offering a catch-up provision for older workers. Most importantly, for our purpose in this book, the Act provided people who were self-employed or who were small-business owners with no employees the same advantages and benefits of a conventional employer 401(k) plan, including the ability to make Roth contributions. Before EGTRRA became effective in 2002, there was no compelling reason for an owner-only business to establish a Solo 401(k) plan because the business owner could generally receive the same benefits by adopting a SEP IRA. One of the most important rules set forth in EGTRRA was the creation of the designated Roth contribution option for 401(k) and 403(b) plans. This provision allows plan participants to designate all or a portion of their employee deferrals as after-tax (Roth) contributions.

"Some people mistakenly believe that there is a pretax or regular Solo 401(k) plan and a Roth Solo 401(k) plan (after-tax). This is not true. The Roth feature is just a component of a Solo 401(k) plan that can be included or not, based on the decision of the employer. The availability of the Roth component is typically designated in the plan-adoption agreement.

"Roth deferral contributions should generally be made to a separate designated account under the plan. This can be done by simply creating a new bank or brokerage account under the plan name and plan employer identification number, if applicable. The reason for establishing a new account for Roth 401(k) plan contributions is so the plan administrator can keep track of and maintain an accounting of the pretax and after-tax contributions and asset values. This becomes especially important in the case of rollovers or distributions.

"The designated Roth 401(k) elective-deferral contributions follow the same rules as a pretax 401(k) plan deferral. However, unlike a pretax deferral, your Roth 401(k) employee deferral is included in your gross income in the year you make the contribution. The tax treatment of a Roth employee deferral is much like a Roth IRA. Unlike a Roth IRA, there are no income restrictions with your 401(k) Roth contribution option as long as your plan offers this feature. Like employee deferrals, Roth employee deferrals and pre-tax employee deferrals together may not exceed the IRC 402(g) limit, which was eighteen thousand dollars (twenty-four thousand dollars if over the age of fifty) for 2015 and 2016. Roth employee deferrals and the allocated earnings must be separately accounted for under a 401(k) plan.

"Your Roth contributions are invested in your retirement-plan account, the same as any pretax contributions you make. But your Roth money is tracked separately than your pretax money and will appear as a separate item on your retirement-plan statements. You can still contribute to a Roth IRA even after maximizing your Roth 401(k) deferral as long as you can satisfy the Roth IRA contribution rules, specifically the income-threshold limitation.

"Many people want to know what the benefits of making Roth 401(k) contributions are, since they are after-tax and do not allow you to defer paying taxes when you contribute them to your Solo 401(k) plan.

"Making a pretax Solo 401(k) plan contribution will give you an immediate tax deduction that can reduce your federal income tax, but it will require you to pay tax and a ten percent early-distribution penalty if you are under 59½, and withdraw the pretax funds in the form of a distribution. (Note: Applicable FICA and self-employment taxes would still be applied to the compensation amount prior to the tax-deductible contribution.)

"In contrast, in the case of an after-tax (Roth) Solo 401(k) plan contribution, no immediate tax deduction would be available. But as long as certain age and holding requirements are met, all contribution amounts, income, and appreciation from the Roth account would come out of the 401(k) plan tax free and penalty free. Roth contributions are subject to federal income tax *before* the money is contributed to your account. This is unlike a traditional IRA or any pretax 401(k) employee contributions, which are made to your account without federal income taxes being deducted. So you defer federal taxes on your before-tax contributions (and any investment earnings) to a later date when you withdraw the funds in the form of a taxable distribution.

"Like traditional contributions made to your retirement plan, your Roth contributions grow without tax until retirement. Unlike before-tax contributions, however, your Roth money can be withdrawn without paying additional federal income tax as long as you meet certain requirements (i.e., qualified Roth distribution). Indeed, you can live off your income and gains from the Roth portion of your Solo 401(k) without ever paying additional tax.

"To qualify for federal tax-free withdrawals of your Roth contributions (and any related investment earnings), there are certain tax-law requirements so that the distribution is treated as a 'qualified distribution':

- Generally, you wait must wait at least five years after January 1 of the year you make your first Roth contribution to the 401(k) plan before taking a withdrawal.
- Your withdrawals must begin after you have reached age 59½, or if you have died or have become disabled." John said.

"Very interesting. I know you mentioned this before, but if I adopted a Solo 401(k) plan for my business, should I make Roth or pretax contributions?" Amy asked.

"Often tax professionals and financial advisors are asked whether it makes sense to make a Roth after-tax contribution or a pretax contribution. The upside with Roth contributions is that your Roth withdrawals in retirement (including any earnings and gains on those contributions) are completely tax free if you meet those requirements listed above," John said. "When deciding whether you should make Roth contributions, before-tax contributions, or a combination of the two, here are some important considerations: If you feel your tax rate in retirement will be higher than it is today, Roth contributions may make sense for you. However, if you expect your tax rate to be lower in retirement than during your working years, you may benefit more from making before-tax contributions and paying taxes when you withdraw your money. It is hard to imagine, but we are currently in a historically low tax-rate environment. For most of the century, including some boom times, top-bracket income-tax rates were much higher than they are today. In fact, during the 1950s and early 1960s, the top-bracket income-tax rate was over ninety percent. In light of our growing deficit, social-security shortfall, and heavy government spending, it is not far off to suggest that income-tax rates will be higher when you retire then they are now. That being said, no one knows what will happen tomorrow when it comes to Congress and taxes, and especially not in twenty or thirty years, so an educated guess is all one can muster."

"So how should I think about it?" Amy asked.

"How confident are you in your expected returns? If you were very confident that your investments and/or cash flow from your investments are relatively secure and will grow over time, a Roth account would make sense. Bear in mind that many people felt that Enron, Lehman Brothers, and Bear Stearns were safe investments and suitable for Roth funds, and we all know how those companies turned out. In general, Roth 401(k) investments seem to work well with real-estate income-producing investments as well as dividend-growth investments where the cash flows are generally perceived as stable.

"The farther away your retirement, the greater opportunity for tax-free growth and the more potential you have for tax-free gains. Basically, if you will not be retiring in the near future, Roth contributions may make a good deal of sense, since your account has more time to potentially grow in value. This may make the tax advantages of Roth contributions even more important to you—although Roth dollars can benefit retirement savers of all ages," John said.

"I really love all those Roth deferral examples you mentioned when we first met, do you have any more for the Roth Solo 401(k) plan so I can get a better handle on how much I can end up with if I was diligent about making Roth Solo 401(k) plan contributions for a number of years?" Amy asked.

"Of course. The following examples should convince you of the enormous benefits of establishing a Solo 401(k) plan with a Roth component and contributing as much as you can to the Roth on an annual basis," John said.

WHAT IS THE ADVANTAGE OF A ROTH CONTRIBUTION?

"In order to get a better handle on the potential advantages of making after-tax Roth contributions, I think the following examples will help convince you of the enormous retirement benefits you would realize by adopting a Solo 401(k) plan with a Roth component for your new business:

- Starting balance: $0
- Annual contribution: $17,500
- Current age: 30
- Age of retirement: 65
- Expected rate of return: 9.77 percent
- Marginal tax rate: 25 percent
- Total amount of contributions: $612,500

"At age 65 with a Roth 401(k) plan, the individual would have $4,733,705 tax free. Whereas if a pretax 401(k) plan was used, the amount of the account at age 65 would be valued at $3,550.279. I used the rate of return of 9.77 percent because that is the average return of the S&P 500 from 1924 through 2014. Now assume that the individual wanted to retire at age of 70:

- Starting balance: $0
- Annual contribution: $17,500
- Current age: 30
- Age of retirement: 70
- Expected rate of return: 9.77 percent
- Marginal tax rate: 25 percent
- Total amount of contributions: $700,000

"At age 70 with a Roth 401(k) plan, the individual would have $7,656,209 tax free. Whereas if a pretax 401(k) plan was used, the amount of the account at age 70 would be valued at $5,742.157," John said.

"That is unbelievable. I should totally be able to max out my Roth 401(k) plan contributions, and if I can generate solid returns over my lifetime, I can't believe I can have around seven million dollars tax free when I retire. Even taking into account inflation and the cost of money, seven million dollars is a ton of money. This is just plain amazing. I can't believe I have never heard of the Solo 401(k) plan before. I am so thankful that you agreed to chat with me about this type of stuff," Amy said.

"It's my pleasure. Here are some more examples. I just hope you share some of this info with your friends and family so that whether they are self-employed and can use a Solo 401(k) plan or have a 401(k) plan with their employer, they understand the enormous benefits of making annual 401(k) plan contributions. Here we go…

- Starting balance: $0
- Annual contribution: $17,500
- Current age: 30
- Age of retirement: 65
- Expected rate of return: 8 percent
- Marginal tax rate: 25 percent
- Total amount of contributions: $612,500

"At age 65 with a Roth 401(k) plan, the individual would have $3,144.681 tax free. Whereas if a pretax 401(k) plan was used, the amount of the account at age 65 would be valued at $2,358.511. Now assume the individual wanted to retire at the age of 70:

- Starting balance: $0
- Annual contribution: $17,500
- Current age: 30
- Age of retirement: 70
- Expected rate of return: 8 percent
- Marginal tax rate: 25 percent
- Total amount of contributions: $700,000

"At age 70 with a Roth 401(k) plan, the individual would have $4,727,630 tax free. Whereas if a pretax 401(k) plan was used, the amount of the account at age 70 would be valued at $3,545.723.

- Starting balance: $0
- Annual contribution: $17,500
- Current age: 40
- Age of retirement: 65
- Expected rate of return: 9.77 percent

- Marginal tax rate: 25 percent
- Total amount of contributions: $437,500

"At age 65 with a Roth 401(k) plan, the individual would have $1,749,385 tax free. Whereas if a pretax 401(k) plan was used, the amount of the account at age 65 would be valued at $1,312.039.

- Starting balance: $0
- Annual contribution: $17,500
- Current age: 40
- Age of retirement: 65
- Expected rate of return: 8 percent
- Marginal tax rate: 25 percent
- Total amount of contributions: $437,500

"At age 65 with a Roth 401(k) plan, the individual would have $1,334,141 tax free. Whereas if a pretax 401(k) plan was used, the amount of the account at age 65 would be valued at $1,000.606.

- Starting balance: $0
- Annual contribution: $18,000
- Current age: 40
- Age of retirement: 60
- Expected rate of return: 8 percent
- Marginal tax rate: 25 percent
- Total amount of contributions: $ $360,000

"At age 70 with a Roth 401(k) plan, the individual would have $2,126,420 tax free. Whereas if a pretax 401(k) plan was used, the amount of the account at age 70 would be valued at $1,594.815."

"Holy cow," Amy said. "I thought the Roth IRA contribution numbers were impressive; the Roth Solo 401(k) numbers blow them away. I could literally end up having many millions tax free in my retirement account if I can max out my Roth Solo 401(k) contributions each year. Hopefully my business continues to do well, and I will be able to max out my Roth 401(k) because the numbers are just ridiculous. I still can't believe more self-employed people don't know about the power of the Solo 401(k) plan and especially the power of the Roth Solo 401(k) plan. I feel that so many millennials and generation Xers are missing out on the opportunity to retire rich and generate tax-free income. I consider myself a relatively educated person who is well read and is pretty up to date with all current events, and I never heard of the Solo 401(k) plan till a few weeks ago when you first mentioned it. I know six or seven friends off hand that are self-employed and would totally get into making Solo 401(k) Roth contributions if they only knew of it. I bet if I sent them an email with the examples you just provided me and showed them how maxing out their annual contributions at their age and continuing to till they retire can get them a few million dollars when they retire, I will get their attention quick. It's almost like the Solo 401(k) plan is a secret that the really well informed are aware of and are almost not willing to share their secret with anyone else. It is just plain unbelievable that if I was able to put away even just $10,000 a year from now until the age of seventy and was able to just get a six percent rate of return that I can end up with around $1.8 million tax free. I know I keep saying it, but this is truly amazing," Amy said.

"I agree. The examples above show the enormous retirement benefits to making Roth-type contributions to a Solo 401(k) plan starting at a young age and on a consistent basis. That being said, there is certainly nothing wrong with having several million dollars in a pretax retirement account, although if your federal and state income-tax rate was at fifty percent when you retired, that million-dollar-plus retirement account would still be nice but definitely not as nice as being able to live off the money tax free and without ever having to pay tax on the money again.

"Taking this a step further, one can argue that with a fifty percent tax rate, having $1 million in a Roth 401(k) plan is like having $1.5 million in a pretax account. Numbers never lie—the hard part is turning down your CPA who is pushing for you to make the pretax contribution so it reduces your current income tax and also makes him or her look better in your eyes. You need to think long term by focusing on the advantages of tapping a tax-free account when you retire, especially if taxes are higher then than they are now.

Whether you make pretax or Roth contributions is not as important as making the contributions. Contributing as much as you can to your Solo 401(k) plan or IRA is the most important action you can take to secure your wealth when you retire. I would argue it is more important than the college you went to or the first job you had. Being diligent about saving for retirement is literally your golden ticket to retiring in style. With federal and state income-tax rates expected to increase in the future, gaining the ability to generate tax-free returns from your retirement investments when you retire is the last surviving legal tax shelter. Imagine if someone told you that if you started making Roth 401(k) contributions in your forties and that by just generating a modest rate of return, you could have over a million dollars tax free when you retire. With a Roth 401(k), you can live off the Roth 401(k) investment income tax free or take a portion of your Roth 401(k) funds and use it for any purpose without ever paying tax," John said.

"Well, you convinced me. Now you got to work on the millions of millennials and generation Xers who have never heard about the Solo 401(k) plan or don't understand the enormous benefits of contributing to a Roth IRA," Amy said.

"Well, I got my work cut out for me. Let's now move on to some of the other benefits of adopting a Roth Solo 401(k) plan," John said.

"OK, works for me," Amy said.

HIGH ROTH CONTRIBUTIONS

A Roth Solo 401(k) combines features of the traditional 401(k) with those of the Roth IRA. Like a Solo 401(k) plan, the Roth Solo 401(k) plan is perfect for any self-employed individual or small-business owner with no employees. The Roth Solo 401(k) plan contains the same advantages as a Solo 401(k) plan, but contributions are made with after-tax dollars as with a Roth IRA. While you don't get an up-front tax-deduction, the Roth 401(k) account grows tax free, and withdrawals taken during retirement aren't subject to income tax, provided you're at least 59½ and have held the account for five years or more.

The Roth Solo 401(k) can offer advantages to self-employed individuals who wish to maximize their ability to generate tax-free retirement savings while receiving the ability to invest in real estate, precious metals, private businesses, or funds tax free and without custodian consent.

Unlike a Roth IRA, which limits individual Roth IRA contributions to $5,500 annually ($6,500 if the individual is fifty years or older) for 2015 and 2016, with a Roth Solo 401(k) account, an individual can make after-tax (Roth) contributions of up to $18,000, or $24,000 for those fifty or older by the end of the year for 2015 and 2016. This allows you to put away thousands of dollars more in tax-free retirement income than you would through a Roth IRA.

"Do the Roth IRA income limits apply to the Roth Solo 401(k) plan?" Amy asked.

"Great question. The IRS has established income rules that govern who is eligible to make after-tax (Roth) IRA contributions. If your income exceeds a certain amount, you will not be allowed to contribute to a Roth IRA. The good news is that this income-threshold requirement does not apply to a Solo 401(k) plan Roth account," John said.

"That is great news. I am loving the Roth Solo 401(k) plan already," Amy laughed.

"I knew you would. A Roth Solo 401(k) is perfect for sole proprietors, small businesses, and independent contractors such as consultants. The Roth Solo 401(k) plan is unique and so popular because it is considered the last-remaining legal tax shelter available. There are so many features of the Roth Solo 401(k) plan that make it so appealing and popular among self-employed business owners."

Unlimited Investment Opportunities

With a Roth 401(k) plan or Roth 401(k) plan subaccount, with the right plan documents, you can invest your after-tax Roth 401(k) plan funds in real estate, precious metals, tax liens, private business investments, and much more tax free. Unlike a pretax 401(k) plan, in a Roth 401(k) account all income and gains flow back tax free to your account. As long as you have reached the age of 59½ and have had the Roth 401(k) account opened at least five years, you can take Roth 401(k) plan distributions tax free. In other words, you can live off your Roth 401(k) plan assets or income tax free. With federal income-tax rates expected to increase, the ability to have a tax-free source of income upon retirement may be the difference between retiring early or not.

LOAN FEATURE

"While an IRA offers no participant-loan feature, the Roth Solo 401(k) allows participants to borrow up to fifty thousand dollars or 50 percent of their account value (whichever is less) for any purpose at a low interest rate (the lowest interest rate is Prime, which is 3.5 percent as of March 2016). This offers a Roth Solo 401(k) plan participant the ability to access up to fifty thousand dollars to use for any purpose, including paying personal debt or funding a business," John said.

"I am just loving the Roth Solo 401(k) plan. I know a while back you talked about the SEP IRA and mentioned that the Solo 401(k) plan is so much of a better retirement plan for the self-employed; can you explain that a bit?" Amy asked.

"As I said earlier, before the EGTRRA became effective in 2002, there was no compelling reason for an owner-only business to establish a Solo 401(k) plan because the business owner could generally receive the same benefits by adopting a profit-sharing plan or a SEP IRA. After 2002, EGTRRA paved the way for an owner-only business to put more money aside for retirement and to operate a more cost-effective retirement plan than a SEP IRA or 401(k) plan. The SEP is a pure profit-sharing employer-sponsored retirement plan that allows for a tax-deductible contribution equal to the smaller of fifty-three thousand dollars or twenty-five percent of compensation for 2016."

"I have heard of the SEP IRA but not the Solo 401(k) plan. I know this may be a bit duplicative, but what are the main advantages of establishing a Solo 401(k) plan over a SEP IRA?" Amy asked.

"The Solo 401(k) has the following advantages:
- Higher maximum contribution. As I've already mentioned, a Solo 401(k) plan allows you to make an employee-salary-deferral contribution and an employee-profit-sharing-deferral contribution. A SEP IRA, on the other hand, only allows for a profit-sharing contribution equal to the lesser of $53,000 or 25 percent (20 percent in the case

of a sole proprietorship or single-member LLC) of the earned income or compensation earned via the business, and it does not have an employee salary-deferral contribution. So if you are sixty years old and have an S corporation from which you earn $100,000 in self-employment wages according to your W-2 form, then you can put $24,000 plus $25,000 (which is 25 percent of $100,000) or approximately $49,000 into your Solo 401(k). Whereas if you establish a SEP IRA, you can only defer 25 percent of $100,000 or $25,000.

- Catch-up contributions. With a Solo 401(k), you can contribute an extra $6,000 if you are over fifty years of age. The SEP IRA does not allow a catch-up contribution.
- Roth feature. A Solo 401(k) plan can be made in either pretax or after-tax (Roth) formats. A SEP IRA only permits pretax contributions.
- Tax-free loan option. A Solo 401(k) permits you to borrow up to $50,000 or 50 percent of your account value, whichever is less. This loan can be used for any purpose. A SEP IRA does not allow you to borrow any money from your account without triggering a prohibited transaction.
- Invest in real estate, and use leverage with no additional tax. With a Solo 401(k), you can make a real-estate investment using nonrecourse funds without triggering the Unrelated Debt Financed Income rules and the Unrelated Business Taxable Income (UBTI) tax (IRC 514). This is not possible with a SEP IRA, as using SEP IRA funds to purchase real estate using a nonrecourse loan would trigger the Unrelated Business Taxable Income tax.

THE ROTH SOLO 401(K) WINS EVERY TIME

When Congress put EGTRRA into effect in 2002, it did a real favor for self-employed Americans. Prior to 2002, there was really not much reason to establish a Solo 401(k) plan versus a SEP IRA, which is why the SEP IRA is so widely known. However, EGTRRA changed all of that. After decades of being disadvantaged when it came to taxation and retirement savings, the Solo 401(k) plan now makes it possible for the self-employed to build their wealth faster than ever. With its high annual contributions, tax advantages, Roth feature, and loan component, EGTRAA paved the way for the Solo 401(k) plan to overtake the SEP IRA as the most popular retirement account for the self-employed. The Solo 401(k) enables you to save far more money than any other retirement-savings plan, while retaining the simplicity, low cost, and flexibility that every self-employed person wants.

"It's not often that the government delivers more than expected, but in the case of the Solo 401(k), we really lucked out. Now let's look first at what you can't do with a Solo 401(k) before we move on to what you can do," John said.

7

THE PROHIBITED-TRANSACTION RULES

T HE NEXT TIME they met, Amy was ready with the question that was first and foremost on her mind.

"Now that I know you can make alternative-asset investments, such as real estate with a self-directed Roth IRA or Roth Solo 401(k) plan, I have a few investment ideas in mind and just wanted to get a better handle on the type of investments I can or can't make with my retirement funds," Amy said.

"You bet," John said. "Now's a perfect time."

"One more question. I assume that if I continued to invest my Roth IRA and 401(k) plan funds into stocks and mutual funds, I would not have to worry about the prohibited-transaction rules you are about to describe?" Amy asked.

"Yes, that is one hundred percent correct. In fact, if you are not interested in making alternative-asset investments with your retirement account and are not interested in learning about the prohibited-transaction rules, please let me know and I can move on to another topic." John said.

"No – I think it I helpful to learn about the prohibited transaction rules because I probably would consider using my IRA to buy real estate down the road at some point, Amy said."

John pulled out some notes and dug in.

THE BASICS OF PROHIBITED TRANSACTIONS

"Even though it sounds daunting," John said, "it's really not. But it is a little fuzzy. The IRC doesn't describe what a self-directed IRA or Solo 401(k) plan can invest in, only what it *cannot* invest in. Specifically, IRC Sections 408 and 4975 prohibit disqualified persons from engaging in certain types of transactions. The purpose of these rules is to encourage the use of IRAs for the accumulation of retirement savings and to prohibit those in control of retirement plans from taking advantage of the tax benefits for their personal accounts."

"So it's sort of protecting my account from me?" Amy asked.

"In a way. Prohibited-transaction rules are based on the premise that investments involving retirement accounts and related parties should be handled in a way that benefits the retirement account and not the retirement-account owner."

"Would the IRS–prohibited transaction rules be different if I did a self-directed Roth IRA or a Solo 401(k) plan?" Amy asked.

"Not really. The main difference is that a Solo 401(k) plan is able to purchase life-insurance contacts but an IRA is not. The IRS–prohibited transaction rules are triggered when IRA funds are used to make an investment, whether or not the investment is made directly by an IRA custodian or a 401(k) plan," John said.

"So if no harm would be coming to anyone except me, by my own hand, why should the IRS be so concerned about investments involving my retirement account and my family members?" Amy asked.

"Basically," John answered, "that's the only way the IRS can protect its very important revenue-generating distribution rules. It needs to make sure that if people want to use their retirement funds for personal purposes, they pay tax and a penalty if they are under the age of 59½. In other words, it's the IRS's position that if you want to use retirement funds for personal purposes, that's OK as long as you pay the appropriate tax and penalty."

"Fair enough, I guess," Amy said. "I'd want to protect my revenue too."

"Exactly," John said. "So, in developing the disqualified-person rules, the IRS is basically saying that it believes a retirement-account holder and his or her lineal descendants are one and the same, and if retirement-account funds are being transferred directly or indirectly to a disqualified person, it is the same as if the retirement-account holder himself or herself were personally benefiting."

"That position makes sense," Amy said.

John nodded. "Yes. If you think about it—by giving money to your parents or children, you are clearly benefiting to some degree because of the close family relationship. For example, using your retirement account to pay your children's tuition or your parents' mortgage is either directly or indirectly benefiting you because if your parents or kids benefit, you are benefiting to some degree. The IRS's position is that if you were able to transact with a disqualified person and use retirement-account funds you could simply transfer the retirement-account funds to a child or parent and that would be just like them taking the money personally, which would eliminate the need to take a taxable distribution. This is something the IRS would definitely not appreciate."

"I think I get it," Amy said. "So if I could take some of my retirement-account funds and give them to my husband and kids, it would be pretty much the same as if I got to use the money personally."

"Right," John said. "The IRS was concerned that if they allowed this, people would be able to circumvent the distribution rules and avoid paying tax on their IRS accounts while simultaneously receiving some degree of benefit from the funds because they were used to help a close family member, such as a parent, child, or spouse."

"Ah, because I wouldn't have paid tax on that money otherwise, and I would still get to use it for my personal benefit."

"Remember, in the case of a traditional pretax IRA or 401(k) plan, you were granted a tax deduction for the IRA or 401(k) plan contribution on the expectation that you would eventually pay tax on the accumulated pretax retirement account value," John said. "If you were able to take the pretax retirement funds and give them to a parent, spouse, or child, it would be like you were gaining use of the retirement funds without having to pay any tax or the ten percent penalty, if applicable."

"And if that were possible, everyone would do it to avoid paying some taxes on that money," Amy said.

"Sure," John said. "And the IRS would be left with very little tax revenue from the pretax retirement account, and it would also lose tax revenue because of the use of the IRS deduction in the year of contribution—a double whammy."

"So prohibited-transaction rules are actually very important for the IRS," Amy said.

"The bottom line," John said, "is that most Americans' largest asset by the time they retire is their retirement account. The self-directed IRA and Solo 401(k) structure has become so popular over the last several years because the 2008 financial crisis hit those retirement assets so hard and showed people how important it is to diversify their retirement investments. The IRS has actually granted retirement investors a wide array of investment options when using retirement funds, but there are a number of important rules the IRS has codified that govern how IRA retirement funds are to be used."

"I never thought of the IRA as being the most important tool in America for retirement," Amy said.

"It really is," John said. "According to the Investment Company Institute November 2013 publication, IRAs represent more than one-quarter of US total retirement-market assets, compared with seventeen percent two decades ago, with $5.7 trillion in assets at the end of the second quarter of 2013. And they've only risen in importance on household balance sheets. In June 2013, IRA assets were nine percent of all household financial assets, up from four percent of assets two decades ago. In May 2013, 46.1 million, or thirty-eight percent of US households reported they owned IRAs. IRAs are such an important asset for retirees that it makes navigating the IRS–prohibited transaction rules even more crucial."

"But like you said," Amy added, "the tricky part is that the IRS doesn't tell you what you can invest in or how you should use your IRA assets; it only tells you what you can't invest in or how you can't use those assets."

"Exactly," John said. "So prohibited transactions are important to follow if you want to gain maximum advantage from the work you are doing to create and grow your IRA retirement assets."

"Are the penalties for violating prohibited-transaction rules harsh enough to be worth worrying about?" Amy asked.

"Yes," John said, "they're steep. And if your IRA is your most valuable asset, as it is for most Americans, it will trigger a hefty tax and penalty with significant financial ramifications to your retirement."

"Are the prohibited-transaction rules the same for traditional and Roth IRAs or Roth 401(k) plan?" Amy asked.

John nodded. "The same rules apply to all IRAs including traditional IRAs, Roth IRAs, SEP IRAs, and SIMPLE IRAs."

"I wonder why I never heard of prohibited-transaction rules before we started talking."

"You're not alone," John said. "Most Americans have never heard of the prohibited-transaction rules for good reason. After all, most retirement investors use their retirement funds to buy traditional financial assets, such as stocks, mutual funds, and ETFs. With those investments, the chance of engaging in a prohibited transaction is slim to none. Hence, for people who are not interested in using retirement funds to make alternative-asset investments, the prohibited transaction riles are not extremely relevant; although, I think they are worth knowing about. For people who are interested in making alternative-asset investments with their retirement accounts such as real estate, the prohibited-transaction rules become very important. The good news is that the harsh penalties are easily avoidable. As long as you stay away from breaking the rules, you have no reason to fear the IRS when making self-directed IRA or Solo 401(k) plan investments."

"OK," Amy said. "So what areas do we need to discuss?"

"Let's look at prohibited transactions that are restricted because they pertain to disqualified persons, conflicts of interest, and self-dealing," John said. "And we should also look at exceptions and exemptions to the restrictions, as well as certain categories of transactions that are not allowed with a retirement account, such as the purchase of collectibles. Though there are many different scenarios stipulated in IRC Section 4975, and extensive case law clarifying those scenarios, the restrictions themselves are not complicated, and I can simplify them as much as possible to make them easier to follow. Even so, it can be helpful to get advice from a tax professional just to make sure you're on the straight and narrow path."

John then explained everything Amy needed to learn about disqualified persons.

DISQUALIFIED PERSONS

If a retirement-account transaction is restricted, it is likely because it pertains to a disqualified person. Who does the IRS consider a disqualified person?

Generally, this is referring to *you* (the IRA holder or 401(k) plan participant) and most of *your immediate family*, including your direct lineal ancestors or descendants as well as *any business* entities that hold a controlling equity or management interest in your retirement account.

Specifically, a disqualified person is

a. *you*, as the retirement-account holder, or any person with authority for making retirement-account investments;

b. *a trustee or custodian*, or a person providing services to the retirement account;

c. *the owner*—this is generally not applicable to IRAs and only really covers 401(k) plans;

d. *an employee organization*—this is generally not applicable to IRAs and only really covers 401(k) plans;

e. *a 50 percent owner* of (c) or (d);

f. *a family member* of (a), (b), (c), or (d), which includes your spouse, your parents and grandparents, your children and grandchildren, and their spouses but not brothers, sisters, aunts, uncles, cousins, step-siblings, or friends;

g. *a partnership, corporation, trust, or estate* more than 50 percent owned or controlled by (a), (b), (c), (d), or (e);

h. *a 10 percent owner, officer, director, or highly compensated employee* of (c), (d), (e), or (g); or

i. *a 10 percent or more partner or joint venture* of (c), (d), (e), or (g).

In order to determine whether a proposed transaction is a prohibited transaction and violates IRC 4975, it is important to examine all the parties engaged in the proposed transaction rather than just the retirement-account owner.

According to IRC Section 4975, a retirement account is prohibited from engaging in certain types of transactions. The types of prohibited transactions can be best understood by dividing them into three categories: (1) direct prohibited transactions, (2) self-dealing prohibited transactions, and (3) conflict-of-interest prohibited transactions.

DIRECT OR INDIRECT PROHIBITED TRANSACTIONS

What is a direct or indirect prohibited transaction? Essentially, it is a transaction between the retirement account and a disqualified person, which either directly or indirectly personally benefits that disqualified person. It is important to remember that the IRS–prohibited transaction rules are primarily in place to ensure that the use of retirement funds is in no way directly or indirectly personally benefiting the plan participant or any of his or her lineal descendants. The reason is clear. The IRS holds that if you wish to make personal use of your retirement funds to help yourself or a close family member, doing so is essentially like helping yourself. Accordingly, you must take a distribution and pay the tax and penalty, if you are under 59½ years old. Those prohibited-transaction rules are basically the way the IRS polices and protects their distribution rules—a significant revenue source for the IRS and Treasury. In addition, when it comes to accumulating 401(k) and IRA funds, most of the funds are in pretax form, meaning the IRS provided the 401(k) plan participant or IRA holder with a tax deduction with the anticipation that the benefit provided to the taxpayer would be paid back in the form of taxation on the appreciated assets of the retirement account at a later time. It makes sense, then, that the IRS is so concerned with making sure that retirement funds are not used for any personal purpose that would allow someone to circumvent the distribution rules and taxation on the funds used. The IRS and Department of Labor need to protect their distribution rules because that is how they ensure that the IRS and Treasury will receive the taxes they believe they deserve from retirement distributions.

Direct and indirect prohibited transactions are different. A direct prohibited transaction is the simplest type of prohibited transaction to uncover because it deals with scenarios involving a disqualified person and the retirement account directly. In contrast, an indirect prohibited transaction concerns transactions that do not appear to directly benefit a disqualified person but could do so indirectly based on certain facts and circumstances. For example, using your self-directed IRA to pay your personal credit-card bill would be a clear direct prohibited transaction. However, using your self-directed IRA to invest in a company in which you own 15 percent might be considered an indirect prohibited transaction based on certain facts and circumstances.

For example, you cannot use your retirement account to do the following with a disqualified person:

- Sell, exchange, or lease property
- Lend money or extend credit
- Furnish goods, services, or facilities
- Transfer income or assets

John handed Amy a copy of IRC 4975 for his review. Here are some scenarios pertaining to IRC 4975(c)(1)(A) that illustrate prohibited transactions to do with directly or indirectly selling, exchanging, or leasing property to a disqualified person.

4975(C)(1)(A): THE DIRECT OR INDIRECT SALE, EXCHANGE, OR LEASING OF PROPERTY BETWEEN A RETIREMENT ACCOUNT AND A DISQUALIFIED PERSON

- Joe sells an interest in a piece of property owned by his retirement account to his son—PROHIBITED
- Beth leases real estate owned by her retirement account to her daughter—PROHIBITED
- Mark uses his retirement-account funds to purchase an LLC interest owned by his mother—PROHIBITED
- Victor leases an interest in a piece of property owned by his retirement account to his son—PROHIBITED

- Tracy sells real estate owned by her retirement account to her father—PROHIBITED
- Ben sells real estate he owns personally to his retirement account—PROHIBITED
- Jason transfers property he owns personally to his retirement account—PROHIBITED
- Katy purchases real estate with her retirement-account funds and leases it to her son—PROHIBITED
- David uses his retirement-account funds to purchase an interest in an entity owned by his father—PROHIBITED
- Ted transfers property he owns personally subject to a mortgage to his retirement account—PROHIBITED
- Sally uses personal funds to pay expenses related to her retirement-account real-estate investment—PROHIBITED
- Jane uses personal funds to pay taxes and expenses related to her retirement-account real-estate investment—PROHIBITED

Here are other scenarios pertaining to IRC 4975(c)(1)(B) that illustrate prohibited transactions to do with directly or indirectly lending money or extending credit to a disqualified person:

4975(C)(1)(B): THE DIRECT OR INDIRECT LENDING OF MONEY OR OTHER EXTENSION OF CREDIT BETWEEN A RETIREMENT ACCOUNT AND A DISQUALIFIED PERSON

- Ted lends his wife $70,000 from his retirement account—PROHIBITED
- Mary personally guarantees a bank loan to her retirement account to purchase real estate—PROHIBITED
- Dan uses his retirement-account funds to lend an entity owned and controlled by his father $18,000—PROHIBITED
- Ken lends his son $4,000 from his retirement account—PROHIBITED

- Rick uses the assets of his retirement account as security for a loan—PROHIBITED
- Brandon uses his personal assets as security for a retirement-account investment—PROHIBITED
- Chuck uses retirement-account funds to lend an entity owned and controlled by his father $45,000—PROHIBITED
- Eric acquires a credit card for his retirement account—PROHIBITED

Real-Life Examples

Here is a real example of how the IRS–prohibited transaction rules work:

Peek v. Commissioner, 140 TC 12 (2013)

In *Peek*, the Tax Court held that a personal guarantee by an IRA owner of a loan to the owner's IRA is a prohibited transaction [since it is a loan of money or extension of credit between a plan and a disqualified person under Code Sec. 4975(c)(1)(B)].

However, what if the loan was not made directly to the IRA but was made instead to an entity owned by the IRA? Is a personal guarantee by the IRA owner of such a loan a prohibited transaction? That was the subject of the Peek case. *Peek* involved two IRA owners (Mr. Fleck and Mr. Peek) who jointly invested in a corporation (FP) formed by them to acquire the assets of another company (AFS). The IRAs were the only shareholders of FP.

FP acquired the assets of AFS in exchange for a combination of cash and notes, including a promissory note from FP to the sellers secured by personal guarantees from both IRA owners. Fleck and Peek were fiduciaries of their respective IRAs due to retaining authority and control over such IRAs and thus were disqualified persons under Code Sec. 4975(c)(1)(A), and each IRA constitutes a "plan" under 4975(e)(1).

Nevertheless, they argued that because their personal guarantees did not involve the plan itself—that is, since the guarantees were between disqualified persons (Fleck and Peek) and an entity (FP) other than the IRAs themselves—the guarantees were not prohibited.

This argument was flatly rejected by the Tax Court, which noted that 4975(c)(1)(B) also prohibits indirect loans and/or extensions of credit between a plan and a disqualified person and that the "obvious and intended meaning" of (c)(1)(B) "prohibited Mr. Fleck and Mr. Peek from making loans or loan guarantees either directly to their IRAs or indirectly to their IRAs by way of the entity owned by the IRAs."

It is also prohibited, according to IRC 4975(c)(1)(C), to use your self-directed IRA to directly or indirectly furnish goods, services, or facilities to a disqualified person.

4975(C)(1)(C): THE DIRECT OR INDIRECT FURNISHING OF GOODS, SERVICES, OR FACILITIES BETWEEN A RETIREMENT ACCOUNT AND A DISQUALIFIED PERSON

- Andrew buys a piece of property with his retirement-account funds and hires his father to work on the property—PROHIBITED
- Rachel buys a condo with her retirement-account funds and personally fixes it up—PROHIBITED
- Betty owns an apartment building with her retirement-account and hires her mother to manage the property—PROHIBITED
- Bill purchases a condo with his retirement-account funds and paints the walls without receiving a fee—PROHIBITED
- Henry buys a piece of property with his retirement-account funds and hires his son to work on the property—PROHIBITED
- Mary buys a home with her retirement account, and her son makes repairs for free—PROHIBITED
- Beth owns an office building with her retirement account and hires her son to manage the property for a fee—PROHIBITED
- Jackie owns an apartment building with her retirement-account funds and has her father manage the property for free—PROHIBITED
- Doug receives compensation from his retirement account for investment advice—PROHIBITED
- Matt acts as the real-estate agent for his retirement account—PROHIBITED

INDIRECT PROHIBITED TRANSACTIONS

Indirect prohibited transactions inspire a lot of debate because the determination of whether a prohibited transaction occurred is largely based on the facts and circumstances.

Indirect prohibited transactions are transactions that may not violate any of the direct prohibited-transaction rules on their face, but still may be considered a prohibited transaction by the IRS. For example, when an individual uses a retirement account to invest in a company in which he owns a 15 percent share, this would not seem to be a prohibited transaction because the individual retirement-account holder owns less than 50 percent of the entity and the entity does not seem to be a disqualified person under IRC 4975. However, if it turned out that the company needed the funds to avoid bankruptcy or the investment was made to secure a job within the company, the IRS could argue that the investment directly or indirectly helped the retirement-account holder personally.

Many tax professionals fail to focus on the indirect prohibited-transaction rules outlined in IRC 4975 and just focus on the direct prohibited-transaction rules. The IRS seems to be using the indirect prohibited-transaction rules as a tool for scrutinizing retirement account transactions that seem to personally benefit the retirement-account holder but don't violate the direct prohibited-transaction rules under IRC 4975.

The following examples below will help illustrate.

Subject to the exemptions under IRC Section 4975(d), an indirect prohibited transaction generally involves one of the following:

4975(C)(1)(D): THE DIRECT OR INDIRECT TRANSFER TO A DISQUALIFIED PERSON OF INCOME OR ASSETS OF A RETIREMENT ACCOUNT

- Ken is in a financial jam and takes $32,000 from his retirement account to pay a personal debt—PROHIBITED
- John uses his retirement account to purchase a rental property and hires his friend to manage the property. The friend then enters

into a contract with John and transfers those funds back to John—PROHIBITED

- Melissa invests her retirement account funds in a real-estate fund and then receives a salary for managing the fund—PROHIBITED
- Jim uses a house owned by his retirement account for personal use—PROHIBITED
- Seth deposits retirement-account funds into his personal bank account—PROHIBITED
- Spencer buys precious metals using his retirement-account funds and uses them for personal gain—PROHIBITED
- Bryan purchases a vacation home with his retirement-account funds and stays in the home on occasion—PROHIBITED
- Elliot buys a cottage with her retirement-account funds on the lake and rents it out to her daughter and son-in-law—PROHIBITED
- Allison purchases a condo using her retirement account on the beach and lets her son use it for free—PROHIBITED
- Kelly invests her retirement-account funds in an investment fund and then receives a salary for managing the fund—PROHIBITED
- Larry uses his retirement-account funds to purchase real estate and earns a commission as the real-estate agent on the sale—PROHIBITED
- Steve uses his retirement-account funds to lend money to a company he owns and controls—PROHIBITED
- Gordon invests his retirement-account funds into a business he owns 75 percent of and manages—PROHIBITED

SELF-DEALING PROHIBITED TRANSACTIONS

Self-dealing is a term for a situation that arises when someone benefits on both sides of a deal. According to 4975(c)(1)(E), self-dealing, which is a form of an indirect prohibited transaction, occurs when you directly or indirectly use the income or assets of your retirement account to further your own interests or benefit your own accounts.

4975(C)(1)(E): THE DIRECT OR INDIRECT ACT BY A DISQUALIFIED PERSON WHO IS A FIDUCIARY WHEREBY HE/SHE DEALS WITH INCOME OR ASSETS OF THE RETIREMENT ACCOUNT IN HIS OR HER OWN INTEREST OR FOR HIS OR HER OWN ACCOUNT

- Debra, who is a real-estate agent, uses her retirement-account funds to buy a piece of property *and* earns a commission from the sale—PROHIBITED
- Ben wants to buy a piece of property for $120,000 and would like to own the property personally but does not have sufficient funds. As a result, Ben uses $110,000 from his retirement account *and* $10,000 personally to make the investment—PROHIBITED
- Nancy uses her retirement-account funds to invest in a real-estate fund managed by her son, *and* Nancy's father receives a bonus for securing Nancy's investment—PROHIBITED
- Karen makes an investment using her retirement-account funds into a company she controls that will benefit her personally—PROHIBITED
- Brett uses his retirement-account funds to invest in a partnership with himself personally in which he and his family will own more than 50 percent of the partnership—PROHIBITED
- Pam uses her retirement-account funds to invest in a business she and her husband own and operate, and she and her husband earn compensation from the business—PROHIBITED
- Rick uses his retirement-account funds to lend money to a business that he controls and manages—PROHIBITED
- Lance invests his retirement-account funds in a trust in which Lance and his wife would gain a personal benefit—PROHIBITED
- Helen uses her retirement-account funds to invest in a real-estate fund managed by her son, who receives a bonus for securing her investment—PROHIBITED
- Stanley invests his retirement-account funds into a real-estate project in which his development company will be involved in order to secure the contract—PROHIBITED

- Warren uses his retirement-account funds to invest in his son's business that is in financial trouble—PROHIBITED
- Alex uses his retirement-account funds to buy a note on a piece of property for which he is the debtor personally—PROHIBITED

Real-Life Examples

Here's a real-life example of a self-dealing prohibited transaction.

Rollins v. Commissioner, **T.C. Memo 2004-60**

Rollins v. Commissioner is an important case because it illustrates how one can engage in a prohibited transaction with an entity even if the entity is not a disqualified entity per se. The Rollins case also is important for examining whether a potential transaction could be considered an indirect prohibited transaction under IRC 4975.

The facts in *Rollins* are as follows: Mr. Rollins owned his own CPA firm. He was sole trustee of its 401(k) plan. Mr. Rollins caused his plan to lend funds to three companies in which he was the largest stockholder (9 percent to 33 percent), but not controlling stockholder. The companies had twenty-eight, seventy, and eighty other stockholders, respectively. Mr. Rollins made the decision for the companies to borrow from his 401(k) plan. The loans were demand loans, secured by each company's assets. The interest rate was market rate or higher. Mr. Rollins signed loan checks for his plan and signed notes for borrowers. All loans were repaid in full.

Mr. Rollins acknowledged that he is a disqualified person with regard to the plan because he owns Rollins, the CPA firm, but he contends that (1) none of the corporations that were the borrowers was a disqualified person, (2) none of the loans was a transaction between him and the plan, and (3) he "did not benefit from these loans, either in income or in his own account."

The Tax Court held that a Code Section 4975(c)(1)(D) indirect prohibition did not require an actual transfer of money or property between the plan and the disqualified person. The fact that a disqualified person could have benefited as a result of the use of plan assets was sufficient. The Tax Court held that the transactions were used by Rollins or for his benefit and were assets of the plan. These assets of the plan were not transferred to Rollins. For each of those transactions, however, Rollins sat on both sides of the table.

Rollins made the decisions to lend the plan's funds, and Rollins signed the promissory notes on behalf of the borrowers.

One of the more interesting parts of the Rollins case was the Tax Court's emphasis that as the taxpayer, the burden of proof is the responsibility of the taxpayer. In other words, at its core, the Rollins case is a burden-of-proof case that illustrates the breadth of the application of 4975(c)(1)(D) as well as the difficulty of meeting that burden of proof. Mr. Rollins was not a majority owner of any of the borrowers, but he was the largest shareholder for each company. And he also signed the notes for each borrower.

Would the same decision have been made if Mr. Rollins was not the largest shareholder or had not, as the court put it, "sat on both sides of the table" (e.g., by not signing the notes on behalf of the borrowers)? It's not entirely clear if that would have influenced the court since it was still Mr. Rollins's burden (as the disqualified person) to prove that the transaction did not enhance or was not intended to enhance the value of his investments in the borrowers. That seems to be a very tough burden to meet. Moreover, as the court noted, the fact that a transaction is a good investment for the plan has nothing to do with the problem.

The lesson is that caution should be exercised whenever a disqualified person is sitting "on both sides of the table."

"Here are a few more real-life example," John said.

T.L. Ellis, TC Memo-2013-245

On October 29, 2013, the Tax Court in *T.L. Ellis*, TC Memo. 2013-245, Dec. 59,674(M), held that establishing a special-purpose limited liability company to make an investment did not trigger a prohibited transaction, as a newly established LLC cannot be deemed a disqualified person pursuant to IRC Section 4975.

In *T.L. Ellis*, TC Memo. 2013-245, Mr. Ellis retired with about $300,000 in his 401(k) retirement plan, which he subsequently rolled over into a newly created self-directed IRA.

The taxpayer then created an LLC taxed as a corporation and had his IRA transfer the $300,000 into the LLC. The LLC was formed to engage in the business of used-car sales. The taxpayer managed the used-car business through the IRA LLC and received a modest salary.

The IRS argued that the formation of the LLC was a prohibited transaction under IRC Section 4975, which prohibits self-dealing. The Tax Court disagreed, holding that even though the taxpayer acted as a fiduciary to the IRA (and was therefore a disqualified person under IRC Section 4975), the LLC itself was not a disqualified person at the time of the transfer. After the transfer, the LLC was a disqualified person because it was owned by Mr. Ellis's IRA, a disqualified person. Additionally, the IRS also claimed that the taxpayer had engaged in a prohibited transaction by receiving a salary from the LLC. The court agreed with the IRS. Although the LLC (and not the IRA) was officially paying the taxpayer's salary, the Tax Court concluded that since the IRA was the sole owner of the LLC, and that the LLC was the IRA's only investment, the taxpayer (a disqualified person) was essentially being paid by his IRA.

The Ellis case is the first case that directly reinforces the legality of using a newly established LLC to make IRA investments without triggering an IRS-prohibited transaction. The Tax Court ruled that a prohibited transaction had occurred because Mr. Ellis received a salary from the LLC, which was wholly owned by his IRA. Of note—the Tax Court confirmed that using a newly established LLC, wholly owned by an IRA and managed by the IRA holder does not in itself trigger a prohibited transaction. In addition, we will soon discuss how using a 401(k) plan to purchase corporate stock could have allowed Mr. Ellis to make the business investment without triggering a prohibited transaction.

ERISA ADVISORY OPINION LETTER 93-33A

In this advisory opinion, an IRA owner proposed to use his IRA to buy land and a building at a high school founded by his daughter and son-in-law and to lease the property back to the school at either fair market rent or lower rent depending on the school's ability to pay. Presumably, this school was a non-profit organization, without stockholders.

The IRA owner, having discretion to invest the IRA's assets, was a fiduciary and a disqualified person. The IRA owner's daughter and son-in-law were the sole directors and officers of the school. As such, by virtue of 4975(e)(2)(F), they also were disqualified persons. Consequently, the Department of Labor concluded that the proposed sale-leaseback transaction would constitute the use of IRA assets for the benefit of disqualified persons (i.e., the IRA owner's daughter and son-in-law) in violation of 4975(c)(1)(D). It seemed that the major factor here was the arrangement to lease back the property at a rent dependent on the school's ability to pay. In fact, the Department of Labor took the broad view that either 4975(c)(1)(D) or (E) would be violated if a transaction were part of an agreement, arrangement, or understanding in which the fiduciary caused plan assets to be used in a manner designed to benefit any person in whom such fiduciary had an interest that would affect the exercise of his or her best judgment as a fiduciary.

CONFLICT-OF-INTEREST PROHIBITED TRANSACTIONS

According to 4975(c)(i)(F), a prohibited transaction also occurs when a disqualified person is connected to a transaction involving the income or assets of the retirement account. This is called a conflict-of-interest prohibited transaction. For example:

4975(C)(I)(F): RECEIPT OF ANY CONSIDERATION BY A DISQUALIFIED PERSON WHO IS A FIDUCIARY FOR HIS OR HER OWN ACCOUNT FROM ANY PARTY DEALING WITH THE RETIREMENT ACCOUNT IN CONNECTION WITH A TRANSACTION INVOLVING INCOME OR ASSETS OF THE RETIREMENT ACCOUNT:

- Jason uses his retirement-account funds to loan money to a company that he manages and controls and also owns a small ownership interest in—PROHIBITED
- Cathy uses her retirement account to lend money to a business that she works for in order to secure a promotion—PROHIBITED

- Eric uses his retirement-account funds to invest in a fund that he manages and where his management fee is based on the total value of the fund's assets—PROHIBITED

Real-Life Examples

And here's a real-life example:

Technical Advice Memorandum 9118001

In this Technical Advice Memorandum, the IRS concluded that loans made by a law firm's pension and profit-sharing plans to its clients to provide those clients with financial support while they were awaiting settlement on their lawsuits were prohibited transactions under both IRC Sections 4975(c)(1)(D) and 4975(c)(1)(E) of the code.

The law firm's partners, who were fiduciaries with authority over plan assets, directed a bank, as the plan trustee, to lend clients money pending the outcome of their suits. The district office contended that this is a transaction prohibited by IRC Section 4975(c)(1)(D) since the partners of the law firm were acting as a lending institution and the law firm was indirectly using and benefiting from plan assets. The taxpayer disagreed, arguing that the loans were made to clients from the plan assets solely to benefit plan participants and that it is a common business practice in personal-injury law firms to advance funds to clients who are awaiting settlement.

The IRS determined that the loans were prohibited under IRC Section 4975(c)(1)(D) because the employer, who is a disqualified person under IRC Section 4975(e)(2)(C), benefited from the use of plan assets. As the IRS stated, the parties benefiting from the loans (i.e., the party whose business object is being served) were the partners in the law firm. It did not matter that the clients could have received loans elsewhere or that the loans were good investments nor did it matter that it was common practice for law firms to advance funds to clients pending the conclusion of their lawsuits. As long as a benefit is derived by a disqualified person through the use of a plan asset, a transaction is prohibited under IRC Section 4975(c)(1)(D).

In addition, the IRS found that the loans were also prohibited under IRC Section 4975(c)(1)(E). The partners of the law firm were fiduciaries since they exercised their authority with respect to the management of plan assets by directing the trustee (the bank) to enter into loans with their clients in conjunction with their legal representation. As such, the partners, in their capacity as plan administrators, dealt with the assets of the plan in their own interest.

"That was really helpful. Just to confirm, if I was only investing into stocks and mutual funds I wouldn't have to worry about all these prohibited-transaction rules?" Amy asked.

"Yes, that is correct. It is close to impossible to for the average American that is using retirement-account funds to buy stocks, such as Apple, or mutual funds to enter into a prohibited transaction. That is why most retirement-account holders have never heard of these rules," John said.

STATUTORY EXEMPTIONS TO THE PROHIBITED-TRANSACTION RULES

Amy was doing a good job taking in all the information that John was giving her.

"There are a lot of situations to consider," Amy said.

"Yes," John said. "Like I said, the IRS doesn't tell you what you can do, only what you can't, and that understanding develops like any tax law."

"But I don't need to be an expert and know everything," Amy said. "I just need to start by thinking about my particular situation or the investments I want to make."

"Exactly," John said. "And then check with a tax attorney or CPA who understands the IRS–prohibited transaction rules to make sure."

"That way I'll have a pretty good idea whether the IRS would be interested in what I want to do."

"Exactly. And Congress has also created several ways to grant exemptions from the very broad prohibited-transaction rules. This allows some wiggle room when it comes to navigating prohibited-transaction rules for certain specific circumstances."

"Oh," Amy said. "Tell me more."

"The most popular way for satisfying a prohibited-transaction exemption is the statutory exemption because anyone who complies with the terms of the statute will be able to benefit from the exemption."

John continued to explain:

In IRC 4975(d), Congress created certain statutory exemptions from the prohibited transactions outlined in 4975(c). These exemptions were made because Congress believed there is a legitimate reason to permit them, as long as certain specified requirements are satisfied. In such situations, Congress has decided to issue blanket prohibited-transaction exemptions permitting certain types of transactions, as long as certain requirements prescribed in the statute are met.

The most common prohibited-transaction exemption involves participant loans from a 401(k) plan, which we discussed in detail the last time we met. Unfortunately, the 401(k) plan loan feature does do not apply to IRAs. IRC 4975(d)(1) describes conditions under which loans are allowable. The majority of the statutory exemptions found under IRC 4975(d) are not commonly applied because of their specific application, such as the ability to invest plan assets in bank-deposit accounts where the bank is the employer or to invest plan assets in life insurance–company products where the company is the employer. However, besides the 401(k) loan exemption, the other common prohibited-transaction exemption often used is IRC 4975(d)(13), which addressed the ability to use a 401(k) plan to buy corporation stock (qualifying employer securities), which is the basis for the ROBS transaction we discussed a few weeks ago.

"Unfortunately the exceptions to the prohibited-transaction rules are so narrow and limited in scope that most self-directed retirement account investors are not able to take advantage of any of them when making self-directed IRA investments."

"That's what I figured," Amy said.

"Yes," John agreed. "Navigating IRS–prohibited transaction rules is complex and requires a thorough examination of the facts and circumstances involved in the retirement account transaction before determining whether a prohibited transaction had occurred. In fact, in addition to the prohibited-transaction rules under IRC 4975, the plan-asset rules is a set of rules that can trigger the prohibited-transaction rules. The plan-asset rules are generally designed to apply 'look-through' rules to interests held by a retirement account in an investment fund, such as a hedge fund. I don't want to get into too many details on the plan-asset rules because it mostly relates to investment funds but just wanted you to be aware of the broad scope of the prohibited-transaction rules."

"OK, I understand and definitely want to stay away from doing any type of transaction with my retirement accounts that could trigger a prohibited transaction," Amy said.

"Unfortunately, there are a number of other categories of investments that are not permitted to be made with retirement accounts."

OTHER PROHIBITED ASSETS

"There are a number of other investments," John continued, "that are not permitted. These investments do not fall under the prohibited-transaction rules under IRC Section 4975 but are outlined under IRC 408. I talked about those in detail already. But just to review, a retirement account can't invest in collectibles such as

- any work of art;
- any metal or gem;
- any alcoholic beverage;
- any rug or antique;
- any stamp; and
- most coins."

"Right," Amy said, "I remember being surprised by that."

"Well," John explained, "the basic reason these types of assets are prohibited from being purchased with retirement funds is that they are generally hard to value and difficult to sell."

"Makes sense," Amy said.

"Remember, though, that .99 percent pure gold, silver, or platinum bullion as well as American Eagle and state-minted coins are approved investments for your retirement account and will not trigger a prohibited transaction."

"Yes, interesting," Amy said.

S AND C CORPORATION INVESTMENTS

"In addition to the IRS–prohibited transaction rules outlined in the IRC Section 4975," John continued, "a retirement account can't own stock in an S corporation."

"Why is that, again?" Amy asked.

"Because of the shareholder restrictions imposed on S corporations," John answered. "S corporations are C corporations that elect to pass corporate income, losses, deductions, and credits through to their shareholders for federal tax purposes. To qualify for S corporation status, the corporation must meet the following requirements:

- be a domestic corporation;
- have only allowable shareholders, including individuals, certain trusts, and estates;
- not include partnerships, corporations, or nonresident alien shareholders;
- have no more than one hundred shareholders; and
- have only one class of stock.

"Because an IRA or 401(k) plan is considered a trust for federal income-tax purposes," John continued, "which is not treated as a permitted shareholder for an S corporation; having a retirement account invest and become a shareholder would violate the S corporation rules and cause the S election to be invalid, making the entity a C corporation again for tax purposes."

"But a retirement-account plan can own stock in a C corporation, right?" Amy asked.

"That's right."

"OK," Amy said, "I understand I can't engage in four categories of transactions with my retirement account:

(1) collectibles, with a special carve-out for precious metals and IRS-approved coins;

(2) life-insurance contracts with my Roth IRA, but may with my 401(k) plan, so long as the plan documents allow it;

(3) S corporation stock; and

(4) any transaction that directly or indirectly personally benefits me or any other disqualified person—the IRC 4975 prohibited transactions."

"You got it," John said.

"I was just wondering something," Amy said. "Who determines whether I've engaged in a prohibited transaction?"

"That's actually a good question," John said. "Through an arrangement between the IRS and the Department of Labor (DOL), it's the DOL's responsibility to determine whether a specific transaction is a prohibited transaction and to issue prohibited-transaction exemptions. When the IRS discovers what appears to be a prohibited transaction in an individual's IRA, it turns the matter over to the DOL to make the determination. The DOL reviews the situation and responds to the IRS, which in turn responds to the taxpayer. If the IRA grantor wants to apply for a prohibited-transaction exemption, he or she must apply to the DOL."

"So does the DOL issue the exemptions?" Amy asked.

"It does have that authority," John said. "What's known as 'prohibitive transaction class exemptions,' or PTCEs, are available for anyone, while another class of exemptions, called individual prohibited-transaction exemptions, or PTEs, are issued only to the applicant."

PENALTIES FOR ENGAGING IN A PROHIBITED TRANSACTION

"This makes sense to me," Amy said, "but I was wondering, what are the IRS penalties if someone does engage in an IRS-prohibited transaction?"

"As you can imagine," John said, "the penalties are quite steep. The IRS needs to make them painful in order to protect the distribution-taxation rules, which are a big revenue source for the government."

"I get it," Amy said.

"In general," John continued, "the penalty under IRC Section 4975 generally starts out at fifteen percent for most types of retirement plans."

"Wow," Amy said, "that is harsh."

"Actually," John said, "it's even harsher for IRAs. In general, if the IRA holder (IRA owner) or IRA beneficiary engages in a transaction that violates the prohibited-transaction rules set forth under IRC Section 4975, the individual's IRA would lose its tax-exempt status and the entire fair market value of the IRA would be treated as a taxable distribution, subject to ordinary income tax. In addition, the IRA holder or beneficiary would be subject to a minimum penalty of fifteen percent as well as a ten percent early-distribution penalty if the IRA holder or beneficiary is under the age of 59½."

"Holy cow," Amy said.

"Yeah," John said. "Although the penalty for engaging in a prohibited transaction generally starts out at fifteen percent for most types of retirement plans, the penalty is more severe for IRAs. The initial tax on a prohibited transaction is fifteen percent of the amount involved for each year (or part of a year) in the taxable period. If the transaction is not corrected within the taxable period, an additional tax of one hundred percent of the amount involved is imposed. Both taxes are payable by any disqualified person who participated in the transaction (other than a fiduciary acting only as such). If more than one person takes part in the transaction, each person can be jointly and severally liable for the entire tax. According to Code Section 408(e), when an IRA is involved in a transaction that is prohibited under Code Section 4975, the IRA loses its tax-exempt status, and the IRA holder is treated as receiving a distribution on the first day of the tax year in which the prohibited transaction occurred. The distribution amount that the IRA holder is deemed to have received is equal to the fair market value of the IRA as of the first day of such tax year. In other words, the entire IRA is blown up and no longer treated as an IRA as of the first day of the taxable year in which the prohibited transaction occurred."

"I want to avoid that," Amy said.

"The good thing when it comes to prohibited-transaction penalties," John said, "is that they are easily avoidable."

"Basically," Amy said, "just don't engage in a prohibited transaction, and you have nothing to worry about."

"Exactly," John said. "For most retirement investors who will be investing in stocks and other traditional financial products, there is really not much to worry about when it comes to a prohibited transaction. The likelihood of engaging in a prohibited transaction in such circumstance is almost impossible, especially if you are buying stocks, mutual funds, and ETFS from a major financial institution. But, for a retirement-account investor looking to make nontraditional investments, such as real estate, private loans, and precious metals, you really need to make yourself aware of the prohibited-transaction rules because of the harsh penalties."

"I get it," Amy said. "Investor beware."

"The prohibited-transaction rules are extremely broad," John noted. "So a retirement-account investor looking to engage in certain nontraditional investments must be especially cautious and should consult a tax attorney or CPA with specific questions."

"I promise," Amy said.

"It's critical to understand what you can't do when it comes to the IRS," John said. "We need this information in advance before making important decisions about how we will invest or allocate our retirement-account assets. But I think it's time we start talking about how to get money out of your retirement account when you are ready to retire. I know it may be a bit premature considering your age, but I want you to understand how the rules work. Specifically, let's talk about the IRA and 401(k) plan distribution rules."

"That sounds great. Same time and place next week," Amy said.

"Perfect." John responded.

8

IRA AND 401(K) PLAN DISTRIBUTIONS AND ROLLOVERS

A MY ARRIVED A few minutes early and waited in line to buy the cappuccinos and muffins. John arrived a few minutes later and they both took a seat at their regular table.

"I know we've spent a lot of time discussing the ins and outs of the IRA, Roth IRA, and Roth 401(k) plan," John said, "including the many tax and retirement-planning advantages."

"It's been very helpful," Amy said.

"Let's now look at how you can take funds out of a Roth IRA or Roth Solo 401(k) plan by way of distribution as well as how you would go about rolling funds out of the structure to a new retirement-account custodian. I think it is important to understand your options so you can plan accordingly. I will start with the Roth IRA and then move on to the Roth Solo 401(k) plan."

DISTRIBUTIONS FROM A TRADITIONAL IRA AND ROTH IRA

"An IRA owner may take distributions from his or her IRA at any time," John said. "The determination of whether the distribution is taxed depends on the type of IRA (i.e., traditional or Roth), the age of the IRA owner, and in the case of a Roth IRA, the duration of time the account has been established.

I know you have a Roth IRA, but I want to briefly discuss the distribution rules for the traditional IRA, which I believe highlights the main advantage of the Roth IRA—no required minimum distribution and no tax on a qualified Roth distribution."

"OK, that makes sense," Amy said.

"The IRA owner is required to include traditional IRA (pretax) distributions in his or her taxable gross income. The IRA owner who receives a distribution will report the distribution on his or her individual federal income-tax return (IRS Form 1040) and pay tax on the distribution based on the individual's federal income-tax rate."

"What kind of IRA-related transactions are *not* treated as distributions subject to tax?" Amy asked.

"Those would be

- rollovers;
- transfers;
- recharacterizations;
- revoked IRA within seven-day period; and
- the portion of a distribution relating to nondeductible traditional IRA contributions."

EXEMPTION FROM THE EARLY-DISTRIBUTION 10 PERCENT TAX

"In general," John said, "traditional IRAs are designed to encourage retirement saving and at the same time discourage people from taking money away from their retirement savings before reaching the age of 59½. The age 59½ was selected by Congress because it was believed to be the age when one began transitioning from active employment to retirement. Remember that early distributions are subject to an additional tax. The IRS assesses a ten percent penalty on the taxable portion of early distributions. However, the ten percent early-distribution penalty does not apply in the following situations."

Death of the IRA Owner

An IRA distribution to beneficiaries is not subject to the 10 percent early-distribution penalty. In other words, upon the death of the IRA owner, the distribution of the owner's IRA to his or her beneficiaries is not subject to the 10 percent penalty.

Disability

Distributions received by a disabled IRA owner are not subject to the 10 percent early-distribution penalty. Prior to making the disability distribution, the financial organization may require written evidence from the disabled IRA owner to verify disability. The IRA owner can demonstrate this by using IRS Form 1040, Schedule R, Credit for the Elderly or Disabled.

Rollovers and Conversions

Amounts rolled over to an IRA or properly converted to an IRA are not subject to the 10 percent early-distribution penalty.

First-Time Homebuyer Expenses

Distributions taken for qualified first-time homebuyer expenses are not subject to the 10 percent early-distribution penalty. There is a $10,000 lifetime limit with this exemption.

Return of Nondeductible Contributions

The 10 percent early-distribution penalty would not apply to the portion of a distribution that represents a return of nondeductible contributions or after-tax assets received through a rollover.

Substantially Equal Periodic Payment

The 10 percent early-distribution penalty shall not apply to distributions that are part of a series of substantially equal periodic payments made at least annually over the IRA owner's life expectancy or joint life expectancy of the IRA owner and his or her beneficiary. The rules that apply to this option can be found in IRC 72(t) and are quite complex.

Health Insurance

An IRA owner who received federal or state unemployment compensation for twelve consecutive weeks may take IRA distributions to pay for health insurance. These distributions are not subject to the 10 percent early-distribution penalty. The IRA owner must take a distribution in the year he received his unemployment or in the year that follows. This exemption does not apply to distributions taken more than sixty days after the IRA owner regains employment.

Medical Expenses

Distributions used for reimbursed medical expenses that exceed 7.5 percent of the IRA owner's adjusted gross income are not subject to the 10 percent early-distribution penalty.

Higher-Education Expenses

IRA distributions used for qualified education expenses of the IRA owner, his or her spouse, spouse's child, or grandchild are not subject to the 10 percent early-distribution penalty.

IRS Levy

Distributions taken because of IRS tax levies imposed on the IRA owner are not subject to the 10 percent early-distribution penalty.

Qualified Reservist Distributions

Qualified reservists (including National Guard personnel) called to active duty after September 11, 2001, for a period of at least 180 days or for an indefinite amount of time are permitted to take penalty-free distributions from their IRA. This applies to distributions taken between the date of the order or call to duty and the end of the active-duty period. **Note:** The distribution taken will still be subject to federal income tax.

TAKING A DISTRIBUTION FROM A ROTH IRA

"The difference between a traditional IRA and a Roth IRA is most evident in the treatment of distributions," John said.

"How so?" Amy asked.

"As a brief reminder, in the case of a traditional IRA, an IRA distribution is taxed as ordinary income unless it is rolled over into another retirement plan. If the individual were under the age of 59½ when the distribution is made, a ten percent excise tax would apply to the distribution in addition to the ordinary income tax due on the value of the distribution. If the individual is over the age of 70½ at the time the distribution is taken, then no excise tax applies; however, the individual is required to pay ordinary income tax on the amount of the traditional IRA distribution. Remember also that an individual over the age of 70½ is required to take minimum annual distributions based on a percentage of the individual's total IRA value at the end of the year. Each year the IRS releases a table that determines the amount of the required minimum distribution. In general, distributions from a Roth IRA that are *not* qualified may be subject to income tax and an additional ten percent early-distribution penalty. A qualified distribution is a distribution from a Roth IRA that meets both of the following two categories of requirements:

1. It occurs at least five years after the Roth IRA was established and the owner funded his or her first Roth IRA.
2. It is distributed under one of the following circumstances:
   - The Roth IRA holder is at least age 59½ when the distribution occurs.
   - The Roth IRA holder becomes disabled before the distribution.
   - The beneficiary of the Roth IRA holder receives the assets after his or her death.

"It's also important to remember that the IRS uses special rules when determining the source of the Roth IRA assets being distributed and the potential tax implications, including funds converted to a Roth IRA," John continued. "Based on the IRS ordering rules, Roth IRA assets are distributed in the following order, keeping in mind that once assets from one source run out, the assets from the next source are distributed:

1. Regular Roth IRA participant contributions
2. Taxable conversion and rollover amounts

3. Nontaxable conversion and rollover amounts
4. Earnings on all Roth IRA assets"

John went on. "In determining what portion of the distribution is considered to come from contributions as opposed to earnings, you must follow the ordering rules outlined above. For example, let's say Jim made a five-thousand-dollar contribution to his Roth IRA in 2010. In 2011, at age forty-five, Jim's Roth IRA was worth six thousand dollars, and he needed the entire amount to pay a personal expense. Based on the Roth IRA ordering rules, Jim would be able to take his five-thousand-dollar Roth contribution back without tax or penalty but would be required to pay tax and a ten percent early-distribution penalty on the one thousand dollars of income. This is in contrast to a Roth 401(k) plan that follows a pro rata basis formula for determining the taxation of Roth 401(k) distributions, which is less taxpayer friendly than the Roth IRA distribution ordering rules discussed above. Also, it is important to remember that the Roth IRA distribution ordering rules apply to all your IRAs in the aggregate."

TAKING EARLY DISTRIBUTIONS FROM FUNDS CONVERTED TO A ROTH IRA

"The penalty rules regarding taking early distributions from Roth IRA conversion funds add a twist. The early-withdrawal penalty applies to a distribution of conversion money from Roth IRA assets if the plan participant is under the age of 59½ in a few situations

1. The distribution is made within the five-tax-year period starting with the year that the conversion was distributed from a pretax IRA and
2. Only to the extent that the distribution is attributable to amounts that were includable in gross income as a result of the conversion."

"In general, when thinking about taking early distribution from funds converted to a Roth IRA, you must realize that there could be a tax implication because of the ordering rules for determining the taxation of a nonqualified Roth distribution."

"Do you have an example?" Amy asked.

"For example, in 2010, Bill converted all sixty thousand dollars in his traditional IRA to his Roth IRA. Jim's Forms 8606 from previous years show that ten thousand dollars of the amount converted is his basis. Bill included fifty thousand dollars ($60,000 – $10,000) in his gross income. In 2014, Bill made a regular contribution of five thousand dollars to a Roth IRA. In early 2015, at age sixty-one, Bill took an eight-thousand-dollar distribution from his Roth IRA. The first five thousand dollars of the distribution is a return of Bill's regular contribution and cannot be included in his income. The next three thousand dollars of the distribution cannot be included in income because it was included previously."

"What about if I do a Roth conversion?" Amy asked. "How do the early-distribution penalties work?"

"The penalty rules regarding conversions are a bit different from those for annual contributions, which may be taken at any time for any purpose free of income taxes and penalty. An early withdrawal of a conversion contribution has a different twist. The early-withdrawal penalty applies to a distribution of conversion money from a Roth IRA from an individual under the age of 59½ in a few situations.

1. The distribution is made within the five-tax-year period starting with the year that the conversion was distributed from a traditional IRA and
2. Only to the extent that the distribution is attributable to amounts that were includable in gross income as a result of the conversion."

"In general," John said, "when doing a Roth conversion, you can take a distribution of the funds that were converted at any time without tax.

However, an early-distribution penalty of ten percent would apply if the five-year holding period from date of conversion was not satisfied and you are under the age of 59½."

"How about an example?" Amy said.

"Let's say Joe made a twenty-thousand-dollar conversion from his regular IRA to a Roth IRA in 2008. The entire amount converted was includable in Joe's income for 2008. Joe made no additional contributions or conversions to a Roth IRA in 2008 or in later years. In 2011, before he is age 59½, Joe withdraws ten thousand dollars from the Roth IRA. Joe will have no tax to pay on this withdrawal because he paid income taxes on the full twenty thousand dollars he converted in 2008; however, he will have to pay a ten percent penalty (or one thousand dollars) unless one of the IRA early-withdrawal exceptions apply. Why? Because Joe was under the age of 59½ when he took the distribution. If Joe, had been over the age of 59½ when he took the distribution, there would have been no tax or ten percent penalty since the amount distributed was part of the taxable Roth IRA conversion. Also keep in mind, the income or gains generated from the Roth IRA conversion amount would be subject to the regular Roth IRA distribution rules."

"So, if you are going to take funds early from your Roth IRA, weigh your conversion decision very carefully," Amy said.

"That's the lesson," John agreed.

"The Roth IRA sounds really good," Amy said. "Can I move from a traditional IRA to a Roth IRA if I am a high-income earner?"

"Yes. Since 2010, there are no longer any income-level thresholds preventing an IRA holder wishing to convert pretax IRA funds to a Roth IRA. In fact, the IRS is more than happy if you do and actually encouraged IRA holders to do it in 2010 when they allowed individuals who elected to do a Roth conversion in that year to spread the tax due over two years. It really just comes down to money like almost everything in life; the 2008 financial crisis really hurt the IRS tax-revenue collection numbers, and ever since 2008 they have been trying to find ways to generate additional tax revenues, and encouraging a Roth conversion to produce immediate tax is one way."

Roth IRA Conversion - What Should I Do?

First thing's first – can you afford to pay the taxes on the conversion?	• Ordinary income • Added to income on IRS Form 1040 • Payable with personal funds ° Paying with converted funds does generally not make tax sense
Your age	• The younger you are more tax free growth is available
Type of investments to be made with Roth IRA funds	• Memories of Enron, Lehman Brothers, etc. • Tax-free income to supplement other sources of income (i.e. real estate rental income)
Higher tax rates in the future increase benefit of having a Roth IRA	• Where will tax rates go? • Power of tax-free compounding
Estate Planning opportunities	• Pay tax now and avoid estate and gift taxes on that amount • Paying the taxes now reduces the size of your estate and any estate tax bill • Conversion can provide lifetime income tax benefits to you that also can benefit your beneficiary • Spouse can live off Roth IRA funds tax-free or can have the Roth IRA grow for children tax-free

TAKING AN IN-KIND DISTRIBUTION FROM AN IRA

"Can I distribute the assets my IRA owns, such as stocks and real estate, or do I need to sell the asset?" Amy asked.

"Great question," John said. "When you take a distribution, you can distribute cash or any IRA asset, which is known as an in-kind distribution. The same would apply to rollovers to another IRA custodian. You can roll over cash or IRA assets, as long as the new IRA custodian will accept that asset category to be held in an IRA. For example, say you had your self-directed IRA account with ABC custodian and owned real estate in the self-directed IRA account. If you wanted to change custodians and move the real estate to a new IRA custodian, you would need to find an IRA custodian that will accept the real estate as an IRA asset. As we discussed, most of the traditional banks will not allow your IRA to own real estate because of the a lack of financial incentive for them, so if you want to roll over a self-directed IRA account that holds alternative assets, such as real estate, you will need to find an IRA custodian that allows an IRA to invest in real estate or the alternative asset in question."

"How would I take an in-kind distribution of real estate?" Amy asked.

"It would pretty much follow the same process as taking a cash distribution," John said, "except there are some minor differences. The first thing you would need to do is value the real-estate asset you will be taking as a distribution. This is especially important if you have a pretax IRA as there would be a tax imposed on the value of the real estate being taken as a distribution, as well as potentially a ten percent early-distribution tax. In the case of a Roth IRA, the in-kind distribution would be exempt from tax so long as the distribution is qualified (over the age of 59½ and Roth IRA has been opened at least five years). Once you get a value for the real estate, you will then need to complete a distribution-request form with the IRA custodian and indicate that you will be taking an in-kind distribution of the real estate. When the distribution process has been completed and submitted to the IRA custodian, you would need to retitle the real estate from the name of the LLC to you own personal name. This can be done via a title company or a real-estate attorney locally. The key is to show that the ownership of the real estate has been changed from the IRA to the IRA holder personally."

"Just to be clear," Amy said, "I'll be responsible for paying tax on the fair market value of the real estate or other asset I take as a distribution if I have a pretax IRA?"

"Yes," John said, "that's one hundred percent correct. The tax due on an in-kind distribution is the fair market value of the asset on the date the distribution was taken and not the price you paid for the asset. For example, if the IRA purchased a home for one hundred thousand dollars and ten years later the house has appreciated to three thousand dollars and if the IRA holder wants to take the house as a distribution, but she wants to live in it, she would be deemed to have taken a three-hundred-thousand-dollar distribution because that is what the house was valued at on the date of the distribution. The same would go for stock, precious metals, or any other alternative asset. Taking cash as a distribution is simple because the distribution equals the amount of cash that was taken as a distribution. This is why obtaining an independent valuation of the in-kind asset that will be taken as a distribution is so important—because the amount of tax due will be directly based on the fair market value of the asset. It's not a surprise that the IRS will pay special attention to the value of any asset being taken as an in-kind distribution."

"OK, that is helpful. I don't currently own any real estate in my Roth IRA but have some really good stocks and mutual funds and for whatever reason I needed to take a distribution, it is nice to know I would not be forced to sell the asset," Amy said.

"That is correct, but having a Roth IRA is like gold so you should be committed to keeping it open as long as you can, most certainly past you are 59½ so you can take advantage of a tax-free distribution of all contributions and earnings. Taking an early distribution kills the benefit of the Roth IRA and should really only be done under dire circumstances," John said.

"I have one last piece of advice on the Roth IRA distribution I want to leave you with. Since the key to the Roth IRA distribution rules is making sure the distribution is qualified, which generally required the Roth IRA holder being over the age of 59½ and the Roth IRA to have been open at least five years at the time of the distribution, I generally encourage anyone interested in a Roth IRA to open a Roth IRA, which can be done for free at most banks and just contribute one dollar. This will start the five-year clock ticking and can help someone satisfy the qualified-distribution rules much quicker, especially if the individual is nearing the age of 59½. In your case, Amy, you took the best approach which was starting a Roth IRA early and continuously contributing to it helping you start building a nice tax-free retirement nest egg," John said.

"Thanks, John. That means a lot coming from you. I am just blessed that I was lucky enough to have talked with you some fifteen years ago, and you mentioned the Roth IRA. It just made a lot of sense to me—kind of a no-brainer," Amy said.

"Agreed. Now let's turn to how one can take distributions from a Solo 401(k) plan."

TAKING DISTRIBUTIONS FROM A ROTH SOLO 401(K) PLAN

"There are only a few established ways to take money out of a Solo 401(k) plan," John said. "The most common method is via a distribution." He went on to describe it.

'Distribution' is essentially a term for taking funds from a retirement account and turning tax-exempt funds into personal funds that are no longer exempt from tax. There are many different reasons for talking a distribution from your 401(k) plan before being required to do at age 70½ via the required minimum distribution rules, but most revolve around the ability to use the funds for personal purposes, such as for paying expenses. (Also, remember that you can use the loan feature as another way to take money out of your plan. Unlike a distribution, there is no tax or penalty on your loan.)

While not ideal, taking a distribution from your 401(k) plan can be a big help if you need a bunch of cash right away. There are a two main negatives for taking a distribution: you will forfeit the benefits of tax-deferred compounding (tax-free growth in the case of a Roth 401(k)) by cashing out the tax-deferred or tax-free amount, and, in the case of a pretax 401(k) account, you'll have to pay income taxes on your distribution for the tax year in which you take it out. In some cases, you'll also incur a 10 percent penalty, which can significantly cut into the amount you would be able to use.

For the most part, most plan documents do not allow one to take a distribution from his or her Solo 401(k) plan until a certain event occurs, often called a 'triggering event.' The actions that trigger a distribution under a Solo 401(k) plan will change depending on the type of plan documents you have adopted. Typically, distributions of elective deferrals cannot be made until one of the following occurs:

- You reach age 59½.
- The plan terminates, and you do not establish or maintain a successor-defined contribution plan.
- You have a severance of employment.
- You become disabled.
- You die.
- You incur a financial hardship.

Depending on the terms of the plan, distributions may be

- nonperiodic, such as lump-sum distributions or
- periodic, such as annuity or installment payments.

Plan Termination

Plan retirement age ranges between 59½ and 65. Your Solo 401(k) plan documents (specifically, your plan-adoption agreement and plan-summary description document) will define the 'normal retirement age' for your plan.

If your Solo 401(k) plan terminates, your plan documents will likely allow you to request distributions from your plan: in other words, the ability to roll over the retirement funds to an IRA or another 401(k) plan. In addition, most Solo 401(k) plans allow a plan participant who has left his or her job with the employer who adopted the plan the ability to receive distributions of the plan's vested account balance. Since in the case of a Solo 401(k) plan, the plan participant and plan owner are generally the same person, this means that if you close or sell your business or stop working, a triggering event occurs that allows you to access the plan funds through distribution.

Disability

You may also begin receiving distributions from your Solo 401(k) plan if you become disabled. It would be up to the plan participant to prove that he or she is disabled by providing supporting medical documentation to the plan administrator.

Death

Of course, all 401(k) plans allow the beneficiaries of a plan participant to begin receiving distributions upon that participant's death. It is common to name your spouse as your primary Solo 401(k) plan beneficiary unless he or she consents to the naming of another beneficiary.

Hardship Distributions

Your Solo 401(k) plan may also provide for hardship distributions if you have an immediate and heavy financial need. This need is determined based on all relevant facts and circumstances. Indeed, your financial need may be considered immediate and heavy by the IRS even if it was reasonably foreseeable or due to your own choices and decisions. Specifically, the IRS regulations consider the following to be financial hardships:

- Expenses for your medical care or the medical care of your spouse or dependents
- Costs directly related to the purchase of your principal residence (but not your mortgage payments)
- Tuition, related educational fees, and room-and-board expenses for the next twelve months of postsecondary education for you, your spouse, your children, or your dependents
- Payments necessary to prevent your eviction from your principal residence or foreclosure on your mortgage on that residence
- Funeral expenses
- Certain expenses relating to the repair of damage to your principal residence

Hardship distributions from a 401(k) plan are generally relegated to the amount of your elective deferrals and generally do not include any income earned on the deferred amounts. However, a plan can permit employer-matching contributions and employer-discretionary contributions to be included in hardship distributions. Hardship distributions cannot be rolled over to another plan or IRA. According to the IRS, a distribution is treated as a hardship distribution only if it is made on account of the hardship to satisfy the immediate and heavy financial need of the employee.

Hardship distributions are a permanent reduction of an account balance and cannot be repaid. They can have a significant impact on a plan participant's retirement-account balance.

Immediate and Heavy Financial Need
You are not permitted to obtain a distribution, however, that exceeds the amount needed to relieve your immediate and heavy financial need. In addition, you are not allowed a distribution if your financial hardship need can be filled by other resources that are reasonably available to you, including:

- Your spouse's assets and any available assets of your children if they are minors
- Resources that could be obtained through reimbursement or compensation by insurance
- By liquidating your assets
- By ceasing to make elective contributions to your plan
- By other distributions or nontaxable loans from your plan
- By borrowing from commercial sources on reasonable terms in an amount sufficient to satisfy the need

After you have elected to take a hardship distribution from your Solo 401(k) plan, you are prohibited from making contributions to your plan and other retirement plans for at least six months after receiving your hardship distribution.

Hardship distributions are includable in gross income unless they consist of designated Roth contributions. They may also be subject to an additional tax on early distributions of elective contributions. Unlike loans, hardship distributions are not repaid to the plan. Thus, a hardship distribution permanently reduces your Solo 401(k) account balance.

To determine whether a hardship distribution is appropriate, the IRS looks at all relevant facts and circumstances. The place to start, of course, is your personal resources. However, your retirement assets are relevant in making an overall determination. Your resources are deemed to include the assets of your spouse and minor children when they are reasonably available to you. Thus, for example, a second home—whether owned by you or your spouse as community property, joint tenants, tenants by the entirety, or tenants in common—generally will be deemed a resource. Interestingly, the amount of an immediate and heavy financial need may include any amounts necessary to pay any federal, state, or local income taxes or penalties reasonably anticipated to result from the distribution.

An immediate and heavy financial need is a hardship that is generally not able to be relieved from other resources reasonably available to the plan participant:

- Through reimbursement or compensation by insurance or otherwise
- By liquidation of the employee's assets
- By cessation of elective contributions or employee contributions under the plan
- By other distributions or nontaxable (at the time of the loan) loans from plans maintained by the employer or by any other employer, or by borrowing from commercial sources on reasonable commercial terms in an amount sufficient to satisfy the need

According to the IRS, a distribution is deemed necessary to satisfy an immediate and heavy financial need if all of the following requirements are satisfied:

- The distribution is not in excess of the amount of your immediate and heavy financial need.
- You have obtained all distributions, other than hardship distributions, and all nontaxable (at the time of the loan) loans currently available under all your plans.
- You are prohibited, under the terms of the plan or an otherwise legally enforceable agreement from making elective contributions and employee contributions to your plan and all other plans for at least six months after receipt of the hardship distribution.

"I know one of my friends was able to take a distribution from her plan while she was still employed, and she is under 59½, and I don't believe she had any hardship—what's the deal?" Amy asked.

"In general, even if no triggering event has occurred, there may be other ways you can take money out of your Solo 401(k) plan as a distribution. These are often referred to as in-service distributions. Generally, there has to be a triggering event in order for you to get access to your retirement funds prior to the age of 59½. There is one major exception to this rule, and that is the in-service distribution option. An in-service distribution is when a participant, who is still employed by the plan sponsor, is allowed to take a distribution from the plan.

"In-service withdrawals from 401(k) plans carry very specific restrictions. Only employer contributions are eligible for in-service distributions and not employee deferrals. What that means is that any employee-deferral contributions made by the plan participant to the plan are *not* eligible for in-service distributions and are subject to the triggering rules described above. Only employer profit-sharing contributions can be used for an in-service distribution. The in-service distribution gets you access to your funds prior to turning 59½ but will still require you to pay tax and penalty on the amount of the distribution.

"In order to be eligible to take an in-service distribution of profit-sharing funds, your plan documents must allow for them. Even if the plan documents allow for in-service distributions, they will generally put restrictions on when the in-service distribution can be made. This could be the plan's normal retirement age, an early retirement age, or any age. It could also be after a fixed period of time. However, in many cases, the contribution must be at least two years old or the account must be at least five years old. It all comes down to the plan documents and what they say. The plan document is basically the bible for your 401(k) plan, and it will determine all the rules with respect to the operation of the plan. Remember, if you are over 59½ or can satisfy one of the triggering events, you will not need to worry about the in-plan service distribution rules, as you will have the ability to take a distribution of vested funds from the plan," John said.

"OK, that is interesting. I understand that I would need to check the plan documents associated with the plan adopted to get the answer, but in general, if under the age of 59½ and I don't want to terminate the plan or leave the business, I cannot not get any of the employee-deferral contributions (pretax or Roth) and would only have access to the employer (profit-sharing) contributions?" Amy asked.

"Yes, that is pretty much it. You would have the benefit of the loan feature to get up to fifty thousand dollars or could generally access any funds rolled into the plan," John said.

"Wait. Are you saying that if I rolled pretax IRA or former employer pretax 401(k) funds into my Solo 401(k) plan, I can take those funds as a distribution anytime without a triggering event?" Amy asked.

"Great question. Again, it all comes down to the plan documents. However, in general, funds rolled into a 401(k) plan can be rolled out of the plan without a triggering event or without the need to satisfy the in-service distribution rules. In other words, since the funds were rolled over to the 401(k) plan and are not employee-deferral contributions, they can be rolled out of the plan into an IRA or taken as a distribution at any time without having to satisfy in-plan service or plan triggering-event rules," John said.

"So how would I actually take a distribution from a Solo 401(k) plan I adopted?" Amy asked.

"Depending on the terms of your plan, the distributions you take may be 'nonperiodic' lump-sum distributions or 'periodic' distributions such as annuity or installment payments. Specifically, if a distribution in excess of one thousand dollars is made and you (or your designated beneficiary) have waived the 'Qualified Joint and Survivor Annuity' option, you may receive the funds as:

- a lump-sum payment;
- a partial payment;
- installments payments not to exceed your life expectancy or the joint and last survivor life expectancy of you and your designated beneficiary; or
- by applying the distribution to a purchase of an annuity contract. Note that most Solo 401(k) plans do not require that plan distributions take the form of a life annuity or joint and survivor annuity as required under the Retirement Equity Act (REA) of 1984."

"I assume I would have to report a distribution from my Solo 401(k) plan to the IRS?" Amy asked.

"Yes. In addition to reporting the amount of the distribution on your personal federal income-tax return (IRS Form 1040), the Solo 401(k) plan administrator will be required to complete and file with the IRS Form 1099-R. A copy form 1099-R will also be sent to the plan participant who took the distribution, which in the case of a Solo 401(k) plan is likely the same person as the plan administrator. The purpose of the 1099-R is to disclose to the

IRS the amount of the distribution taken from the Solo 401(k) plan so that the IRS can verify that the amount is properly reported on the individual's personal-tax return," John said.

"Do the same RMD rules that apply to traditional IRAs apply to funds in a Solo 401(k) plan?" Amy asked.

"Yes, pretty much. Unfortunately, you can't keep your retirement funds in your account indefinitely. The RMD rules are in place to stop you from accumulating wealth in your Solo 401(k) without tax. Interestingly, unlike a Roth IRA, which does not require a Roth IRA holder to take RMDs, a Roth Solo 401(k) account is subject to RMDs even though no tax may be due because the RMD distribution will likely be a qualified distribution," John said.

"That is interesting. Is there a reason why the Roth IRA is not subject to the RMD rules and a Roth 401(k) plan is?" Amy asked.

"I have not been able to find a good reason, but I think just like the estate tax, the RMD rules are seen as a way of preventing wealth inequality, which could impact the overall economy. From the IRS's position, it would cause a major burden on the operation of the government if individuals were able to receive a tax deduction when making an IRA or 401(k) plan contribution, providing him or her with an immediate tax benefit as well as gaining the ability to generate tax-deferred growth for an unlimited period time. Therefore, it is only fair that the period of tax-deferred growth be capped at some point and require you to pay tax on a percentage of the income that has grown tax deferred each year. Without the RMD rules, too much wealth would be concentrated in tax-exempt accounts, making it very difficult for the government to operate and offer the necessary services that our society needs and expects. Don't worry; there is a way to get around the Roth Solo 401(k) plan RMD rules, which I will discuss shortly," John said.

"I know this is a bit premature since I am only in my thirties, but when would I have to start taking RMD?" Amy asked.

"Generally, you have to start taking withdrawals from your retirement-plan account when you reach age 70½. For a Solo 401(k) plan, the RMD amount for a plan participant is equal to the plan-account balance as of the last valuation date in the calendar year immediately preceding a year for which an RMD is due. However, if you are a participant in a 401(k) qualified retirement plan and are not a five percent or greater owner of the company sponsoring the plan, then you might be able to delay taking your distribution until you retire (even if you retire after age 70½). Unfortunately, in the case of a Solo 401(k) plan, the plan participant is generally more than a five percent owner of the company adopting the plan, so this exception to the RMD rules is generally not applicable," John said.

"If I have traditional IRA funds, can I use those funds to satisfy the RMD amount for my Solo 401(k) plan?" Amy asked.

"Yes. You could use IRA funds to satisfy an RMD from your Solo 401(k) plan, but if you had two 401(k) plans, you would have to satisfy the RMD amount for each plan separately. Let me explain further. The required distribution rules apply only to your Solo 401(k) plan. In other words, you cannot satisfy your required minimum distribution by making a distribution from another plan. These rules are different than the rules that apply to satisfying RMD payments for an IRA. In the case of an IRA, the total RMD amount is calculated and can be satisfied from any IRA account.

For example, if you have three IRAs, each with a value of $30,000, and the annual RMD amount is $4,000, you can satisfy the RMD payment from any of the three IRA accounts and in any percentage. Your plan document ensures that these rules override any inconsistent distribution options available to you previously. As the plan administrator, you must determine the minimum amount required to be distributed each calendar year. You can obtain information to help you calculate the minimum distribution amount in IRS Publication 575, *Pension and Annuity Income*.

The 'beginning date' for your required minimum distribution is April 1 of the first year after whichever of the following events is latest:

- The calendar year in which you reach age 70½
- The calendar year in which you retire
- If you reach age 70½ on the date that is six calendar months after your seventieth birthday

"I touched on the RMD when we first met, and they are quite complex. The good part is that your 401(k) plan administrator or bank where the 401(k) plan is held should be able to help you navigate through the rules. In addition, there is ton of information on the IRS website. For this reason coupled with the fact that you have a Roth IRA, I am going to move on to how to avoid the RMD rules with your Roth Solo 401(k) plan," John said.

"Thank you. The RMD rules are pretty complicated, and I don't have to worry about them for another fifty or so years, so I think I am OK," Amy said.

"Good. Let's now turn to how to avoid RMDs with a Roth Solo 401(k) plan. Like a pretax Solo 401(k) plan, a plan participant over the age of 70½ must take RMDs from their Roth 401(k) account. This is quite different from the Roth IRA, which does not require RMDs."

"So how could you circumvent the RMDs rules in the case of a Roth Solo 401(k) plan?"

"First, a 401(k) plan participant with Roth funds that is nearing the age of 70 should start thinking about rolling the Roth 401(k) plan funds into a Roth IRA. In general, you are able to roll retirement funds out of a 401(k) plan after reaching the age of 59½. The key is making sure that Roth 401(k) plan rollover to a Roth IRA is done prior to the plan participant reaching the age of 70. For example, if you have a Roth 401(k) Plan and are going to reach the age of 70 in 2016, you want to make sure that you have rolled the Roth 401(k) plan funds into a Roth IRA prior to December 31, 2015. The reason for this is that the RMD amount is based off the value of the retirement account as of 12/31 of the prior year. So if you left the Roth 401(k) plan funds in the 401(k) plan and rolled the funds into a Roth IRA in 2015, because there was a balance in the Roth 401(k) plan as of 12/31/2014, an RMD would be due from the Roth 401(k) plan in 2015. Going forward, after the Roth 401(k) plan participant reaches the age of 70½, he or she can simply roll the Roth 401(k) funds into a Roth IRA and make sure that the Roth 401(k) plan balance is zero as of 12/31."

"OK," Amy said.

"The fact that a Roth IRA holder is not required to take RMDs when reaching the age of 70½ offers Roth 401(k) plan participants a convenient way to circumvent the Roth 401(k) plan RMD rules and allow their Roth funds to keep growing tax free," John continued. "The key is making sure that the initial rollover to a Roth IRA is done prior to 12/31 of the year before the Roth 401(k) plan participant reaches the age of 70½ as well as making sure that in all subsequent years, the balance of the Roth 401(k) plan is zero as of December 31.

"It is important to keep in mind that a Roth IRA has a separate five-year clock from the 401(k) plan for purposes of satisfying the Roth qualified distribution rules. Therefore, if one has not established a Roth IRA prior to the rollover, that individual would be required to keep the rollover funds in the Roth IRA for five additional years before the Roth IRA funds can be distributed tax free," John said.

"OK, thankfully I don't have to worry about the RMD rules for quite some time. Other than taking a taxable distribution, is there any other way to pull retirement funds out of an IRA or Solo 401(k) plan without tax?" Amy asked.

"Unfortunately, if you had a pretax IRA you would not be able to use those funds for any personal purpose without paying a tax, or ten percent early-distribution penalty if you were under the age of 59½. Having a Roth IRA, would allow you to pull money out without tax assuming the Roth IRA distribution is 'qualified' (you are over the age of 59½ and the Roth IRA account has been opened at least five years) or you are taking out only what you had contributed to the Roth IRA. However, as we previously discussed, a Solo 401(k) plan does have a loan feature that will allow the plan participant to borrow up to fifty thousand dollars and use the funds for any purpose without triggering a tax or penalty. This exception to the distribution rules applies only to 401(k) plans and not IRAs. Even better, there is no need for any triggering event or age requirement. As long as the plan documents include the loan option and it has been adopted as part of the plan, you can use the loan feature to pull money out of your Solo 401(k) plan without a triggering event and without any tax or penalty. Generally, if permitted by the plan, you may borrow up to fifty percent of your vested account balance up to a maximum of fifty thousand dollars. The loan must be repaid within five years, unless the loan is used to buy your main home. The loan repayments must be made in substantially level payments, at least quarterly, over the life of the loan," John said.

"I love the Solo 401(k) plan loan feature. For me that's a prominent reason why I would consider adopting one over a SEP IRA. The Solo 401(k) loan feature seems like a great vehicle for getting access to retirement funds without paying tax or penalty. This seems especially true if you are under the age of 59½ and don't qualify for any of the hardship-distribution exceptions. In addition to getting access to your Solo 401(k) plan funds, using the loan feature will also allow me to grow my retirement account since the interest I pay back on the loan will go back to the plan," Amy said.

"Yes, exactly. The Solo 401(k) plan loan feature is really the only legal way one can get access to their retirement funds and use the funds for any purpose without tax or penalty," John said.

"In contrast, I assume I would have to pay tax and penalty if I took an early distribution from my Solo 401(k) plan?" Amy asked.

"Yes. The first thing to remember is that you need a plan-triggering event before taking an early distribution from a 401(k) plan, so early distributions are not very common in a 401(k) plan. In general, the only way a plan participant can get access to their 401(k) funds before the age of 59½ is to terminate employment or the company terminates the plan creating a triggering event. Taking an early distribution from a 401(k) plan does not make a lot of sense because of the twenty percent withholding tax. You would be better off rolling the funds to an IRA, if possible, and then taking a distribution from an IRA, which does not impose a withholding tax."

"OK," Amy said.

"There is a twenty percent mandatory federal income withholding tax that is applied to taxable distributions. If you elect to receive a check directly from your employer, you will only receive eighty percent of your distribution. In essence, if you expect to receive a check for $200,000, your employer will withhold twenty percent, or $40,000, and send you a check for $160,000. In addition, if a distribution is made before you reach age 59½, you may be liable for a ten percent additional tax on the distribution. This tax applies to the amount received that an employee must include in income."

"Are there any exceptions?"

"Yes. The ten percent tax will *not* apply if distributions before age 59½ are made in any of the following circumstances:

- Made to a beneficiary (or to your estate) on or after your death
- Made because you have a qualifying disability

— 231 —

- Made as part of a series of substantially equal periodic payments beginning after separation from service (termination of employment) and made at least annually for your life or life expectancy or the joint lives or life expectancies of you and your designated beneficiary (the payments under this exception, unless death or disability come into play, must continue for at least five years or until you reach age 59½, whichever is the longer period)
- Made to you after separation from service if the separation occurred during or after the calendar year in which you reached age fifty-five
- Made to an alternate payee under a 'qualified domestic relations order' (QDRO)
- Made to you for medical care up to the amount allowable as a medical expense deduction (determined without regard to whether you itemize deductions)
- Timely made to reduce excess contributions
- Timely made to reduce excess employee or matching employer contributions
- Timely made to reduce excess elective deferrals
- Made because of an IRS levy on your Solo 401(k) plan
- Made on account of certain disasters for which IRS relief has been granted

"Interestingly, unlike an IRA, there is no exception to the ten percent early-distribution penalty for a 401(k) plan for (i) qualified first-time home-buyers, up to ten thousand dollars, (ii) qualified higher-education expenses, and (iii) health-insurance premiums paid while unemployed," John said.

"If I did establish a Solo 401(k) plan with a Roth component, I would obviously try my best to never take an early distribution," Amy said.

"That would be very wise. In the case of a Roth 401(k) account, distributions from a Roth 401(k) account that are not qualified may be subject to income tax and an additional ten percent early-distribution penalty. A qualified distribution from a designated Roth account is not included in gross income. A qualified distribution is a distribution from a Roth 401(k) plan that meets both of the following two categories of requirements:

1. It occurs at least five years after the Roth 401(k) participant established and funded his or her first Roth 401(k) account.
2. It is distributed under one of the following circumstances:
   - The Roth 401(k) plan participant is at least age 59½ when the distribution occurs.
   - The Roth 401(k) holder becomes disabled before the distribution.
   - The beneficiary of the Roth 401(k) plan participant receives the assets after the participant's death."

In the case of a Roth Solo 401(k) plan distribution that is not qualified, the following chart summarizes the tax implications.

Roth 401(k) Distribution Scenario	Taxation
Under 59½ and Roth 401(k) account opened and funded less than five years	Income tax and 10 percent penalty calculated on a pro rata basis between contributions and earnings
Under 59½ and Roth 401(k) account open and funded more than five years	Income tax and 10 percent penalty calculated on a pro rata basis between contributions and earnings
Over 59½ and Roth 401(k) account open and funded less than five years	Income Tax calculated on a pro rata basis between contributions and earnings
Over 59½ and Roth 401(k) account open and funded more than five years	No tax

In the case of a nonqualified Roth 401(k) distribution, in determining what portion of the distribution is considered to come from contributions as opposed to earnings, each distribution is simply treated on a pro rata basis. If a Roth 401(k) distribution is a nonqualified distribution:

- the portion of the distribution that represents contributions to the account will be nontaxable (and not subject to the 10 percent penalty) and
- the portion of the distribution that represents earnings (i.e., growth) will be taxable and *potentially* subject to the 10 percent penalty.

"This is in contrast to a Roth IRA that uses specific ordering rules to determine the tax treatment of Roth IRA nonqualified distributions," John said.

"Got an example?"

"Sure," John said. "Jim currently has twenty thousand dollars in his Roth 401(k), of which eighteen thousand dollars is from contributions and two thousand dollars is from earnings; any distribution will be considered to come ninety percent from contributions and ten percent from earnings—meaning that ninety percent of the distribution will be nontaxable, and ten percent will be taxable and possibly subject to a ten percent penalty if Jim is under the age of 59½."

"OK, this is a bit confusing, and I hope I never have to take early distributions from my retirement account, but if I did, I guess it is important to understand the rules. Just to be clear, early distributions from a pretax IRA would be subject to tax and a ten percent early-distribution penalty, whereas, for a Roth IRA, I can always take my Roth contributions without tax or penalty, but the earnings would be subject to tax and penalty if the distribution is not qualified," Amy said.

"Yes, that is accurate. But remember, in the case of a 401(k) plan, you would need a plan-triggering event to get your funds out of the plan if you are under 59½, and those funds could be subject to tax and penalty, in addition to required withholding by the employer. However, like an IRA, taking a distribution of converted Roth 401(K) funds add a twist. The early-withdrawal penalty applies to a distribution of conversion money from a Roth 401(k) assets if the plan participant is under the age of 59½ in a few situations.

1. The distribution is made within the five-tax-year period starting with the year that the conversion was distributed from a pretax 401(k) account *and*
2. Only to the extent that the distribution is attributable to amounts that were includable in gross income as a result of the conversion"

"In general, when thinking about taking early distribution from funds converted to a Roth 401(k) plan, you must consider that there could be a tax implication because of how the source of the Roth distributions is determined.

For example, Bill made a twenty-thousand-dollar conversion from his pretax 401(k) account to a Roth 401(k) in 2008. The entire amount converted was includable in Bill's income for 2008. Bill made no additional contributions or conversions to a Roth 401(k) in 2008 or in later years. In 2011, at the age of sixty-five, Bill's 401(k) account was valued at forty thousand dollars. Bill withdraws ten thousand dollars from the Roth 401(k). In order to determine what Bill would pay on the Roth 401(k) plan, the following distribution would be used: first, Bill would take the conversion amount (basis) and divide it by the total value of the 401(k) plan. Then Bill would multiply that percentage by the amount of the distribution. Based on our example, fifty percent of the ten thousand dollars would be basis and fifty percent would be subject to income tax. Remember, no ten percent early-distribution penalty would apply because Bill is over the age of 59½."

"OK," Amy said.

"It is important to remember that just because you made a Roth 401(k) contribution or did an in-plan Roth conversion, you are not able to make tax-free withdrawals from your designated Roth account at any time. Remember the same plan-triggering rules that apply to pretax elective contributions also apply to designated Roth contributions. If your plan permits distributions from accounts because of hardship, you may choose to receive a hardship distribution from your designated Roth account. The hardship distribution will consist of a pro rata share of earnings and basis, and the earnings portion will be included in gross income unless you have had the designated Roth account for five years and are either disabled or over age 59½," John said.

"OK, that makes sense. I assume you would have to report the distribution amount on my individual federal income-tax return (IRS Form 1040) in the year after the distribution is taken. For example, if the early distribution was taken in 2015, the income must be reported by April 15, 2016. The early-distribution penalty must also be reported on IRS Form 5329—Additional Taxes on Qualified Plans (Including IRAs) and Other Tax-Favored Accounts—if the distribution will be taxable."

"Distributions from a qualified retirement plan are subject to federal income tax withholding. However, if your distribution is subject to the ten percent additional tax, your withholding may not be enough."

"Thanks so much for taking the time to explain the IRA and 401(k) plan distribution rules, but if I can be honest, I hope that I never have to take a distribution from either my Roth IRA or 401(k) plan until I am over the age of 59½, which will allow me to circumvent any early-distribution penalty or tax in the case of my Roth IRA. The RMD rules are pretty complex, which is another great reason for having a Roth IRA. The one thing I really have to consider and talk over with my husband is doing a conversion of my 401(k) plan funds to either a Roth IRA or Roth Solo 401(k) plan," Amy said.

"That makes sense. Just remember that Roth IRA funds cannot be rolled into a 401(k) plan, so if you do a Roth conversion, the funds cannot be rolled into a Solo 401(k) plan you establish. You can always roll the 401(k) plan funds from your former employer into your new Solo 401(k) plan and then do an in-plan conversion. In both cases you will have a Roth account, it is just a matter of where you want the funds to sit for investment purposes," John said.

"Got it. If it is OK with you John, can we do one more quick meeting where we can kind of put everything you discussed together and I can try to come up with a game plan going forward for my retirement accounts?" Amy said.

"For sure. I am really going to miss our meetings. It's been fun, and I love helping young people who are motivated to learn more about the benefits of retirement planning and especially interested in exploring the power of the Roth," John said.

"Awesome. See you next week," Amy said.

9

PUTTING IT ALL TOGETHER

Amy showed up for her meeting with John, but this time she brought her younger sister Cindy and her boyfriend, Chad, along. Amy had been speaking with Cindy, who is twenty-five years old, and had just started a job with a start-up Internet company, about the need to start saving for retirement. Amy had described her experience and how easy it can be to start saving with a Roth IRA. She also mentioned that all it took was putting away just four to five dollars a day, basically one Grande Caramel Macchiato, and she could potentially end up with a million dollars tax free when she retired. Cindy was intrigued and thought it would make sense for her boyfriend, Chad, to come along since he worked in the city and at age thirty-five needed to start focusing on retirement saving. Amy agreed and thought it was a really great idea. Amy texted Cindy the time and date and encouraged her and Chad to join.

John showed up a few minutes late and was surprised to see Amy with Cindy, who he knew, and another person who he did not. Amy introduced John to Chad and explained that Cindy and Chad both were intrigued by the prospect of using a Roth-type of account to help bolster retirement wealth. Amy mentioned how blown away Cindy was that just by just saving a couple of dollars a day she could end up with significant tax-free wealth upon retirement. John asked how old Cindy and Chad were, and when Amy mentioned that Cindy was twenty-five and Chad was thirty-five he was even more excited because Cindy was a millennial and Chad was a generation Xer, and it would be a great way to highlight the advantages of the Roth retirement account for both generations.

"That sounds great," Amy said.

"OK, let's get started. I think it may make sense to do a quick overview of the two main types of Roth retirement accounts, the Roth IRA and Roth Solo 401(k) plan, for Cindy and Chad so that they have a deeper understanding of how they work, which will make our discussion on the concept of tax deferral and tax-free investing more meaningful," John said.

THE ROTH IRA

In 1997, Congress, under the Taxpayer Relief Act, introduced the Roth IRA to function like a traditional IRA, but with a few attractive modifications. The big advantage of a Roth IRA is that if you qualify to make contributions, all distributions from the Roth IRA are tax free—even the investment returns—as long as the distributions meet certain requirements. In addition, unlike traditional IRAs, you may contribute to a Roth IRA for as long as you continue to have earned income (in the case of a traditional IRA, you can't make contributions after you reach age 70½). The rules for the Roth IRA are found in the IRC under Section 408A.

A Roth IRA is an IRA that the owner designates as a Roth IRA. An individual and not a business must establish a Roth IRA. A Roth IRA is generally subject to the rules for traditional IRAs. For example, traditional and Roth IRAs and their owners are identically affected by the rules treating an IRA as distributing its assets if the IRA engages in a prohibited transaction or the owner borrows against it. The reporting requirements for IRAs also apply to Roth IRAs. However, several rules, described below, apply uniquely to Roth IRAs.

The most attractive feature of the Roth IRA is that even though contributions are not deductible, all distributions, including the earnings and appreciation on all Roth contributions, are tax free if certain conditions are met.

Roth IRA Characteristics

The following is an overview of the tax characteristics of the Roth IRA:

- Contributions are not tax deductible. Unlike a traditional IRA, an individual is not permitted to take an income-tax deduction for their Roth IRA contributions. All Roth IRA contributions are made with after-tax dollars. This means that the amount of the contribution is treated as basis in the IRA.
- Earnings are tax deferred. Earnings and gains from a Roth IRA are tax deferred and may be tax exempt if certain conditions are met. This means that all income and gains generated by a Roth IRA investment are not subject to income tax.
- Tax-free earnings. The attraction to the Roth IRA is based on the fact that qualified distributions of Roth earnings are tax free. As long as certain conditions are met and the distribution is a qualified distribution, the Roth IRA owner will never pay tax on any Roth distributions received.

The advantage of contributing to a Roth IRA is that income and gains generated by the Roth IRA investment can be tax free and penalty free so long as certain requirements are satisfied. Unlike a traditional IRA, contributions to a Roth IRA are not tax deductible.

Unlike the Traditional IRA, there is no 70½ age limit on making contributions. Individuals of any age with compensation are eligible to contribute to a Roth IRA. The total amount you may contribute to a Roth IRA for 2014 cannot exceed the lesser of $5,500 ($6500 if over the age of fifty) or 100 percent of compensation ($11,000 for married couples, $13,000 if over the age of fifty).

If you maintain a traditional IRA, the maximum contribution to your Roth IRA is reduced by any contributions made to your traditional IRAs.

Distributions from a Roth IRA that are not qualified may be subject to income tax and an additional 10 percent early-distribution penalty. A qualified distribution meets both of the following two categories of requirements:

1. It occurs at least five years after the Roth IRA owner established and funded his or her first Roth IRA.
2. It is distributed under one of the following circumstances:

- The Roth IRA holder is at least age 59½ when the distribution occurs.
- The Roth IRA holder becomes disabled before the distribution.
- The beneficiary of the Roth IRA holder receives the assets after his or her death.
- The distributed assets will be used toward the purchase or rebuilding of a first home for the Roth IRA holder or a qualified family member. This is limited to $10,000 per lifetime. Qualified family members include the following:
  - the Roth IRA holder;
  - the Roth IRA holder's spouse;
  - the children of the Roth IRA holder and/or his or her spouse;
  - the grandchild of the Roth IRA holder and/or his or her spouse; and
  - the parent or other ancestor of the Roth IRA holder and/or his or her spouse.

ROTH SOLO 401(K) PLAN

The Roth 401(k) plan or Roth Solo 401(k) plan is a retirement plan that must be established by a business. The Roth Solo 401(k) plan is not a different type of 401(k) plan but is simply referring to a plan that includes a Roth deferral option. In the case of a Roth Solo 401(k) plan, the business cannot have any full-time employees other than the owners and spouses. An individual who has no self-employment income or business income is not eligible to adopt a 401(k) plan and must use a Roth IRA to make Roth contributions. In 2001, Congress passed EGTRRA as part of the so-called "Bush tax cuts." The Act provided people who were self-employed or who were small-business owners with no employees the same advantages and benefits of a conventional employer 401(k) plan, including the ability to make Roth contributions. Before EGTRRA became effective in 2002, there was no compelling reason for an owner-only business to establish a Solo 401(k) plan because the business owner could generally receive the same benefits by adopting a SEP IRA. The Roth Solo 401(k) follows the same tax characteristics as the Roth IRA, except the contribution amount is far greater than a Roth IRA. For 2015 and 2016, the Solo 401(k) Roth employee-deferral contribution maximum amount is $18,000 or $24,000 if over the age of fifty, whereas a Roth IRA is just $5500 or $6500 if over the age of fifty. The Roth Solo 401(k) and Roth IRA both offer the advantages of tax-free growth, but the distribution rules differ slightly.

Both the Roth IRA and Roth Solo 401(k) plan require that a distribution be qualified in order for all Roth funds to be distributed tax free. A qualified Roth distribution is essentially a distribution of a Roth account open at least five years and the individual account holder being over the age of 59½. Where the Roth IRA and Roth Solo 401(k) plan distribution rules differ is that to determine the tax treatment of a distribution rules, a Roth IRA follows a set of ordering rules whereas the Roth Solo 401(k) plan follows a pro rata formula. In general, using the ordering rules formula is more taxpayer friendly. Other than that, the Roth IRA and Roth Solo 401(k) plan pretty much operate the same way.

"I don't want to get caught in the details of the Roth IRA and Roth 401(k) plan because Amy and I spent so much time discussing it. Cindy and Chad, you can always contact me with questions on the Roth IRA or go online to the IRS website, including IRS Publication 590," John said.

"OK, that makes sense." Cindy said.

"I know the Roth IRA and Roth 401(k) plan tax rules seem a bit confusing, but for our purposes, the most important feature of the Roth IRA or Roth 401(k) plan is the ability to make tax-free investments and generate tax-free wealth. Let me explain further. Much of what I am about to discuss now I have spent time chatting before with Amy, so this may be a bit of recap for you Amy, but it is very important that Cindy and Chad truly understand the advantages of tax-free investing with a Roth retirement account, which I like to call the last, best legal tax shelter."

THE ADVANTAGE OF RETIREMENT SAVING

John continued, "The foundation of retirement investing is based on the concept of tax deferral. Tax deferral means that you can postpone taxes on any earnings you make on the money in your tax-deferred accounts. That means your money is growing each year without having to remove any funds to pay tax. For example, if you contributed $2,000 to an IRA each year for ten years and averaged a 7 percent annual rate of return, assuming a 25 percent income-tax rate, your IRA would be worth $31,291, whereas if you invested the funds personally, you would have just $23,468. Now, imagine that instead of contributing over ten years, you contributed over thirty years. Assuming the same facts, your IRA would be worth $244,692 versus just $183,519. Now, further assume that you were able to save $10 a day or $3560 over the year and started making contributions starting at twenty-five through the age of seventy. Let's further assume you were able to generate a 7.5 percent rate of return over the forty-five years, you would have around $1.2 million when you retired at age seventy. Pretty impressive numbers for just saving a little bit each day."

"Yeah, that is just amazing. I am twenty-five years old, have a college degree, and consider myself pretty intelligent, and this is the first time that someone explained to me how tax deferral works. I have heard of the concept and am aware of the benefits of retirement planning, but when you put it into numbers, it is just so impressive, and it is a shame that more of my friends don't know about this," Cindy said.

"I agree with Cindy. I am a bit older and am considered a generation Xer because I was born in the early eighties, but this is really the first time I actually grasped the concept of tax deferral. I am a fairly successful guy and have a college degree as well as a master's degree and never really fully understood how tax deferral works. If I did, I would have certainly started using a Roth IRA sooner considering I started working over twelve years ago, at least part-time, and had extra money to save," Chad said.

"Well, Chad and Cindy, as I mentioned to Amy when we first spoke, you are not alone and should not feel embarrassed that you have not fully understood the power of a Roth retirement account and the power of tax-free investing. After speaking with tens of thousands of American retirement investors of all ages over the last several years, I kept hearing the same from them—I only wish I started saving for my retirement early, and I wish I knew then what I know now about the power of the Roth retirement account and tax-free investing. Then I give them the numbers on how saving just a few dollars a day can turn into hundreds of thousands of tax-free dollars at retirement, and they get even more frustrated. The good news for all three of you is that you are young enough to get started now and still reap the huge benefits of a Roth IRA. I will start with Cindy's situation since she is the youngest, and then we will move to Chad."

The others waited eagerly.

MILLENNIALS, GENERATION X, AND RETIREMENT SAVING

"It may be hard for someone who is just twenty-five to start thinking about retiring, especially when there is so much interesting stuff to check out on Facebook, Instagram, or Twitter, but this is exactly the time that you should start preparing for retirement. As you probably know you are considered a millennial. Millennials (also known as the millennial generation or generation Y) are the demographic group following generation X. There are no precise dates when the generation starts and ends. Most researchers and commentators use birth years ranging from the early 1980s to the early 2000s. The millennials or generation Y folks are certainly the most savvy and well-informed generation ever, but if they just added the concept of 'tax deferral' to their vocabulary, they could also end up being the richest generation. Let me give you an example.

"Let's assume that Michelle is twenty-five years old and saves $5 a day or $1,825 a year, which she contributes to a Roth IRA. Let's also assume that Michelle was able to save $1,825 a year until she reached the age of seventy. Not a very unrealistic assumption. Let's also assume that Michelle was able to average eight percent annually on her Roth IRA investments, which is actually below the average S&P 500 return since its inception through 2014, which is close to ten percent. Let's further assume that the tax rate stayed static at twenty-five percent. Based on the facts, Michelle would have $761,803 in her Roth IRA at age seventy, versus just $411,552 had she made the investments personally. Alternatively, let's say Michelle was able to save $10 a day or $3650, assuming the same prior facts, Michelle would have $1,523,605 in a Roth IRA versus just $823,105 if she had invested personally," John said.

"That is awesome. I can totally put away five dollars a day now and hopefully when I get older I can make it to ten dollars a day. The numbers seem attainable, and if I invest the funds for the next forty-five years, I assume I will be able to get between a seven and eight percent rate of return that should make me pretty comfortable when I retire," Cindy said.

"Yes, that is right. It's all about consistency, but once you see and understand the power of tax-free investing, trust me you will find a way to put the money in a Roth IRA each year. You may not be able to max out, but whatever you put in is great. The key is starting early and making IRA contributions on a consistent basis. Let's now turn to Chad, who is thirty-five and can still take full advantage of saving for retirement"

Chad nodded.

"Since Chad was born in the early 1980s, he is considered to be part of the generation X, commonly abbreviated to gen X. That's the generation born after the post–World War II baby boom. Gen Xers are often called the MTV generation. Although, Chad is a bit older than Cindy, as part of generation X he is still in a great position to take advantage of the power of the Roth retirement account and tax-free investing. Let's take the example of Matt. Matt is thirty-five years old and has not yet started saving for retirement. If Matt was able to contribute $4,000 a year to a Roth IRA until he reached the age of seventy, then, assuming the same eight percent rate of return as our example with Michelle and the same twenty-five percent tax rate, Matt would have $744,409 in his Roth IRA at age seventy, but only $472,483 if he had made the investments personally. As you can see, from a retirement standpoint, Michelle is much better off than Matt because she started making Roth IRA contributions at a younger age. Even though Matt contributed $4000 a year and Michelle contributed just $1825 in the second example and Michelle's Roth IRA contributions equaled $82,125, whereas Matt's contributions equaled $140,000, yet, because Matt's Roth IRA funds has less tax-deferral power behind them, his Roth IRA was valued less than Michelle's. Now, if you take the second example for Michelle where she was able to contribute $3560 a year from twenty-five through seventy and with an eight percent rate of return generated a Roth IRA worth $1,523,605, Matt's Roth IRA account would be worth close to $800,000 less than

Michelle's even though he contributed more than Michelle for thirty-five years," John said.

"Holy cow, that is incredible. I am happy that I met you at twenty-five," Cindy laughed.

"And I am happy I met you in my teens," Amy joked.

"Well, I am happy I met you now because even though I am thirty-five, if I start contributing to a Roth now until I am seventy and generate a solid rate of return, I can have a good amount of money when I retire. John, can you tell me how much I would have at age seventy if I saved fifty-five hundred dollars a year from now until age seventy, assuming a seven percent annual rate of return, just to be conservative," Chad asked.

"Of course. So if you made $5500 contributions to a Roth IRA from the age of thirty-five to seventy and continued to make the annual $5500 Roth IRA contribution through the age of seventy even though the IRA contribution maximum will certainly increase in the future, assuming a seven percent annual rate of return, you will have around $813,524 at retirement, which is still great. When you consider that as of 2015, the average American has around $200,000 when they retire between age sixty-five and eighty,[28] having over $800,000 in a tax-free Roth IRA is pretty good. Now, I don't mean to be a party pooper, but if you had started a Roth IRA at twenty-five like Cindy and were able to put in $5500 a year, which is only about $15 a day, $105 a week, or $458 a month, assuming a seven percent annual rate of return your Roth IRA would be worth $1,681,635 at age seventy, which is real money," John said.

"Thanks for ruining my day," Chad laughed.

"And making mine," Cindy joked.

"The bottom line is that when it comes to generating retirement wealth, the most important factors are starting young, being consistent, and making good investments. The first two you can control, and if you work with a good financial advisor, history shows us that you should be able to generate at least

---

28 http://www.fool.com/investing/general/2015/01/05/the-average-american-has-this-much-saved-in-a-401k.aspx.

a seven percent rate of return over the life of your Roth retirement account, if not more, which based on the numbers I just presented will still allow you to retire comfortably," John said.

"Should we blow them away with some numbers for a Roth Solo 401(k) plan?" Amy asked.

"Ha-ha. I don't want to get Cindy and Chad really riled up, but we will shortly," John laughed.

"I told you Cindy and Chad that you would be blown away by the numbers. Another cool thing with a Roth IRA is that you are not stuck just making traditional investments, such as stocks and mutual funds; you can always establish a self-directed Roth IRA and buy real estate or other alternative-asset investments so long as it is not prohibited by the IRS," Amy said.

"That is right. Thanks for reminding me, Amy. The IRC does not describe what a self-directed IRA can invest in, only what it *cannot* invest in. Internal Revenue Code sections 408 and 4975 prohibit disqualified persons from engaging in certain types of transactions. The foundation of the prohibited-transaction rules is based on the premise that investments involving IRA and related parties are handled in a way that benefits the retirement account and not the IRA owner. The rules prohibit transactions between the IRA and certain individuals known as 'disqualified persons,' which are essentially the IRA holder and his or her lineal descendants. I spent a good amount of time discussing the rules with Amy, but just in keep in mind that if you felt you could generate stronger returns investing in what you know and understand, such as real estate, tax liens, precious metals, and hard money lending versus buying stocks or mutual funds, the option exists," John said.

"OK, that is cool. This really won't be an issue for Cindy and me right now because we are just starting, but maybe in ten or fifteen years when our Roth IRAs have increased in value, we would consider the self-directed Roth IRA. One last question; why do you think that there is not more attention spent by the government or educational institutions to inform teenagers and young adults about the benefits of retirement planning and especially the Roth IRA?" Chad asked.

RETIREMENT SAVING AND RECENT DEVELOPMENTS

"I wish I knew. But things are starting to change. Recently, as of September 2015, three states, Illinois, Washington, and Oregon, have begun to authorize a state-run retirement-savings program for a broad spectrum of the population. The goal: to get small businesses, many of which don't currently offer retirement plans, to deduct contributions from employees' paychecks and funnel them into individual retirement accounts, where money can grow tax deferred until retirement. The problem is that it is really not enough. The government and educational institutions need to start focusing their attention on educating students and new entrants into the workforce about the power of starting an IRA or Roth IRA at a young age. The flip side is having a population that will not have enough money when they retire and be completely dependent upon government safety-net programs, which looks a lot like our current predicament. The *Wall Street Journal* in a 2011 article titled, "Retiring Boomers Find 401(k) Plans Fall Short"[29] detailed how using data from the Center for Retirement Research at Boston College, it calculated that households had a median household income of $87,700 in 2009. If people need eight-five percent of their income for retirement, this means they need to have $74,545 a year. Experts estimate that social security provides as much as forty percent of preretirement income, or $35,080 per year. That leaves a gap of $39,465, and most 401(k) plans don't come close to making that up. According to the article, only eight percent of households have the $636,673 in their 401(k) plans needed to generate that amount. Some families do have other sources of income, but you get the point. Social security plans for solvency for the next seventy-five years, but according to the *New York Times*,[30] it is currently solvent only until 2033 because of demographic pressures and the weak economy. And without reforms, it will pay only about seventy-five

---

29 E. S. Browning, "Retiring Boomers Find 401(k) Plans Fall Short," *Wall Street Journal*, February 19, 2011.

30 New York Times Editorial Board, "Social Security, Present and Future," *New York Times*, March 30, 2013.

percent of the promised benefits. Meanwhile, the nation is experiencing a retirement crisis. Less than half of households ages fifty-five to sixty-four have retirement savings, and of those, half have less than $120,000. Most retirees will be heavily reliant on social security, which currently pays on average $1,265 a month.

"The majority of retirees with annual incomes up to $32,600 get two-thirds to all of their income from social security. Even at higher incomes (up to $57,960), social security is the single biggest source of retirement income, accounting for almost half. Only the top one-fifth of seniors, with incomes above $57,960, do not rely on social security as their largest source of income, and most of them are still working.

So what does all this tell us? Americans need to do a better job of proactively saving for retirement. The IRS has given us the tools. It's my hope that this conversation will help motivate you to get started or, if you have started making IRA contributions, to keep making contributions on a continual basis," John said.

"That is some scary stuff. It is clear that every American needs to do a better job taking care of their own retirement planning and not just relying on the government for support. I just wish this was taught to us in school or at some point while I was in college. I was lucky that I spoke with you at a dinner party at my parents' home back when I was eighteen, but most people my age or even Cindy's age won't be so lucky," Amy said.

"I know. Americans have one of the lowest savings rates for developed countries. Americans are the ultimate consumers, and that definitely plays a role. The problem is that most young people do not understand that saving just a few dollars a day in a Roth IRA can make them wealthy when they retire. Of course, it is difficult for a young person to think or even care about what will happen when they are seventy or older since the belief is that retirement is so far away, why worry now. I totally understand where the millennials and generation Xers are coming from as I have two kids myself who are more focused on what they will be doing on the weekend than on concerning themselves with how much money they will have in fifty years, but unfortunately our actions today have a direct correlation with the wealth we have at retirement. I wish this wasn't the case, but the reality is that what we do from a retirement standpoint starting at a young age impacts the amount of wealth we have when we retire. Sure, there are always ways to catch-up as you make more money later in life, but as my example of Michelle and Matt showed, there is really no substitute for starting to save for retirement at a young age and continuing to make annual retirement-account contributions. This is why educating our young generations about the importance of retirement saving and the power of tax deferral is so important. I am confident that if we can show the young millennial and gen X generations the enormous benefits of retirement savings at a young age and make Roth IRA savings easy and seamless, then more and more Americans will be in a better place when retirement hits than their parents. For example, assume Jane started a Roth IRA at the age of twenty-five. Her starting balance is $0. If she made annual contributions of just $3500 or about $10 a day until she retired at age seventy and was able to generate a rate of return eight percent, Jane would have approximately $1,460,991 in tax-free retirement funds. In contrast, if she invested outside of a retirement account, assuming a twenty-five percent tax rate, she would have just $789,278. Hence, the Roth IRA allowed the individual to accumulate an extra $671,713.

"I believe, however, if the millennials or generation Xers are informed and shown the benefits of retirement planning at a young age and specifically the Roth IRA, they can become the generations most prepared for retirement and actually surpass their parents in the quality of their retirement lifestyle. At the age of retirement, they will actually be in a position to stop working, be more independent, enjoy a high quality of life, and even pass the funds on to a spouse or children—all for just starting a free Roth IRA and putting in a few dollars a day. It's not hard or painful, but it can be the difference between retiring rich and having to work all your life," John said.

"I know; I get it and think my sister and Chad also get it."

"We do," Chad said. "You could not have made it clearer on how establishing a Roth IRA and contributing to it each year on a consistent basis will be the best decision we ever make."

"Trust me, it will be. I know it is really hard to think of your retirement when you have your entire life ahead of you and retiring seems so distant, but it does creep up on you. I am in my forties, and I still think of myself as a kid, but the reality is that as we get older time goes quicker, so it is imperative to start as early as you can and begin contributing to a Roth IRA or any retirement account for that matter. The gist of the matter is the actions we take or don't take at a young age have a great impact on our entire lives and retirement. Whether that is doing well in high school and getting into a good university, or pursuing a skill set that becomes highly sought after, which leads to a high-paying job, saving for retirement can have the same impact in your life. I now it's hard to worry about the future especially some forty years in the future, but trust me you will be happy you did when you see the amount you have in your retirement account. It's probably not fair that you have to worry about retirement when you are just starting to enter the workforce, but that is just how the system works. Just like it's not fair how your score on a standardized test at age sixteen can determine what university you attend and potentially what type of job you get, the same goes about retirement saving. I wish it was a more even playing field where everyone was informed and educated about the importance of saving for retirement, but this is unfortunately not the case, and those that are uninformed unfortunately are significantly disadvantaged when it comes to retirement saving since the most important thing is starting to save for retirement at an early age and making contributions on a consistent annual basis. I don't want to sound like a broken record, but the fact is what I am saying is so important that it can literally change your entire life as you get older. It is just a shame that more people your age don't know about the power of the Roth IRA and tax deferral," John said.

"I think we get it," Amy laughed. "Now can we focus a bit on me and talk about what type of retirement plan I should adopt for my business?"

"OK," John said. "Sorry about being so annoying and harping on the benefits of the Roth IRA; I promise I am almost done. Cindy and Chad, I am now going to spend some time discussing the benefits of the Roth Solo 401(k) plan for Amy's business. Since you are both not self-employed, feel free to tune out or check your emails for the next few minutes," John said.

"Actually, I have the potential opportunity to do some independent consulting down the road and would be interested in learning more about the Solo 401(k) plan if you don't mind," Chad said.

"Not at all. As a quick summary, the Solo 401(k) plan, also known as the Individual 401(k) or self-directed 401(k) Plan, is an IRS-approved type of qualified retirement plan that is suited for business owners who do not have any employees other than themselves and perhaps their spouse. The Solo 401(k) plan is not a new type of plan. It is a traditional 401(k) plan covering only one employee. The Solo 401(k) is perfect for sole proprietors, small businesses and independent contractors such as consultants. A Solo 401(k) plan can be adopted by any business with no employees other than the owner(s). The business can be established as a sole proprietorship, LLC, corporation, or partnership. The Solo 401(k) plan is unique and so popular because it is designed explicitly for small, owner-only businesses. In 2001, Congress passed EGTRRA as part of the so-called 'Bush tax cuts.' The act provided people who were self-employed or who were small-business owners with no employees the same advantages and benefits of a conventional employer 401(k) plan, including the ability to make Roth contributions. Before EGTRRA became effective in 2002, there was no compelling reason for an owner-only business to establish a Solo 401(k) plan because the business owner could generally receive the same benefits by adopting a SEP IRA. The Roth Solo 401(k) follows the same tax characteristics as the Roth IRA, except the contribution amount is far greater than a Roth IRA. For 2015 and 2016, the Solo 401(k) Roth employee-deferral contribution maximum amount is eighteen thousand dollars or twenty-four thousand dollars if over the age of fifty, whereas a Roth IRA is just fifty-five hundred dollars or sixty-five hundred dollars if over the age of fifty," John said.

"OK, that is really helpful. I am sorry if you already went through this with Amy, but I assume the Roth Solo 401(k) plan is not a separate 401(k) plan?" Chad asked.

"That is correct. Depending on the plan documents and where you establish your Solo 401(k) plan, the plan-adoption agreement should offer you the option of including a Roth component in the plan. Essentially, it all comes down to the plan documents. The adoption agreement indicates what options in the plan documents will apply to your Solo 401(k) plan. For example, I have some clients that don't want to include the loan feature, so their plan

ADAM BERGMAN, ESQ.

documents will not include the loan feature even if the plan documents allow for it," John said.

"OK, that makes sense. I assume I can only contribute what I earn from my business to the Solo 401(k) plan and not dividends or gains from selling my Apple stock?" Chad said.

"That is correct. You need to generate earned income from the business that has adopted the Solo 401(k) plan in order to make contributions. According to the IRS, taxable earned income includes:

- wages, salaries, and tips;
- union strike benefits;
- long-term disability benefits received prior to minimum retirement age; and
- net earnings from self-employment.

"However, the following are examples of income that are *not* considered earned:

- Pay received for work while an inmate in a penal institution
- Interest and dividends
- Retirement income
- Social security
- Unemployment benefits
- Alimony
- Child support"

"OK, that makes sense. Can you just quickly go over how much I would be able to contribute to my Solo 401(k) plan if I set it up this year?" Chad asked.

"That is exactly the question I was waiting to ask," Amy said.

THE ROTH SOLO 401(K) PLAN ASSESSED

"Under the 2015 and 2016 Solo 401(k) contribution rules, a plan participant under the age of fifty can make a maximum employee-deferral contribution in the amount of eighteen thousand dollars. That amount can be made in pretax or Roth, so long as the plan includes the Roth option. On the profit-sharing side, the business can make a twenty-five percent (twenty percent in the case of a sole proprietorship or single-member LLC) profit-sharing contribution up to a combined maximum, including the employee deferral, of fifty-three thousand dollars.

"For plan participants over the age of fifty, an individual can make a maximum employee-deferral contribution in the amount of twenty-four thousand dollars. That amount can be made in pretax or Roth so long as the plan includes the Roth option. On the profit-sharing side, the business can make a twenty-five percent (twenty percent in the case of a sole proprietorship or single-member LLC) profit-sharing contribution up to a combined maximum, including the employee deferral, of fifty-nine thousand dollars.

"Before the Economic Growth and Tax Relief Reconciliation Act of 2001 (EGTRRA) became effective in 2002, there was no incentive for an owner-only business to establish a 401(k) plan because the business owner could generally receive the same benefits by adopting a profit-sharing plan or SEP IRA. However, EGTRRA changed everything and turned the Solo 401(k) plan into the most popular retirement plan for the self-employed. EGTRRA cleared the way for an owner-only business to defer more money into a retirement plan and to operate a more cost-effective, less complex type of plan. One of the key features of EGTRRA was that it added the employee-deferral feature founded in a traditional multiple employee 401(k) plan to the Solo 401(k) plan. This feature turned the Solo 401(k) plan into the retirement vehicle that provided the highest contribution benefits to the self-employed.

"A Solo 401k participant can contribute to the plan as an employee and as employer."

Employee Deferrals

For 2015 and 2016, up to $18,000 per year can be contributed by the participant through employee elective deferrals. An additional $6,000 can be contributed for persons over age fifty. These contributions can be up to 100 percent of the participant's self-employment compensation and can be made in pretax or Roth.

Employer Profit-Sharing Contributions

Through the role of employer, an additional contribution can be made to the plan in an amount up to 25 percent of the participant's self-employment compensation (20 percent in the case of a Sole Proprietor or a Schedule C Tax Payer). The employer profit-sharing contributions must be made in pretax but can be converted to Roth if the plan includes a Roth feature.

Total Limit

The sum of both contributions can be a maximum of $53,000 per year (for 2015 and 2016) or $59,000 for persons over age fifty.

If the business owner's spouse elects to participate in the Solo 401(k) and earns compensation from the business, the spouse is allowed to make separate and equal contributions increasing the couples' annual total contribution to $106,000 for 2015 and 2016 or $118,000 if both spouses are over age fifty.

"Solo 401k contributions are flexible. Both the salary deferral and the profit-sharing contributions are optional and can be changed at any time based on business profitability," John said.

"How about some examples," Amy asked.

"OK, no problem. Here we go."

Example 1

Joe, who is thirty-five, is the sole owner of ABC, Inc. Joe receives $100,000 of compensation from the corporation. The maximum deductible contribution Joe can make to his Solo 401(k) account in 2016 would be a whopping $43,000 ($18,000 + [25 percent of $100,000]).

Example 2

Joe, who is thirty-five, is a sole proprietor. Joe earns $100,000 from his sole proprietorship. For 2016, the maximum deductible contribution Joe can make to his Solo 401(k) account would be a whopping $38,000 ($18,000 + [20 percent of $100,000]).

Example 3

Joe, who is forty-two, is the owner of a single-member LLC. Joe earns $100,000 from his LLC from self-employment earnings. For 2016, the maximum deductible contribution Joe can make to his Solo 401(k) account would be a whopping $38,000 ($18,000 + [20 percent of $100,000]).

Example 4

Joe, who is fifty-five, is the sole owner of ABC, Inc. Joe receives $100,000 of compensation from the corporation. In 2016, the maximum deductible contribution Joe can make to his Solo 401(k) account would be a whopping $49,000 ($24,000 + [25 percent of $100,000]).

Example 5

Joe and Kim are married. Joe, who is thirty-five, is the sole owner of ABC, Inc. Joe and Kim each receive $100,000 of compensation from the corporation. For 2016, the maximum deductible contribution Joe can make to his Solo 401(k) account would be $43,000 ($18,000 + [25 percent of $100,000]), and the maximum deductible contribution Kim can make to her Solo 401(k) account would be $43,000, for a total of a whopping $86,000.

"That would be really nice for me. I should have about ninety thousand dollars or so of Schedule C income for 2016, so adopting a Solo 401(k) plan should allow me to put a bundle away into a Roth Solo 401(k) plan," Amy said.

"It may also work for me as I am seriously considering doing some consulting work on the side, and I think I can generate about fifteen thousand dollars or so of additional income, which I would totally contribute to a Solo 401(k) plan adopted by my sole proprietorship business," Chad said.

"Here comes the great news. Now let's look at what you can have when you retire assuming you made annual contributions to your Solo 401(k) plan. We touched on some of this before when I first introduced the Roth Solo 401(k) plan to you, Amy, several weeks ago, but I think Chad and Cindy will be really shocked at the numbers," John said.

"OK, sounds awesome," Chad said.

"Now let's have some fun. Here are some examples of the power of making Roth Solo 401(k) plan contributions over a period of time. I will use different starting ages and annual contribution amounts, but I think the numbers will speak for themselves. I this is really going to amaze all of you."

- Starting balance: $0
- Annual contribution: $10,000
- Current age: 30
- Age of retirement: 70
- Expected rate of return: 7 percent
- Marginal tax rate: 25 percent
- Total amount of contributions: $400,000

At age 70 with a Roth 401(k) plan, the individual would have $2.071,255 tax free.

- Starting balance: $0
- Annual contribution: $15,000
- Current age: 35
- Age of retirement: 70
- Expected rate of return: 7 percent
- Marginal tax rate: 25 percent
- Total amount of contributions: $525,000

At age 70 with a Roth 401(k) plan, the individual would have $2.581,635 tax free.

- Starting balance: $0
- Annual contribution: $18,000
- Current age: 32
- Age of retirement: 70
- Expected rate of return: 7 percent
- Marginal tax rate: 25 percent
- Total amount of contributions: $684,000

At age 70 with a Roth 401(k) plan, the individual would have $3.759,763 tax free.

- Starting balance: $0
- Annual contribution: $18,000
- Current age: 32
- Age of retirement: 70
- Expected rate of return: 5 percent
- Marginal tax rate: 25 percent
- Total amount of contributions: $684,000

At age 70 with a Roth 401(k) plan, the individual would have $2,322,704 tax free.

"Holy cow, that is crazy. I can literally be a multimillionaire if I just can save around one thousand dollars a month or ten thousand dollars a year in Roth Solo 401(k) plan. I know I can do it now, and my business is pretty much a start-up, so I am pretty confident I would be able to increase my annual contributions going forward. The numbers are just incredible. I can't imagine why anyone who is self-employed or has a small business with no full-time employees would not set up a Solo 401(k) plan. Just doesn't make sense, unless people are just not aware of it," Amy said.

"I know, these numbers are outrageous. This would make earning some extra consulting income even more attractive as I can dump it all into a Roth Solo 401(k) plan and watch it grow tax free. It is just unbelievable that this is the first I have heard of a Solo 401(k) plan. I have a bunch of friends that are self-employed, and I know they have no idea about the huge advantages of adopting a Solo 401(k) plan. Just don't understand why the Solo 401(k) plan is not better known," Chad said.

"Well, I think you hit the nail on the head. Many sole proprietors and small-business owners are for some reason not being exposed to the benefits of the Solo 401(k) plan. Considering that a Solo 401(k) plan can pretty much be set up for free at a local bank and doesn't have any administration if the plan assets are less than $250,000, you are right there is no reason why more small business are not using the Solo 401(k) plan," John said.

"Just doesn't make sense. Plus the fact that the Solo 401(k) plan also comes with a loan option that allows a plan participant to borrow up to the lesser of fifty thousand dollars or fifty percent of their plan value and use the funds for any purpose, including for personal or business purposes, there is really no excuse for not establishing a Solo 401(k) plan," Amy said.

"Couldn't agree with you more," John said.

"Me too. I f I do end up starting my own consulting business I will one hundred percent establish a Solo 401(k) plan. Your examples sold me on the value of the Roth Solo 401(k) plan," Chad said.

"OK, so I think we have come to a consensus. Cindy and Chad are going to establish Roth IRAs this year and start making annual Roth IRA contributions from their income. Amy will adopt a Solo 401(k) plan for her new business that includes a Roth component and begin making annual Roth contributions to the Plan. Amy will also keep her Roth IRA open since Roth IRA funds cannot be rolled into a 401(k) plan and continue to make Roth IRA contributions so long as her income allows for it," John said.

"I think you got it. The only thing I would add is that I may consider doing a self-directed Roth IRA with 'checkbook control' at some point to add some diversification to my retirement account portfolio," Amy added.

"OK, that works," John said.

"Thanks so much, John for all taking so much time out of your busy day to chat with me about the Roth retirement account as well as an array of other really interesting retirement topics. I can't thank you enough. I really do appreciate it," Amy said.

"Chad and I also really appreciate you letting us crash your meeting with Amy and teaching us about the importance of the Roth IRA, the exciting benefits of a Roth Solo 401(k) plan, and the power of tax-free retirement savings. I know this is a lesson that will serve us well for our entire life. We really owe you big time," Cindy said.

"No problem. It was really my pleasure. I get a lot of satisfaction talking with young people about the power of the Roth IRA and the importance of starting to plan for retirement at an early age. I hope everything we discussed will motivate you to continue to save for retirement on a yearly basis as well as strongly consider using a Roth IRA or Roth 401(k) plan, if applicable. Saving for retirement does not have to be scary or difficult and actually should be fun as you can watch your money grow without tax and your retirement nest egg get bigger and bigger each year. It really can be one of the most valuable decisions you make in your entire life, and it is free to set up and very simple to do. In fact, there are new online and mobile-device applications out there that will automatically take a set amount of money from your personal account at a set frequency and then automatically contribute those funds to your IRA. I know it is expensive to live, including paying for rent, mortgage, food, credit-card bills, student debt, but I think most of us can save a few dollars a day and put toward retirement, and if you start doing this at an early age and make some wise investment decisions you can come close to having a million dollars tax free when you retire. It is hard to comprehend, but the numbers don't lie. I just hope more young people are exposed to the benefits of retirement planning and especially the Roth IRA because it can literally mean the difference of retiring wealthy or having to work you entire life," John said.

"Thanks again. I am going to post some of these examples on my Facebook page and also tweet them out to all my friends, so hopefully I can help educate some of my friends about the power of the Roth IRA," Cindy said.

"That would be great. Best of luck to the three of you and if you ever have any additional questions on retirement accounts just let me know," John said.

"Will do and thanks again," Amy said.

CONCLUSION

I T MAY BE hard for someone in their twenties or early thirties to start thinking about retiring, especially when there is so much interesting stuff to check out on Facebook, Instagram, or Twitter, and so many expenses to think about, such as rent, mortgage, food, credit cards, and even student debt, but this is exactly the time that a millennial or generation Xer should start preparing for retirement if one wants to have the chance to enjoy retirement without having to save a lot of money each year.

Americans love to spend and hate to save. About 40 percent of working households with those aged between twenty-five and sixty-four have no retirement savings according to a study released last spring by the nonprofit National Institute on Retirement Security. Americans have one of the lowest savings rates for developed countries. However, I believe that education—or its lack thereof—is a big factor. Most people don't understand the basic concepts of retirement planning and how crucial it is largely because it's not widely taught in our high schools or even our colleges and universities. It is my hope that this book will begin to educate Americans, especially the generation X and generation Y, about the significant importance of saving for retirement and can begin the process of increasing the number of young working households with retirement accounts.

The primary objective of the book is to reveal to the millennials and generation Xers the exciting benefits of starting to plan for retirement at a young age as well as uncover the power of the Roth IRA and Roth 401(k). I used the characters of Amy, John, Cindy, and Chad to illustrate the kind of dialogue I have experienced talking with over fifteen thousand retirement investors about the ins and outs of the Roth IRA and Roth 401(k) plan. Amy and

John and the fictitious questions and answers they exchanged were designed to educate and inform the millennials and generation Xers on the enormous benefits of the Roth IRA and Roth 401(k) plan, specifically (i) the importance of starting to plan for retirement at a young age; (ii) the ins and outs of the different types of popular retirement accounts for individuals and small businesses, including the Roth IRA and Roth Solo 401(k); (iii) the power of tax deferral and tax-free investing; (iv) how easy and fun retirement saving can be if you start young; (v) the supremacy of the Roth Solo 401(k) plan for the self-employed or small-business owner; (vi) the ability to buy alternative assets with retirement funds and invest in what you know and understand; and most importantly (vii) how saving just a few dollars a day can lead to millions when you retire if you start young, make annual contributions consistently, and invest wisely.

Amy represented the typical millennial who is smart, well informed, and technologically savvy. However, unlike the typical millennial, Amy has taken a proactive approach to retirement and started contributing to a Roth IRA at age eighteen and consistently made annual Roth IRA contributions going forward. I chose the example of Amy because I wanted to show the power of tax deferral and tax-free investing and how fast the contributions can turn into real wealth. I also wanted to show how just saving a few dollars a day can make the difference between retiring with wealth or having to work the rest of your life. The government has given all of us the power to take control our retirement destiny and build tax-free wealth for our retirement with the advent of the IRA and 401(k) plan; the problem is that too many young Americans do not understand the power of tax deferral or tax-free investing, and once they do, in some cases, it is too late. No one is trying to blame the millennials or generation Xers. The blame lies squarely on us, as a society, who for some reason have not pushed for greater education on the power of retirement saving at our schools and universities. I have many friends who are doctors, lawyers, engineers, who stayed in school until their late twenties and who took hundreds of university- and graduate-level classes on a wide array of subjects but were never once offered the opportunity to learn about how to save for retirement. Many of these very well-educated and successful people couldn't tell you what a Roth IRA is or how the power of tax deferral works.

I know this firsthand because when I am out socializing and I mention that I help people establish self-directed retirement accounts, they look at me dumbfounded and have generally no idea about what I am talking about. This is certainly not a knock on any of my friends or anyone else; it is just an example of how our society, from the rich to the not so rich and the highly educated to the not so educated, is failing to take advantage of the very valuable retirement tools Congress is offering us, which unfortunately can have dire consequences. Imagine if you bought a house but no one told you that you could take a deduction for your mortgage interest payments on your income-tax return. That is kind of like working and earning income and not using a retirement account for your savings. Unfortunately, it is happening far too frequently, especially with the millennials and generation Xers mostly because they are not well informed about the enormous benefits of retirement saving and the huge advantage of starting early. Just imagine if someone who is twenty-five years old was shown that if he or she began funding a Roth IRA with just a few dollars a day or $2000 a year and continued on through age seventy, he or she would wind up with over $1.5 million at retirement (assuming they earn the long-run annual compound growth rate in stocks, which was 9.88 percent from 1926 to 2011). Not a bad result for investing only $2,000 a year or $5.60 a day—basically the cost of a Grande Caramel Macchiato at Starbucks. Hopefully this book will help educate and inform the millennials and generation Xers of the importance of saving for retirement and the value of starting early and using a Roth IRA or 401(k) plan on a consistent annual basis.

Hopefully, I've helped you understand the different types of retirement accounts available for the employed and self-employed and some of their advantages and disadvantages. Most importantly, I hope the book has been able to show you the enormous benefits of having and growing a retirement account and some of the ways you can accomplish this. Whether you have a pretax traditional IRA or an after-tax Roth IRA, or convert from a pretax IRA to a Roth IRA, taking the time to focus on growing your retirement account through contributions and investments could very well be the difference between retiring rich and working the rest of your life.

The key is starting young, being consistent in making annual retirement-account contributions, and investing wisely. Hopefully, this book has shown you the enormous benefits of retirement savings and how easy and simple it can be. You don't need to make a six-figure salary to be able to afford to contribute to an IRA or 401(k) plan. Even one dollar a day starting at an early age can generate hundreds of thousands of wealth when you retire. In fact, Congress is encouraging you to do this by offering a tax deduction in the case of a pretax retirement account or tax-free growth in the case of a Roth retirement account, while your employer may offer you a matching contribution to your 401(k) plan helping to grow your account. The tools for all Americans to retire with wealth have been given to all of us. It is my hope that this book has been able to show you how attainable it is and how easy and rewarding it can be.

I understand that not everyone is able to save thousands of dollars a year for their retirement especially the millennials who are just starting their careers and have the burden of paying rent or a mortgage, car payments, gas, insurance, credit-card payments, student debt, and still have some money left over for entertainment, but I think most millennials can put away a few dollars a day, if that means skipping one afternoon cappuccino, or buying a less expensive bottle of wine for dinner, not ordering the dessert at dinner, or simply being more conscious of expenses. It can be done, and it doesn't have to be burdensome. The same goes for the generation Xers who are likely only starting to get their working careers on track and at the same time have probably more expenses than the millennials. Saving a couple of dollars is something that is certainly realistic and more than doable and can really mean the difference of retiring with wealth or having to work the rest of your life.

It is my hope that I have been able to unravel the common misconception that one needs to make a lot of money in order to save for retirement and retire with wealth. This concept is 100 percent not true and is actually a common statement many young people make when asked why they are not saving for retirement. I hope this book has shown that even saving $1 a day or $365 a year starting at age twenty-one all the way to age seventy can generate close to $175,000 in tax-free wealth at retirement (assuming a 7.5 percent annual rate of return). This figure doesn't taken into account your ability to save more as you get older and hopefully earn more money, but I think it clearly demonstrates that you don't have to be a high earner to start saving for retirement.

I know many millennials who work minimum-wage jobs on a part-time basis who are still able to save a few hundred of dollars a year in a Roth IRA. The power of tax deferral compensates for small annual retirement contributions by turning a small amount of funds into a bundle of retirement wealth over time, assuming wise investment decisions. By deferring or not paying taxes on the returns of an investment, in the case of a Roth retirement account, you are able to benefit from tax-free growth. Therefore, instead of paying tax on the returns of an investment, tax is paid only at a later date, or not at all in the case of a Roth, leaving the investment to grow unhindered. This is why you can turn just a few thousand dollars a year over a period of time into millions at retirement, assuming solid investment returns. If you take away one thing from this book, I hope it is the concept of tax deferral and tax-free investing. It is really the last great legal tax-shelter available to all Americans but even more vital for millennials and generation Xers who because of their age are in the best position to reap its benefits.

The millenniums or generation Y folks are certainly the most savvy and well-informed generation ever, but if they just added the concept of "tax deferral" to their vocabulary to go along with "tweet," "face time," or "WhatsApp," they could also end up retiring with the most money.

www.ingramcontent.com/pod-product-compliance
Lightning Source LLC
Chambersburg PA
CBHW070225190526
45169CB00001B/77